ISBN: 978-0-9858718-4-0
Library of Congress Control Number: 2012953598

Published in the United States of America by:
No Waste Publishing
1568 Fencorp Drive
Fenton, Missouri, 63026, USA

Dedicated to Johannes, of course, and to all of my courageous ancestors who left unique footprints before me. I salute you.

Acknowledgements

My cousin Becky (Mary Rebecca) who spent countless hours compiling all of the letters.

My dear Uncle Buxie for his remembrances.

My cousins, John and Ellen, for copies of the letters, photographs, and access to the Johnson family bible.

My cousin, Rosemary, for photographs and her remembrances of Grandpa Johannes.

The staff at the Goodhue County Historical Society for written material and photographs.

The Red Wing Republican Eagle, for permission to reprint the letters.

Last, but never least, my wonderful son, Thomas, for his expert technology support - at all hours of the day and night.

Thank you all so very much. I am deeply grateful.

Nancy

Circa 1930s at the home he built for Mary

Table of Contents

'The Forgotten'

- Preface
- The Immigrant -
  - Homeland and family
  - A man at 14
  - Fever
- Establishment
  - Red Wing, Minnesota – adopted home
  - Jobs and pay
  - Sickness
  - Mary
  - The 'stone house'
  - The 'Swedish castle'
- The Philospher
  - Introduction
  - Letters – 1 through 217
  - Twilight
- A little more

The 'Forgotten'

I've been stalking my ancestors far and near
To bring into perspective and help to make clear
What manner of people came to this land
In families, alone, or two hand in hand.

Sweden and Norway are special to me
From their ports my ancestors sailed out to sea
Their possessions were few, their future unknown
With babies in arms and children half grown

Young America was the land they did seek
It welcomed the strong and sheltered the weak
They married, they settled, they laughed and they cried
They loved and they worked and they played and they died

To counties, cemeteries, and down 'memory lane'
I've found those who were gentle and some not quite sane
Gangsters, bootleggers, common-law wives
Some led very colorful lives

One was a judge, there were farmers and stonemasons
From illness and epidemics to graves some did hasten
A nurse, a grocer, and veterans of war
Spinsters and bachelors and so many more.

Some remain hidden from my wide-seeking eyes
Their escapades made them hide behind lies
Some I have found by luck or with ease
And then for myself, I feel very pleased

My search is not over, it has not yet finished
My desire to continue will never diminish
The chain was started a long time ago
I am but a link, while the chain ever grows.

nancy elizabeth blondell
1975

-PREFACE-

Where to begin. I hardly know. How to convey the essence of a man I never met. Are there a handful of people left who knew Johannes? They would have been very young children at the time, and now grown old. Of those remaining, would they, and could they come close to agreeing on who he really was? A daunting task I have set for myself, but for all the things Johannes was, or was not, he made his mark and, as the song lyrics go, not in a shy way. Johannes did it his way.

Who was Johannes? – Johannes was an immigrant, poor, but not humble. No, certainly not that. Uneducated yes, but smart about life, certainly. Trusting, but too much so as you will come to see. Deeply religious, although not in a go-to-church-every-Sunday sort of way. A champion of women, to my very unexpected but welcome surprise. Hardworking and determined. Outspoken, to the point of embarrassing his adult children more often than not. Sick in body as a young adult, but strong enough in mind to live to near 84 years during a time when longevity was not a given. Yes, he was all of these things but most of all I found that Johannes was lonely, so very lonely.

How do I know all of this. He was long in heaven before I was born. Family lore provides a small glimpse through that shrouded window, but most of these observations have become apparent through his own writings. During the last dozen years of his life he reached out for companionship in his adopted hometown of Red Wing, Minnesota, by writing random thoughts on many aspects of his personal experiences in life and sending them to the local newspaper, the Republican. The newspaper began publishing them for the enjoyment of the readership. The letters caused no end of embarrassment to his adult daughters, who begged the newspaper not to print them. Their plea was denied, as the readership enjoyed them. The letters were always very opinionated, a few probably never saw the light of day. The majority, however, were published and, fortunately for us, they have been retrieved.

Physically, Johannes was an unhandsome fellow with a prominent nose, who stood about 5 feet 9 inches. He was multifaceted, with a good business head, considerable mechanical skills, shrewd, and with a very strong political view. There is no doubt Johannes was colorful and, in the end, that is what made him a person so interesting for all to know. To lose him to the past does not seem right. He does not deserve to be lost to time.

324

-THE IMMIGRANT-

Homeland and family

Johannes Johnson, born March 14, 1858, in his father's dwelling house on a mountain top near a small village in Sweden. Too small to find on a map, it was in the province of Varmland, north and a bit east of Karlstad, near Lake Grässjön, south of Hagfurs. It was no mansion, even though the kitchen was 'large enough to hold a team of horses'* *(as my father, Johannes' grandson, related to me on more than one occasion).* Farm animals were kept in the lower level of the house where the family also stored the food necessary to survive the harsh Swedish winters. The kitchen held a large fireplace where a fire was kept burning for cooking, summer and winter alike.

Johannes'parents, Johannes Johnsson and Maria Svensdötter farmed, if you could call it that. More, they eked out a living on the rock-infested soil. Neither of his parents had received any schooling.

Johannes was one of five brothers (one dying at age 5 months) and three sisters: Kajsa born Aug 13, 1853; Maria, born Jul 15, 1855; Johannes born Mar 14, 1858; Nils Magnus born Nov 11, 1860/died Apr 25, 1861; Sven born Apr 22, 1862, Kristina born Feb 13, 1865, Nils Magnus (same name as deceased older brother) born Oct 16, 1867; Otto Arvid born Aug 31, 1871; and Anders Gustaf born May 16, 1874. Johannes claimed he would take any licking from his father for all of his brothers and, reflecting back in later years, felt it made him the better person for it.

By his own account his schoolroom education totaled only 60 days! However, even though he lacked a regulation school primer, Johannes learned to read from the old family bible, the so-called "Charles the Twelfth Bible of 1736".

*(Author note: In 1999 when I was fortunate enough to visit this very old and long abandoned structure, I was particularly curious to check out this statement. Much to my amazement, it was true!)

His mother spun and wove their cloth. She made stockings for all 7 children. They never had a store bought pair. To obtain a nice suit from the local tailor a bushel of potatoes would have to be paid. To survive the long harsh Swedish winters they stored a thousand bushels of potatoes in the cellar, two barrels of Norwegian herring, 'enough lutefisk as a horse could pull over a strong road', a good sized pig, 'a couple of pigs dried as hard as basswood', and countless wild berries. Johannes never wore a pair of gloves or mittens on his hands in the old country. Hard to fathom in the bitter cold climate of his Scandinavian homeland. As very young children, all the siblings helped cut and dry hay for their sheep.

At the age of seven or eight to earn money, and knowing he wanted to be rich, Johannes pulled bark off of trees he burned to sell (a barker), and read for the local minister, walking miles to do this.

Johannes' birthplace, Värmland province, bordering Norway.

The family dwelling place, still standing,
on a mountain top, near Gräsmark,
Värmland, Sweden.
(Photo taken by author 1999).

Church in Gräsmark. Family members
buried in the cemetery. Johannes' family
would travel down the mountain to worship

A man at 14

On turning 14 years and able to read and write, Johannes thought himself a man and left home to look for work. Work meant money and earning it was his dream. He packed what little he owned into a cloth sack, with food for one meal, and told his mother not to cry because he would be back.

Heading north, he traveled 300 miles, going into Lapland where he helped to make charcoal, staying in unheated cabins where the morning frost covered everything, even the workmen's beards. Not much of a dream job. Making coal was about as far down on the scale as one could get.

In his own words Johannes explained he went so far north he could see the sun at 12:00 o'clock at night; so far south he could see the cattle feeding in the pastures on Christmas Day, so far east he could see the icebergs in Russia, and so far west they had goats instead of cows feeding on brush and moss.

His early years of wandering left plenty of time to reflect on those at home and what a good mother he had.

Fever

Returning on his 20th birthday, he was eagerly welcomed home. His mother was so proud of how he now looked in the nicer clothes he had acquired. She soon made arrangements for Johannes to begin studying to become a Lutheran minister, her dream for Johannes. (Johannes had a strong faith throughout his life which began at his mother's knee.) However, on the day he was to start school Johannes decided to follow his own dream, to become rich. On October 7, 1878 he left for America, his possessions few, future unknown. His father's last words to him as he left were 'don't give up my boy, whatever meets you in the new world.' He never saw his beloved mother or father again.

Along the way Johannes met up with a man he knew that would sneak tobacco over from Norway, Traveling with him to Christiana (now Oslo), Norway, the man kindly bought him a ticket to America and soon he was sailing on the North Sea, hanging over the rail and throwing up. Sailing for 24 days, he and the rest of the passangers had plenty of time to talk about home and mother.

-Establishment-

Red Wing, Minnesota – adopted home

Landing in Quebec, Johannes next rode in a cattle car heading west and south. Eventually he arrived in Milwaukee, Wisconsin where he boarded yet another train. He had intended to settle at Point Douglas on the Mississippi River, but since he knew no English he mistakenly got off the train at Red Wing, Minnesota. It was June 2, 1879. Johannes was 21 years old. He arrived with $6.00 in his pocket and a knapsack on his back. Walking in mud up to his ankles, he stopped at the Svea Hotel where he was charged $1.00 a day to stay.

Red Wing, a Mississippi River town. It evolved from being inhabited by Native Americans, to further discovery by white explorers, followed by missionaries, and then its first white settlers coming mostly from New England. It was in 1853 that the legal opening of the land for white settlement occurred and, thus, the influx of immigrants. It was made the county seat of Goodhue County in 1854, and was incorporated as a city in 1857.

By 1860 Red Wing had grown to a city of 1,251.

The 1870s brought the building of a railroad through town, and thus Red Wing's world prominence as a market for wheat. However, this soon declined when the railroad reached deeper into the prairies. Local clays provided a strong clay industry for the newly growing city, making stoneware from the high-grade clay, and bricks and sewer tiles from the lower grade of clay. Tanneries provided leather for shoemakers, and limestone quarries aided the local building industry.

In the early years of the 1880s disastrous fires occurred in Red Wing.

The year 1890 brought the greatest tragedy in the history of Red Wing, when the steamboat the Sea Wing, carrying approximately 200 passengers, capsized in a storm. The Mississippi River was patrolled for three days to recover bodies. Of the 98 people who perished, 71 of those were citizens of Red Wing. Funerals in Red Wing were held for four straight days, with the tolling of church bells practically constant.

Red Wing – 1875 and 1877

Red Wing mud blocadeon Christmas Day 1877
Mercury 44degrees below zero on Christmas Day 1879

Otto Arvid, Nils Magnus, Kristina, Anders Gustaf, Johannes
The five siblings who emigrated to America.

Jobs and pay

Johannes worked many jobs when he first arrived in Red Wing: as a farmhand, carpenter, stone mason, anything to make a living. He was hired out by a man called Pat for the railroad for three weeks at $1.25 a day. Farming came next for $3.00 a day and board to help with the harvest. On to Wisconsin where he cut cord wood for $.60 a cord. But now it is spring, so back to Red Wing. He looked into becoming a shoemaker but the wages wouldn't have been more than $7.50 a week so instead Johannes bought carpenter tools and taught himself carpentry. From carpentry he moved on to being a contractor, taking the job to remodel the Svea Hotel for $1.00 a day ($.50 in cash and $.50 in lumber).

Johannes also found time to 'rip rap' a 36-mile stretch of railroad track along Lake Pepin; to supply farmers in western Minnesota with snow fences; and to build some of the first boats in Red Wing, as he was a wonderful carver. These boats were Viking boats, row boats. The boats had sails, as well as four oars on each side so when he took someone out for a ride on Sunday, that person had to row if there wasn't any wind. He also built a replica of a Viking ship, complete with a dragon's head prow and tail at the stern.

Johannes eventually bought land on Sorin's bluff where he operated a quarry, not for the production of lime but for the production of stone. Many tons of stone were sold to the government for rip rap used along the river bank. Stones were carried down the quarry in very low wagons called stone bolts. This was a wagon with its bed only a foot above the ground for easy loading. While coming down the steep and winding quarry road, one of the wagon wheels would be chained so that it would not turn. This caused the team of horses to have to pull a little bit to get the load down the hill.

Working at the stone quarry. Johannes to the right of the horses, with the pointed hat, posing with arm in jacket.

Johannes, left side of picture, next to horse. Pointed hat, posing with arm in jacket.

RED WING STONE QUARRY

Johannes, farthest right, trowel in hand at a job site.

Sickness

Consumption! At the age of 21 and very sick, Johannes went to the doctor. The doctor listened to his chest and gave him a bottle of medicine (cod liver oil) and sent him on his way with no further explanation. Returning to the doctor the next day, Johannes demanded 'what is wrong with me?' The doctor finally confessed he had consumption (maybe cancer?). His life span would be very limited as one lung was gone and the other was diseased. On hearing this Johannes cried, but by that night he had decided not to feed his consumption/possible cancer with cod liver oil so he threw the bottle out the window, where it hit a wagon and shattered. He then began his own cure by taking up an outdoor life and cutting timber. He also turned to his faith, asking - no begging - God for just another 10 years. Johannes got those 10 years that he prayed for, and many more.

Mary

I have found two versions of when Johannes first saw his future wife. The first, a Sunday morning at the Vasa church (a small town settled by Swedes in 1853 about 12½ miles southwest of Red Wing), where he saw a 'beautiful girl' in a new lumber wagon with wooden spring seats, sitting next to her father, Bjorn Haller, who was dressed in clean overalls and holding the reins as tight as he could. To Johannes, Mary looked like a canary bird, dressed in calico with homespun woolen yarn trimming and, **most** importantly, 'without any red paint and flour on the cheek'.

In the second version, Johannes saw 'a pretty girl walking down the street' in Red Wing, 'the best looking girl I ever see in this world.' (Mary had come to Red Wing from her father's farm in Wanamingo, Minnesota, seeking employment as a seamstress. She learned sewing from her father who had been a tailor in Sweden.)

Whichever story it really was, Johannes told himself, "I am going to marry her." According to Johannes, Mary's reply when he asked her was, 'So far as I know, I can marry you tomorrow.' Johannes replied, 'Thank you.' They were married in Red Wing in April 1883 at the Swedish Evangelical Lutheran Mission church.

As was Johannes, Mary was also a native of Varmland, Sweden, born on April 15, 1860. She emigrated with her parents and siblings when she was just a child. One of her siblings died on the voyage, and was buried off the coast of Newfoundland. Another sibling was born on the journey.

Mary was, quite simply, the love of Johannes' life. She was a helpmate, a wonderful mother to their children, and kind to all with whom she came in contact, even to strangers who appeared at their door on a regular basis. There were 'hobo camps' along the river in those days where the homeless would sleep, using a stone under their heads. When they wanted something to eat, they would walk around town looking for a mark on the sidewalk, hobo language meaning a good place to ask for a meal. Mary had someone at her house all the time. She fed everybody, native Americans, homeless, all were made welcome. A fellow came to the house one time, wanting something to eat as he had not eaten for a couple of days, but he wanted to work for his meal. He insisted he would not eat unless she got some work out of him, so he cut the grass, on his knees using a sickle. Only then would he accept the food offered.

Johannes and Mary brought into the world 7 children, carefully choosing their names from the relations of the biblical Abraham – Rachel Marie, John Ephraim, Rebecca Elizabeth, Enoch Bjorn, Ruth Naomi, Gustave Emanual (who died in early childhood) and Martha Teresa.

When Johannes built Mary the home that was ever after known to all of us that followed as 'the big stone house', there was a nice birch tree where Johannes intended to put the front porch of the home. Here, in Johannes' own words (and his unique phonetic spellings): *"And when I kum to the porch the old burch tree was in the way so I giv orders to kut down. But then mi wife kum and said, "bild as yu plees, but I am the bos over the burch tree" and we chewed rags for a few minutes and I said, "if yu dont giv me ani reason that wil go down" and she said, "that tree is going to watch yu when I am gone," so that burch tre has watched me better than the chief and al the poleesemen in Red Wing. That only tuk a nap once and that was when I married the second time."**

*(Author note: A second marriage for Johannes in 1920, more than likely entered into out of shear loneliness, was shortlived, lasting less than a year. Johannes was to lament the remainder of his days about this being one of his biggest mistakes in life.)

In the fall of 1915 Mary went to the local doctor about a small sore on her upper left gum. It was diagnosed as a malignancy. In March Mary received treatment at Mayo Clinic in Rochester, Minnesota, 50 miles away. Again, in the summer of 1916 with increased pain, Mary was hospitalized in Rochester at Mayo's hospital for surgery. She had an uneventful recovery and returned home. However, the cancer continued to spread, causing her to lose one eye, and she died May 18, 1917, leaving Johannes behind, and forever after very lonely.

Johannes and Mary

Wedding 1883

His Beloved Mary

. . . a young girl - 1877

...before her death in 1917 from epithelioma of the upper jaw and cheek, which extended upward and destroyed her eye.

… with her youngest son, Enoch.

… with her oldest grandchild, Sam Blondell.

… with her oldest daughter, Rachel Johnson Callender.

Johannes Johnson's Family

back left:
Enoch, Rachel, Ephraim

front left:
Rebbecca, Mary (wife), Johannes, Martha (on lap), Ruth

The five adult children of Johannes and Mary.
L to R: Martha Teresa, Ruth Naomi, Enoch Bjorn, Rebecca Elizabeth, Rachel Marie
(Son John W Ephraim died in the 1918 swine flu epidemic)
Date: circa 1960s

The Stone House

The house at 657 East Seventh Street, just east of Memorial Drive, was built for his wife Mary in the early 1900s.

As a young 'newcomer' to Red Wing Johannes noticed a large old birch tree growing on a knoll on East 7th street and he thought to himself, "here is where I wish to build my home."

Twenty years later, after much hard work, he bought the knoll, along with the lime quarries on Sorin's bluff above it. The stone used in the house came from the quarry. He put 50 windows in to allow as much light and sunshine as possible into his home. One of the downstairs rooms had 7 windows. The glass was shipped from France. He put 32 corners on the roof and two sets of wide cornice to protect the walls from both snow and rain. He made the front door of 2 inch thick solid oak. The hearth in the fireplace downstairs was raised.

The big stone house Johannes built in1905 for Mary. The stone came from the quarry on the bluff behind the house.

Located behind the stone house, Johannes lived here in 1935 and 1936. Referred to as stüga (cottage). Photo taken early 1940s.

The Castle

Johannes was greatly interested in collecting antiques and coins and owned an extensive collection of Swedish relics, displayed in the 'Swedish Castle" which he had built on the summit of Sorin's Bluff. Reference has been made that Johannes was the first antique collector in that town. The 'castle' was a duplicate of a Norwegian stave church he had once seen. Johannes carried all of the material needed to build the structure up to the top of the bluff on his back.

Many parties were held at the Swedish Castle by Johannes' daughters, with Chinese lanterns strung along the road leading up to the structure. The parties consisted of plain simple games and good clean fun. Johannes also used the 'castle' to entertain local elected officials – the mayor, the city council, etc. All of the food and utensils necessary for these social gatherings were carried up to the top of the bluff by his wife, Mary.

Because of it's location the structure was difficult to patrol by the city police. The building was vandalized many times, and valuable relics were stolen. One story told by his son Enoch related to a banjo from the 'castle'. 'Nick' came across a fellow in Red Wing one day attempting to sell a banjo. Nick, himself a musician, knew there weren't many banjos in town in those days and asked him where he got it. He replied some kids had stolen it from the 'castle' and sold it to him. Nick took the banjo from him and smashed it against a tree and said, "Go and get your money back. I know where that banjo came from! It came from the top of the hill."

The structure eventually fell into disrepair, and Johannes had it torn down. All that remains of it today is its stone foundation.

"SWEDISH CASTLE" - Orville Keiran
(also called "Johannes' Castle")

-The Philospher-

Introduction

Enjoy the following letters* for their down to earth simplicity, yet timeless common sense. Find in them something of value, or find nothing in them but rants from an old man. Call him smart, stupid, funny, crazy, foolish, childish or any other term you wish. Johannes is long beyond caring.

Two personal notes to you the reader from Johannes, foreseeing the future -

". . . and to yu peepel that dont want to reed mi leters, the generashuns that aint born yet mite want to reed it." (1934)

"I meen wel and I want to be a frend to yu al and mi leter mite be reeded when neether me nor Republican isn't here." – Thursday, June 14, 1934

*Author note: It appears that during the early days of publishing the letters, the newspaper edited them to some extent for spelling and punctuation. However, when the newspaper gave Johannes his 'own' column in the Red Wing paper, called "Johannes Says" the editing of his letters pretty much ceased and were published exactly as Johannes wrote them, using his own phonetic spellings. He wrote just the way he spoke. Additionally, although many of the letters are dated and are presented chronologically, a good number are not dated and are presented in no particular order.

Also note Johannes uses the word 'forout' numerous times throughout. He means to say 'without'.

Johannes Johnson,

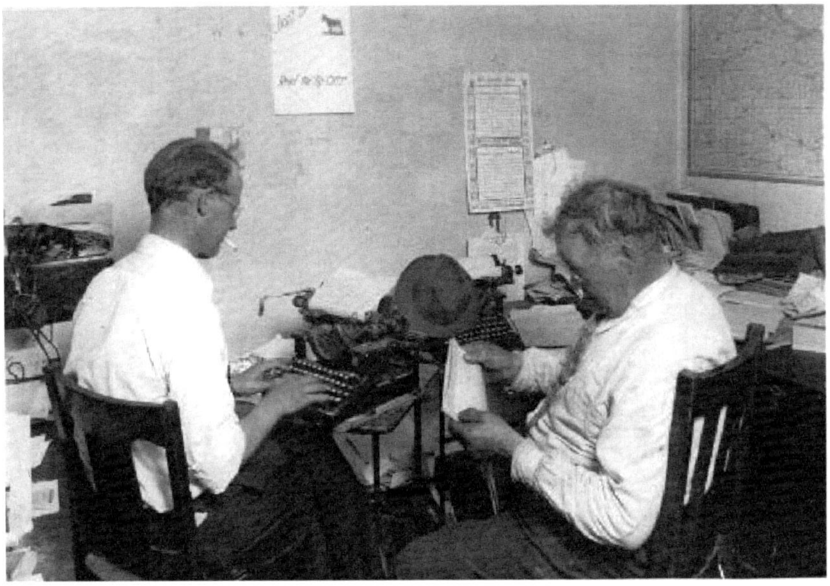

the immigrant philosopher

1858-1942

The Letters

1.
Wednesday, September 3, 1930
Mr. Republican
I wish to write something that will be some good after I'm gone. I been a landlord in Red Wing for more than 45 years and lots of tenants wouldn't pay, and lots owe me for building material and work. Here is the receipt in full for all that's over five years old. I wish you will take care of it. The way it looks, my children are going to be better collectors than I be. And if I happen to meet some of you in the coming world, I don't want you to owe me anything and we are just as good friends. And those little things don't amount to much a hundred years from now, just so we got the understanding. And to you that pay me the rent, I appreciate it. You are the ones that feed me and pay my taxes and bought gas for my car and grease it when it gets dry.

With love to you,
Johannes Johnson

2.
There is one word that I hear wherever I go.

"That's different now." Last week I was up to the cities and I went into a church and the last word in every song was "There is difference now." And when the minister started to preach there was the same thing, "There is difference now." That made me think back half a hundred years when I was young, good-looking boy and had a good bright voice in my throat. But that's different now.

That world is now behind, and she was full of sorrow and hard labor. Fifty years ago, we used to travel fifty miles to hear a good minister, but there is difference now. We can sit in our room and hear the best minister in the country. We can grab the phone and talk to anyone we want to. A wonderful world. Fifty years ago, we used to have a wheelbarrow in every back yard. Now we got a thousand dollar car. And we pay so much a month. Horses and pigs ride better than they used to fifty years ago. Fifty years ago, the ships used to sail on water. There is difference now, they sail in the air. But for all the wonderful things I see and hear about, my mother told me as a child, that God sent His only Son down to a sinful world to save us. I can't understand it and sometimes hard to believe it and God said it Himself, and if I get into Heaven, that will be wonderful to see. But the most wonderful will be that I am there, myself. But some of you folks that can read Greek and Latin, you might understand it better.

Johannes Johnson

3.

Editor The Republican

I am proud to have been under your press twice, and I will try the third time with my sixty days education. Don't ask so much, but I feel it will be fun for you to listen to an old man. How different we can see and how different ideas we have. I can see dust in my minister's eye, but I can't see and know that I got a big square timber in my own eye. Millions are spent and good brains working to find a way to make the world bone dry.

Now I want to tell you my idea. If I had the power, I would set a barrel of good whiskey with the dipper hanging on the outside on the best business corner in town and tell the drinkers to drink all they want. If they got drunk I would not tell the policemen to pick them up and instead of bringing them to jail and spend an attendance bill on them, I would take them back to the barrel and make them drink more. If they wouldn't mind, I would give them the same medicine as gave the mules in the olden times, the best my father gave me was the licking. We were six boys and I took the lickings for all of them, but I think I am the best boy of them all. Every time I got a licking I felt like a new boy. Lick your boys first, teach them to work. When they have learned what the dollar is worth, help them all you can, and don't be stingy.

I don't think that it does any good to the moonshiners to go to jail and let them rest up for a couple of months. To build additions to jails and to hire officers cost money. And that will take up more such bad people. They have as many good sides as you and me. I see drinkers staggering along the sidewalks, stopping for a blind man or a Salvation Armyist, giving them a quarter, maybe their last one.

After him comes a minister or a professor walking by so straight as their backbones were cast in one piece. The drunkards are related to Adam and Eve. What we can't get, we want. They had two boys. One of them would mind and the other wouldn't. Maybe one got the licking for both of them, and that time hasn't changed so much as women's dresses and the drinks. Fifty years ago the ladies dresses dragged three feet behind and wide as a box car. Now when the ladies sit down, they have to pull with both hands and the best they can do is get their skirt three inches above the knee. Where is the rest of the clothing? The millionaires got that and built sky-scrapers and chain stores with them. Fifty years ago our drinks were good, big and cheap. Now they are a thimbleful. Just like poison. But we got to have it because we can't get it. Where is the rest of our drinks? The lawyers and judges and all kinds of officers got them and stocked in their storeroom for a rainy day.

How many lawbreakers did we have when it was wet? How many have we got now? How many saloons did we have? How many we got now? How many breweries did we have and how many have we go to now? How many officers have we got and where do they get their pay? The fines don't pay it. The only thing we got left is the church member. When is that going to be wet? When the ministers and best church members go together and vote just as hard to get it wet as they did to get it dry? This is my belief but you folks don't need to believe the same as I. The times will tell and heal up all the sores.

Johannes Johnson

4.

Mister Republican

When we go out on a clear evening, we can see seven stars together. They represent seven men in the war who were tired out and crawled into a cave and went to sleep for 700 years. When they woke up, they went down town to buy something to eat. They didn't know the town. They didn't know the clothes on the people. When they was paying for the meal, they shook their heads when they found out their money was no good.

Now-a-days, we don't need to sleep more than overnight. When we wake up, the whole town might be swept away. A fast, wonderful world, but dreaming. Fifty years ago, we moved a bluff with wheelbarrows and we got many acres cut down fifty feet that prove that can be done. Now we wash them down with water. If we can't we put the harness on the lightning (*dynamite*) and tear out a thousand tons at a time. A fast, wonderful world, but dreaming.

You take six months trip through the country where a mountain sheep can't walk. You come back and ride on a paved road in a glass cage ten times better than the Queen of Sheba had when she came to Solomon to find out if it was true that she heard about him. A fast, wonderful world, but dreaming.

When we get the evening of our life and look back, it looks like a dream, and we can dream and dream and dream us into Hell, but we can never dream us into Heaven. We got to be awake and watch every step and dress in the right clothing and show the right paper from the right judge.

The next neighbor to lovers' park.
Johannes Johnson

5.
Mr. Republican
Will you please tell your readers how I feel on my 71st birthday?

The first birthday I can remember, I was sitting beside my Mother and the spinning wheel. She told me about old man Abraham, not Abraham Lincoln. My mother did not know anything about him, but that old Abraham that did everything that God told him to do. One time, God told him to kill his only son and he grabbed a knife and was ready to do it, so God had to tell an angel to grab his hand, and gave him a buck to kill instead. My Mother said, "I want to do all that God wants me to do but I could never kill you."

On my 14th birthday, I thought I was a man and as a man, that it was my duty to pull out of the nest and make my own living. I had a sixty day education. I could read and write just as good as my father. Everything was packed in a sack. I kind of looked it over. There was the book about Abraham and his own relation.

I landed 300 miles in the north with Laplanders and Finlanders. So I had plenty of time to think over, I had a good mother. So I got pretty good posted (*educated*), way back in time.

On my 20th birthday I was back to my mother and she was proud of me and my clothes. She said I should be a minister and everything was ready to start the school, but I seen that there was so many rich people in that Abraham relation and I desired to be rich. The same day I should start the school, I took a sneak to America. Here I have half a hundred birthdays, but not one so good as with my mother and the spinning wheel.

I brought into this world six children. I picked out the names from Abraham's relations but they (the grandsons' names) are more stylish. They (my children) call their children Sammy, Buxie and Seetsie, but I am proud of my birthday. I think I can beat anyone in my relation cutting cord wood. I just finished six cords, and pulling it home with a cow rope. So I got wood to the next birthday, if I live.

In the afternoon of my birthday I was surprised by six good ladies. They brought cake and sunshine. In the evening I was surprised by a dozen men. They brought Copenhagen snuff and drinks. They wish me some ten and some fifteen birthdays, but I wish 72 more.

I suppose my report isn't worth much to the most of you. But a pail of water isn't worth much in the middle of the ocean, but in Hell it is worth one million for a drop.

Johannes Johnson

6.

Mr. Republican

Would you please let me in one of your outside corners? I want to tell your readers about my third vacation. I went east as far as Chicago, and six miles inside the city limits. And I got cold feet and cleared out and looked at the cars. It seems to me that half of Chicago was filled with cars and policemen. And I didn't see more than two old cars. And one of them was mine. He (my car) wasn't used to those red and green lights. He got excited and jumped like a rabbit. But we both pulled out and next was Milwaukee where I got two daughters *(Ruth Johnson and Rachel Johnson Callender)* and a son-in-law *(Billy Callender)* that runs a factory with 150 employees. But no, he said, "I got only one made besides the watchman." So I didn't ask him about the time. I asked about the good beer they used to have. "We got it," he said, and opened a bottle and asked, "How did you like it?" The beer is alright to get for nothing, but it is only imitation. We stayed in Milwaukee seven days and looked at red and green lights 'til the eyes got sore.

And that was all we had time to see and I thought to myself I would sooner be a king with the pigs than a pig with the kings. And I carry respect for Red Wing, Hager, and Wacouta. We don't need to sleep half way to the moon *(in tall buildings)* and if we want to go out of town we don't need to drive for eight or ten miles. I'm like a rabbit. I like my home. And so far, I see no place nicer than Red Wing. Now we get the old car and go home. He went 50 or 55 miles and our next stop was Eau Claire, where I bought my first wedding suit 48 years ago. And that part of town where I got my suit is getting old, but the other part of town has improved wonderful. So has the graveyard. Couple hours later, we stop at Hager hill and when I saw Red Wing I thought it was Jerusalem and I told the old car to go slow, we got plenty of time.

Half an hour later we were home and we were glad. And now to you farmers, be proud over your farm and home, but don't forget the one that chops the wood and hauls it for two dollars a cord, and grubs the stumps by hand, who makes it smooth for your machinery,. To you citizens, be proud over your parks and public buildings but don't forget the one that sent you money and gave you a lift. And to you church members, be proud over your church. That is the best place to go Sunday, when you got the best clothes on. But don't forget the old honest people that laid the foundation. To you poker players and moonshiners, quit your business and stay home with your family and don't forget that you'll have more money and a better home.

Johannes Johnson

7.

To the Editor of the Republican

I am more than thankful to you for letting me talk to the young people. When we get old, we want to talk so much and it is so easy to remember fifty years ago, and I want to tell the boys where we used to find the best and nicest girls at that time. We used to go out Sunday morning to the Vasa church and see the well fed and lively horses come pulling a new lumber wagon with wooden spring seats. Up in the air setting a stylish father dressed in clean overalls, holding the reins as tight as he could. Beside him sat a girl like a canary bird, dressed in calico with homespun woolen yarn trimming without any red paid and flour on the cheek. I picked out the best one, I think.

I used to tread in the mud over my ankles when I went to see her. I asked her if she would come to Red Wing to marry me. "Yes, but that cost money." "I know it, but I have a foreman's job at Foot's shop and I get seven and one-half dollars a week, so I can take care of you." "Yes," she said. "I can get a place to work down there for a dollar and a half a week, but there are six children in the family, so there would be lots to do, but I will come if you want me." And in six months we were ready for marriage and she had a couple of trunks full of things a good lady needs for housekeeping. I had made most of the furniture we needed, and we both were satisfied and thought we were rich. The honeymoon lasted clos to 40 years. After that was the end of my good life. I was left alone and all my children grew up and left. I wasn't so well acquainted in the church as I was forty years ago. That long honeymoon made one forget the church, so I picked up one *(another marriage)* on the road between the moonshiner and the poker player, and I wasn't any good at those places. It takes educated and smart people in that company.

There was a call for (*the new wife wanted*) an electric stove, electric iron, electric washer, electric curling iron, and the hair was cut off the same as mine. Electric pancake turner I couldn't find. New Studebaker sedan so they could be acquainted in Wisconsin and Minnesota. Boys, it cost more to get rid of them (*divorce*). Boys, I hope you don't make any mistake like I did. It took me half of my life to know I had a good mother and father. But you boys who had to go to war, it didn't take you long to learn that. And that is a good thing to know at home.

I sit her alone on my 71st birthday, thinking if some of those wise men could find a way through the skies to Heaven. So I wouldn't have to die. That would save trouble for those who have so much to do.

Johannes Johnson

8.
To the Editor of the Republican
As I am a half a hundred years' settler of Red Wing, wouldn't you please let me talk to the public? Don't do like you used to do and throw me in your waste basket. I want to be responsible for my talk. Even if you do with me the same as you did with our Saviour. I haven't got so far to go so that won't make so much difference. I want to tell the young generation when I had the best time in this city.

Forty-eight years ago, I worked for ninety cents a day, chopped wood for sixty cents a cord, got seven pounds of sugar for one dollar, ten cents a box for matches, but one match was enough to light the pipes of three Irishmen and five Swedes, and I didn't owe one dollar in the city. I could afford to buy a three dollar doll for my baby. Today, I got thirty thousand dollars worth of property in Red Wing. I have a hard time to buy hard bread for my two dogs, but I do like you folks do, ride in a swell car. Today, I had a letter from the bankers, grocers, water bill, gas bill, and a whole lot of other trash, I did the same as you folks do. I took the money I had and went and paid on my car. I know they can take the car, but the groceries, gas and water are all gone. If you young folks will take the advice of an old man who went through the mill, never lie for a banker or a banker's robber. If the banker said he'd help you out he will do so. If the robber said he would kill you, you can depend on him. I have lots to say, but I hate the big waste basket the wise men have, and some of them use tobacco too. I have built many homes in Red Wing. I tried to level off the south side of Barns Bluff and the north side of Sorin's Bluff. Now I live where my cow used to live and all who want to call on me are welcome. And I can show you some coins, some are three hundred years old.

Johannes Johnson

9.
Mr. Republican
One evening a friend came and call on me. He feel good but I don't think he had what some call "a bean on" (*drunk*). I told him to sit down. He said, "Here you built this house and put seven windows in one room. What did you do that for if you wasn't dumb?" "The light doesn't cost me anything and I figure it would be just as light outside." He said, "You can never sell this house." That might be, but my kids are pretty good to sell what they don't like, and the bankers is good to sell and the county got a man that we call the sheriff. He can sell most anything."
He said, "All those old bugs know is to drive an ox team and tell other things about 50 years ago." Now, that's more than you young folks can do. And what Red Wing will look 50 years from now, we don't know either of us.

But if you sit down a few minutes more I will tell difference 50 years ago and now. Fifty years ago one father could support ten children. Now ten children can't support one father. Fifty years ago we never used to cook lots and throw it in the back yard and hire an officer (*garbage collector*) to haul it away so we don't get sick from the smell. And we used to read at the table and thank God for giving us the food. Now we have to listen to the radio advertising face powder, tooth powder and fly powder, and ladies' stockings in 127 different colors.

Fifty years ago when we got our pay we used to go to the grocery store. Now we go to the filling station and tire shop and garages. If we got any money left when we go home we stop (at a bar) and if we don't we go pass by. And if Mr. Grondahl (*the editor of The Republican*) don't choke me to death in the waste basket, I will tell more of the same thing the next time.

Good luck and best wishes to all The Republican readers.

Johannes Johnson

10.
Dear Mister Republican
We had a conference in Swede Hill about all kind of drinking. And how peeple get snakes and I was acting as the judge and I want to give my report to my good friend Republikan.
Alkohol is the cleanest and most necessary for our body and we can not live without it but we can not drink it like water. It is to good and to rich. If we drink to much of it we get snakes and we dy. Kafe is a good drink especially in the morning, but we cannit drink six or ten cups of it at once and wash our head with what we get left in the can. We get dark as an Indian and we get snakes an we dy. Beer is a good drink but we kannit drink a barrel at once, that is so weak it takes up so much room so we get stomach layk a cow and our kidneys wear out an d we get snakes and we dy. And a hundred other drinks that I aint eduket enough to describe, but I know that they are all good if you don't misuse them and if you thank God for your drink and use them rayt Uncle Sam would not take no drinks away from you. I had snakes myself so I know something about it, but not from drinking, but from work. I had plenty property and I did want 20 more. I was in such a hurry and I went up to my own table hungry when I had plenty to eat. That was nothing more than snakes that bothered me, but the assessor of Red Wing and what some call deadbeats they cure me so I am through and now I thank God for what I got and for what I get. A young healthy calf drink so much he gets snakes and die, but we will excuse him for a man got his brain in good order.

Johannes Johnson

11.
Mister Republican
Would you please let me talk to some truck drivers and some speed drivers and some that think they are high-toned sports? The way you look when you are driving is like you are seven years old. You think you own the street. I just want to tell you the streets are for the public and you are supposed to look out for everybody but everybody has to look out for you. You don't need to show us that you got four-wheel brakes. Lots of church members have depended on the church and the minister and landed in Hell and lots of drivers have depended on four-wheel brakes and landed in the same place.

Fifty years ago we had an old shoe (*break*) rubbing on the five-feet high wheel and we was high up in the air and we didn't need to be scared. If we promised to be to a place we was there just the same.

Now if you should like to know who paid for the streets the way they look. It was a whole lot of old gubs like me that paid the taxes for a half a hundred years. Now they make machines to do the work with. This is good works and an easy life as long as they last.

Johannes Johnson

12.
I took a day off to try to figure out the reasons we can't pay our bills and I started with the farmers. They all refused to pay. My table was covered with figures and I was tired and went to sleep. And when I wake up it was like a crow been walking under my fingers. And I wiped my glasses and put them on. There stood too big farms, too much machinery, too much lazy people and too much money.

I started off to figure out what the big farmers wanted, according to time and that amounted to be between eight and 10 thousand dollars and that farmer had much money, too good credit or else couldn't buy so much. The first farmers God sent out, Adam and Eve, He give them orders to work, sweat and worry and he gave them Canada thistle instead of machinery. I don't think that God made machinery to crawl on the bottom of the sea or to fly in the air. I think some one made them that fooled Adam and Eve. God helps the ones that helps themselves. He made the machines for the fish and the birds and they get along good and he gave me two good legs and feet. And they was good so long as I used them but the last ten years I had to do as the rest of the people do. I got too much money. I burn up two dollars a week for gas and wear out the car every two years. If I don't wear them out, somebody knocks them out (*runs into them*).
How can I pay my bills? And what I drink I don't want to say anything about, but 50 years ago they could sell two good glasses of beer for five cents. Now you pay 25 cents and you have to have the hook on the door and look through the windows before you straighten your neck and drink it out. Fifty years ago you could get a barrel of flour ground for a dollar. Now according to the price you pay $3.50 and give away three grades of lower flour and give away screenings, shorts and the bran.

There must be something wrong in Denmark when all get so much money. And to you who read it that don't like to hear 50 years ago, please excuse me. I will tell some reason. I was 14 pounds when I was born and I had to be born straight and no professor has cultivated my brain. My eyes and ears and my mouth being a good helper. I always been quick to say no when most of them say, "Yes, yes, that's right."

With love to you all, the prisoner of Swede Hill.
Johannes Johnson

13.

Dear Mr. Republican

I have been in the cities (*Twin Cities*) for a few days looking up old friends and hunting for antiques. I bought some and when I got home and look it up, some of it wasn't older than my baby, but the business men call it antique and that past to a Swede at that. My friend said, "They got smarter people up here." They thought that would be a better place to live. I said, "Don't the people do any mistakes up here?" I don't know any certain mistake. I look through the window over the Mississippi River and said, "What became of them piers that used to stand in the river so many years?" He answered, "They tore them down." "Do you know how much that cost?" "Yes, that cost 16,000 dollars." "How much did that cost to build it?" "That cost 85,000 dollars." "Who paid for it?" "Oh, I don't know. Lots of people, poor working men got jobs." "Don't you think that Kaiser made a mistake when he tried to lick the whole world?" "He couldn't lick the American boys. He killed a few of them." One fellow bust out and left and said, "If you are interested in mistakes, I like to tell you one! We got a nice farm that we call the poor farm. A wonderful place for poor people. They bought a bull for 2,000 dollars, and sold it for 90 dollars. And the calf they traded away to other farmers for scrub stock. Now they are going to quit the farm and pay the poor people so much a day." I said, "That would be fine if they get a good bookkeeper."

Now we are on the depot waiting for the train. My friend begged me to move up there. I said, "When I move from Red Wing, I move to Heaven." He said, "Maybe you will have to move to the rich man that asked Lasarus for a drop of water." I said, "You know the rich man had five brothers and he wanted Lasarus to give warning. You are an educated man, can you tell me the name of them five?" I can tell you my belief. One I call Prohibition, one I call Bankers, one I call Lawyers, one I call Doctors. How about the young brother? I think I would call him a Plumber. Here comes a stylish man hollering like he had his head in an empty barrel, going east to Hastings and Red Wing. Then I took my junk and run. Now I am home carrying spilt milk.

Your friend,
Johannes Johnson

14.
Mister Republican
Last Sunday I took the day off to think about olden times and look at the now days traffic. My cat has crossed the street and it took her half an hour and she had to risk her life to get back. It seems to me that young folks got the pleasure to turn the wheel to a cat or a dog, and sing a daily song, "Step on the Gas". There are lots of roads but our life got only two, one to Heaven and the other to Hell and you get fast enough down hill for to step so hard on the gas. And the other road goes up. Be sure to have plenty gas and good breaks so you don't go backwards.
A half of hundred years ago we wasn't in such a hurry. We used to walk up to the gashouse and city hall and throw stones at the wild ducks. Walking East Seventh Street down to Sand Brook.
In Swede Hill stood the birch tree that leads up to my porch today that had three signs on. "Go to Foot for boots and shoes," and one below, "Go to Clauson for dry goods and carpets," and the third one "Go to Ingseth for fly powder."

Then I build my porch and I was going to cut that old homely birch tree out, but my wife, Mary, said "NO". I want her to give the reason. She said, "That birch tree are going to watch you when I am gone." The birch tree and me had many hard storms, but so old and homely, we are both here. I think the birch tree took a nap when I married the second time.

Johannes Johnson

15.
Mr. Republican
I want to thank you for being so good to me when I get my talking spells and thank you for what you drop in the waste basket. I don't want to hurt your family. You know it takes all kinds of people to make a whole world. Some of your readers come and shake my hand and tell me to keep on telling the truth and we know that children and fools always tell the truth.
Some of my relations don't want to know the difference between 50 years and now. I want to tell so they all hear it and I want Hell and Heaven to hear it.
Fifty years ago, I was a bright-looking man, well-known by lots of ministers and church members, who had will and power to build the foundation for the church and pay for it, and furnish the minister and his wife with all the shoes he could wear. Me and my wife could afford to pay a weekly salary to the church. I had time to go to the hospital and see the sick, and to the poor and give him a lift. And the world was full of honest people. Now I hunt for them. They are hard to get acquainted with. They are so quiet and the world think they know so little. And I am forgetting of both ministers and church members. And the poker player I never got acquainted with. I am without education and it takes a smart man to make a living playing poker.
My treasury is empty and I become property poor. That's the same as walking on crutches and carrying a sore leg. Maybe it will heal up and maybe not. That depends on the chain bank and how much money the robbers get out of the bank. And the wine barrel can get empty if everybody knows where it is. Now the young educated people take up your pencils and figure the reason I want to mention 50 years ago. I wish to have money so I could offer to live 50 years more to see how you boys get along, but if Goodhue County raise the taxes the next 50 year the same as they did the last fifty, I think you boys wouldn't ride so fast as you do now.

Johannes Johnson

16.
Mr. Republican
I got an extension to my writing 50 years ago and now I want to mention four girls. A boy asked a girl to go with him to a dance. She said, "I should say not." He want to know the reason.
"You smell whiskey. I will not go with a drunkard and I will not marry one."
The girl could smell good 50 years ago. Her neighbor friend asked the same from their friends. She said, "No, the last time was enough for me."
"What's the reason?"
"You drove too fast. You lick the horse and you was mean to both the horse and me."
Them two girls had a home education from the first members of the Vasa Church.

Fifty years later I listened to two other girls. When all liquor was strictly forbidden by United States law. The boys said, "Would you please go with me to a barn dance?" "Have you got the bottle? Let me see. Have you got plenty of cigarettes. I think I'll go with the other fellow. He's got a bigger bottle and a better car."
The other girl was asked by a boy to dance, she said, "Where is your car?"
"Right there." "What you take me for? Do you think I will ride in a Ford? I can go with a moonshiner that got a Hudson six. He can go 70 miles an hour and kill all the people and chickens in the road, and wreck a fender off your car and don't need to stop."
Who is to blame for the difference in those two girls? I think those later girls had too good a mother and they quit to go to church too soon. Some people get so educated so they don't want any religion. And they don't need it to rob a bank, but if you want to go to Heaven you got to be religious.

So far as I know the Devil, I can't blame him for all the bad that goes on. He don't lie every word. He makes it through mixing together for to get us to believe it. That is from him, so the milk men learn to mix the milk.

We remember those temperance speakers some years ago. What they promise. There was a good mixture. Figure out if it went as they said. The Devil said to them, take the drinks away from the people, you can chase them like sheep into Heaven. Now you can't chase them or beg them to go to church.

Give the people freedom. Let those that want to drink, drink, and there would not be half the drinking there is now. And we better quit trying selling hats to the Eskimos.

Johannes Johnson

Author note: Hereafter the letters were published as written by Johannes, without editing.

17.
Mr. Republican
I haven't had a yob for 15 yers. I getting too old and nobody want me. I tol I kud yust as well figure out how many kind of rich people we got in dis kuntry. I started wid figures that I lerned from fader and muder, but dey didn't go up high nuf. So I trid those big machines that take 8 yard of dirt in der mout and spit it out over de hill.

And den I trid de oder new small machin but I had to have a rist watch and a diamond ring. And I didn't have eider one, so I found an old machin that most of de olde settlers brot wid (*a wheelbarrow*). Dat didn't take up much room and anybody dat wanted to use it kud use it widout big education and day used to kall it commen sense. And now I going to giv yu the figures and if yu don't lik it, yu do like the big machin and spit it out over do hill.

Der is only 2 kind of rich peepel. One kind got mor big American dollars dat the kuntryu got blackbirds. But dey isn't satisfied. Dy vish for mortgag in both Heaven and Hel.

By dey are smart. Dey vant one place for deir friends and one for deir enemies. De oder kind got al de muney dey tink dey need, so dey aint so particular if dey giv avay a dolar to de von dey no ned it and dey are satisfied. And yo always find dey got gud healt and bot God and de poepel like dem.

And ve vish dey wud nefer die. Now if you vant to be rich, wich part wud yu study for? And we got only 2 kinds of por peepel. One kind ve kal por and de oder kind ve kal property por. Vun kind of por peepel nefer had anything and nefer tried to get anything. Dey handle de big American dolar like it was a broken pants buten, but dey drink for de last quarter dey got and expect de kuntry to feed deir kids and bi silk stockings for de muder.

De oder kind of por peepel hav vorked hard al deir lives, safed every nickel, paid deir bills and bot a farm for $20,000 and paid de $10,000 cash. Now de farm is wirt $5,000 and what dey raise on de farm is wirt next to nutin. And de taxes isn't paid and de land goes bak to de state. What simpati have de officers for dose por peepel and what are de stat goin to do wid de land? When our stumick gets empty and our kids holler for bred what kan we do? Let us tri sumting, even if ve hav to close up de oil stations and start saloon instead. I tink de prohibition maid a mistak when dey tied up the peepel and let de Devil loose. And I tink ve better send de steam shovel back de vay it kum frum and mak dem giv us de weelbarrow back. Kaiser make a mistak when started to lik de hole wurld and I tink ve maid a mistak when ve run our kuntry wid gas and electric and let de por wuking man stand and luk and cri when the work goes on.
And to you readers deir is hard to explain tings to a edukated wurld when I aint got any education miself but if you don't lik *(what I write)* do lik dat big machin, let yur jaw drop and spit it over de hill and if you find sum gud let dem read it in Washington.

With luv to de hole territory of De Republican.
Johannes Johnson

18.
Master Republikan
I heard so much talk and so much ideas about the swimming pool in Colville Park so I think that it is a fool's duty to butt in and let the public know what you tink about it. You all know what I tink do not amount to much. I getting old and don't care what you think. If I am dumb I want you all to know it because that don't make no difference 100 years from now. I look after the work free of charge. I like to learn and according to the time and style I think that it couldn't be made any better, all is made by figures and hard labor. I look for some lazy man but didn't see one. They all poured concrete like mules. But I for my part, I do not believe in either concrete or iron. I never see iron that wouldn't rust or concrete that wasn't imitation stone and peole after us are going to see many fall like taor of babble *(Tower of Babel)* fall and in our future we are going to learn from the old Romans build stone and piers over all opening. I like to invite you all to the first building on the State School. That is Roman style and the man that builded it loosed all that he earned all of his life, but if he could look up of his grave and see the building he would say I made a good job anyhow. If I and the poser and the saying like some of you folks got, I would put the swimming pool on the west of Sorin Bluff close to the water tank, use the same water and according to my figures, the cost would be half and the mosquito wouldn't be one tenth. They aint so much trick to get what our neighbor got, but get what our neighbor can't get. If we had it over the city hanging in iron chains from one bluff to the other, the people would come from Jerusalem and Alaska to take a swim. Now days it got to be something extra and some humbug with if we going to get any kick out of it. I wish you all will excuse me, a fool always wants to come back.

Johannes Johnson

19.
Mister Republican
We had a confrence in east end a few days ago – different men, boys and women. We try to figure out between ourself who had be the best yob in the state. Sum said the governor and sum said de judges, sum said the moonshiner because the officer give dem chance to rest up and ve cud not agree.

Ve vas clos to get in a fite. Deir sat de old man in de corner – too old to raise up, and moss starts to gro on his bak. And he said deir aint any use to fite about dat. I kan tel yu whogot de best and de wurst yobs. De best yob is hed engineer for de highway department. He goes wherever he please. He don't need to kare for de kost. He pay what he wants and nobody kno what mistake he made and everybodi thik he no it al. De von dat got the wurst yob Is de *(h)*onest minister. He works for one dat nos everything. He nos even what he tinks. He have to be in de cort if he leads any church member on de sideroad and he got only von tool to work with, dat old sord dat is sharp on bot edges. But peepel get so use to it dat dey pay no attention to it and de hiest professor vant to tak it avay frum him. And sum of de church members vant him to hide it and kep it under de koat. And his rite pay check he dont get befor he is thru wid de yob and dat vil be accordin to how faitful he been in his work.

Wid love to yu al,
Johannes Johnson

20.
Mister Republican
Would you please let me tell the public some of my wishes. When we get old we get some funny wishes and we want to put our nose in everything and you all now that don't do us any good. But we wish, just the same.

I wish that the ambulance would be free that everybody that need him 15 miles around our home town. I wish when a doctor get called to go and help a child to be born in this world and he refused to go, he shall lose his license forever. And I wish that the ministers be more carful who they marry and never refuse to bury anybody.

And I wish when a mother had ten children, she should have a thousand dollars apiece for what she have more. And every lady who wouldn't be a mother, she should pay a fine to the government, and a man that got a good wife and he is mean to her, I wish to see him licked with a black-snake (*whip*). And I wish that we got the best officers in Red Wing and the new courthouse would be big enough and I could live till its paid for. And I wish to see very steam shovel and caterpillar and truck blow up and the wheel barrows come back like mosquitoes. I wish to see young ladies sit down and milk a jersey cow and the big milk company be used for rags and scrap iron. I wish to see the big bread truck so small as the bee when she sting out the eye of a rabbit.

I wish I never see a drunk man driving a car. I wish that everybody that drives carry protection for the one he meets. I got lots of wishes left but my last wish now is to hear a tune of that nice pipe organ some of you young people bought for the Auditorium.

My wishes might seem funny to you, but they are with love to all of you.

Johannes Johnson

21. Mister Republican
I been in a kind of high school for half a hundred years to try to learn to vote for the right and best man, but now I see that I am absolutely a failure. I don't think I know anymore now than I did the first day. That make me think about the olden times. When God send a man out with a horn full of oil and when found the right man, he put it on his head and rub it and it was up to him to pick out the congress. I don't think there was so much about it and I think that was a whole lot cheaper.

Now days, we don't look for any sheep herders but we want to know how many schools they went through and what they know about those big companies and millionaires and what they need to know.

They need to know something about the poor people and to figure out to get something to do *(make jobs for people)* so they can feed their family for not to be law breakers. That cost money to build all those big buildings and hire all those high priced officers to take care of those that take the wrong road when they are out hunting for Heaven.

And now to you officers of Red Wing and Goodhue County, we give you the job because we thought you were the best men and we pay you good. Don't forget that you work for us and that God sees you. When you read the law, read the same for the dark man as for the rest of us. This country is built up from the whole word and we all are looking for our rights and our protection. I suppose you read about that God had an officer in Heaven *(Lucifer, also called Satan)*. He got proud, so God threw him out and Red Wing and Goodhue County can do the same with you.

And that don't 'make any difference who salt the meat if it's needed and salt is good for the President as well as the beggar. And with our talk we fish the big dollar and with our hard labor we get healthy and happy and some get well fixed.

Don't forget that a hundred pennies make the big dollar.

With love to all that get the Republican and pay for him if you read it or not.
Johannes Johnson

22.
As the talk goes over town that the Red Dragon* is a rough place, it is my duty as the owner of the place to give the public my report what I know. When I rented the place, I gave order to keep clean house. So both high and low could go in and have a good meal so none be ashamed. I sleep thirty feet away from the building. I have never been bothered. Some time I can hear a car start up late. But that's all. I asked the next neighbor. They don't know of any disturbance. I ask across the street and all I ask in the neighborhood report the same thing.

But we don't expect the hotels and restaurants and soft drink parlors down town to boost the place. But I expect as an old settle and tax payer of Red Wing to have protection so those big nice boys that the mothers think are so good, don't tear the stone wall down. They carry away cut stone for two men to handle; flower boxes with half a load of dirt in and they jerked the eyes out of the Red Dragon, and took the horn along.

He had clear eyes for 40 years. I would advise you boys to haul back what you took away. I'm getting old and ain't much good, but next time you try to destroy myk home, I will help the boys *(who work there)* and we will do a still better job.

There is a law to protect an old man's home. Years ago I stood back kof a boy when he shot out 22 window lights in Swede castle. I took the boy and brought him down to the police station and we let him go, but neither him nor the mother said thank you. I think it is a sin to be too good to the boys.

With love to you all,
Johannes Johnson

**Author note – the Red Dragon is the stone house Johannes built for Mary on East 7th Street. It got the name from the carved dragon head Johannes removed from the prow of a boat he had built and placed at the entrance. Johannes rented out the house near the end of the prohibition period, to some questionable renters. Johannes moved into the carriage house (stüga) at the back of the property and lived there during the time the stone house was rented, to keep on eye on things.*

23.

Mister Republican

I have been writing so much about 50 years ago, so maybe some of you got tired. I better move back to Columbus' time and how that happened that he discovered America. He was stranded on an island. He discovered a cave and he went down and found a road to another island two miles away. He crossed two rivers with stone arch bridges and on the other island he found a map that he followed and then he found America.

Columbus took two men in the boat and went ashore. Then he said, "Hello, Indians." And they hollered, "We are discovered." The chief came to Columbus and hollered, "Hello, Columbus." Columbus said, "How do you know my name?" "Oh, there was a fellow here two weeks ago and sold your picture."

King Solomon said when he lived, that there was nothing new under the sun and Hell could never be full, and of books was no end. Its no wonder that so many ladies get smart and thay got plenty time to read. The books we got in Minnesota will side by side go around the state and build a bridge across the Mississippi River higher than the one we got of hanging iron. I don't want to force you to believe this.

I learned that as a kid, but there is always somebody believes it.

The world is trying to show something new and if it can't think anything else they climb up on a 250 foot flagpole and hang for a month and a half. And then they go up in trees. I used to climb in trees 60 years ago, but I wasn't 'foolish enough to hang so long. That took me 50 years to know that I was a fool, but when I married the second time I found that out.

Johannes Johnson

24.
Mister Republican
I take me off an hour to write another letter and thank you all for reading my letters. It pays to advertise in a good paper. I got so many friends so I don't care if I never die. South and west-end and business part of the city want me to keep writing. East-end and Swede Hill hasn't said anything. But you know they never think of a prophet in their home town.

I have listened to advertisements on the radio. Gun powder, face powder and tooth powder, and I aint used anything of it. I think I am good looking according to my age as those that use a barrel of it. And I can clean the neck bone just as good as my dog and if a mouse gets into my house I can hear it just as good as my cat. I think that is money thrown away and to you that have advertised on the radio, I think that the same as if you pound with a hammer inside the barrel that is half full of tin plates and bumble-bees. But I suppose that's the style. And for to fight for the style is going to cost more money for the country than fight the Germans.

We get so stylish so I think it would be hard for our children to get along when they get old. Now we got nothing more to do than to be stylish and that wouldn't pay poor people long. And if poor people forget to work what are they good for? But Red Wing is a good town else I would not stay here so long.
East-end takes care of the mean boys and West-end takes care of the old goobs and the central of the town takes care of the taxes. I don't know they are high and I know I can't help it. But I'm sorry that I send my money down East to the wagon makers, they would be handy to have this Spring. The way it looks to me know, we poor people will soon have our one-wheel buggy back and then we get on our feet. I wish I could write longer letter, but I have to hire for my spelling and I wouldn't tire my secretary.

With a smile and love to you all,
Johannes Johnson

25.
Mister Republican
Some time ago 20 people that didn't have work registered. There was ten that had a bad habit, and all that meets me asks me if I got the bad habit and to tell the truth. I better tell you all about my habit. Those that I quit and those that I got. I had a bad habit to go down town and sit in the grocery store, talking and smoking, so my wife smelled the smoke of the flour when she baked. I quit that habit and I am not sorry,. I had the habit to go into Remmlers and take a good glass of beer when I quit work. I quit that 14 days before they got dry. Now I don't know what I drink. I have to drink what they give me and maybe the next day I can't tell anything about it. The heart might stop and then you can't find out much.

I got one habit I tried to quit for 30 years and that's to chew snuff. If I quit one week, I eat so much more the next week. And I think that's good for two things – no germs on my teeth and no loss to my stomach. I had a bad habit to believe that everybody was honest. That cost me lots of money.

I had the habit to go to church three times on a Sunday and I am sorry I quit that. If you go that habit, don't quit. If a girl happened to marry a drunkard or a lazy man, marry the drunkard in the church and let the lazy man be alone in the castle. A lazy man is less than nothing and a good woman and a good man is the next neighbor to Heaven. A drunkard can be cured if he has snakes a couple of times, but a lazy man will be a burden to the world.

With love from the old man,
Johannes Johnson

26.

Master Republiken

I am sitting now in the old chair that used to belong to old man Tufeson. The best chair I ever own. I always sitting in that when I think back a half a hundred years. Now I thinking about those great good hearted men of Red Wing, that left us and a beautiful mark to look at. Mr. Betcher, Lawther, Sheldon and John Rich. I think it would be right of us Red Wing people to take a day off every year and talk good about them. If they can't hear us there is always some of the younger generation that got the good heart and if we are thankful and the time come they might want to do the same as Pa and Grandpa. Those that help to support the public after they are left *(died)* shall be remembered for hundreds of years. I had a good heart some for over 70 years. Dr. Johnson told me that when I was sick. But I never had any money and that is an awful drawback on a person. Now I am sitting resting good and I am in my dreaming mind, building a tower 12 stories high, maybe of wind, but I wish that would be stone. That don't need to be any polish stone, do like the Roman did, lay one flat stone on two flat stones and that lasted for 1,000 years with no concrete or iron and are still stately fenced in with stone and some old goobs laid them that know how to lay them. Here is a chance for a good heart and money that aint needed to build the first story and I will gladly fill the first story with antiques that I gather up for 50 years. I don't like to have the day coming when a man *(an auctioneer)* holler how much can I get, when some cannot get replaced with money. The 11 stories is easy to get. Mr. Ford had lived long enough to build one story and Rockefeller one story and Northern States one and we will make them put up a light on the top so we can see a fly on a church steeple in Red Wing. I just want to get acquainted with the man that the best heart and most money to give for the first story and now to you readers that get tired of my writing. I daze and thinking I don't expect for you to think I am right and the only one, but I am a whole lot cheaper man than Amos and Andy and you don't need to wait till 11 o'clock at night and the sound like you had a horse and bee swarm in front room *(a radio)* and who you learn the most from is up to you.

Johannes Johnson

27.

Mister Republican

I promise in my last letter if I get good luck, I will be back and put little salt on richer meat. I know I have to be carful so I just want to tell what I have known and seen through my life. Rich people are all good-looking and smart and the reason they are they got their own time to wash the dirt off, and they got money to buy nice clean clothes, and they can keep them clean. God lifted them out of the ash pile, but they had to wash themselves.

A certain percent of rich people got a good heart, and that God and the poor people like. Christmas I went into two room house. A 29 year old mother and nine small children were sitting in the corner, all was quiet and satisfied and more satisfied than Mr. Ford or Rochefeller. The mother was busy cleaning the pantry. The rich good hearted had been there and the road was so narrow that they had to back up for a block to get back. But those people can find the right place, even if the road is narrow.

The roads to Heaven are narrow and if we are on the same road, let us talk good about those people whenever we stood. And there is a certain percent of rich people that go 60 miles an hour. And they can't see the poor people and if some happen to be in the road, they want to give them sixty days In jail. They think the road belongs to them. I think the wider the roads are, the more public the roads are.

And a certain percent of rich people are so busy with figures to get the last cent from the poor people, spending millions trying to learn them bad habits, chew gum, smoke cigarettes and make imitation alcohol, and invent machinery to do the work. So all they want the poor people for is the bad habits. They can't stand to see an old man selling pop corn on the street.

And then to the last they try to figure out a short cut to Heaven, but let me tell you that can't be done, but easy to figure one to Hell.

28.

Dear Mister Republican

One day this spring when I work on the Swede castle, one neighbor came up to me and stood back of me and his thought was so strong that I could hear him plain. When the thought get strong, the lips have to start in. And I want to tell the public what he said. We was only three, him and me and the bluff, and the bluff don't say much. He said, "For all I've seen of fools, I never seen any bigger fool than you. You build a house thirty steps up in the bluff. Who do you think will go up here? And you with your 70 year old limbs and one foot in the grave, now jump around like you are trying to save butter out of fire."

And so he took a big bite of a nice apple he had in his hand. I said that looked to be a good apple. "Yes, that's good," he said. I said, "Do you know that apple is a gift from a time that's gone by? This house must be good to somebody so much as the apple to you. And when I get both feet in the grave, I shall not kick on Red Wing because I did not have nothing to do. And you can't say I've been a lazy man."

And that's our old people's duty to see so you young folks get roof over your head. Them castles you build out of wind and sunshine give you rheumatism in early years and paper collar without a dollar, that's what the dude is made of. But when a fox get hungry he can see the longest distance in the wood and when you get older, you can see that your life aint always fun.

With love to both old and young,
Johannes Johnson

29.
Mister Republican
I found through my life that cats and dogs and human beings are the most jealous of any that are living. If I take up the cat and tickle her, the dog starts to bark. If I talk nice to the dog, the cat gets mad and starts to spit. And if I write a few words in the paper somebody gets jealous and feel ashamed.

The world aint stylish enough. The world ain't big enough. I can't stand on a step ladder with a dictionary in my hand and write big words enough for some of you. I ain't got the time. If you don't like to read it, let your children read it. They might get a kick out of it.

I been wondering why the newspaper man gets grey hair in early years, but now I found out. They try to suit thousands of people every day.

I build Swede castle in the highest point in the county and free for public, and nothing too good for the public. Then some get jealous and knock the windows out. Some took the frames and some took the doors and what was left, I took and moved below the hill so I could watch it better. Now somebody is jealous for that I had gasoline boats of all kinds and Viking boats and I tried to be good to the public.

Now I got only two small Iceland goats left which I tied over in the park road to let them eat the dry grass between the stones, but somebody got jealous and now I invite the public to come and see the damage.

With love to you all but mostly to those that made the complaint. The time will heal up all sores and a hundred years from now all is forgotten.

30.
Mister Republican
According to my sheet that is missing in my book I wrote many letters in the Republican and there isn't many that dried up on the hook. But before I get discharged, I want to show my figures for the last year, 1930. One to nine is ten and three to ten is thirteen. And thirteen is an unlucky number. I found that out the other day I had a toothache. And I asked a neighbor how much they charge to pull a tooth and they told me $2.50. And I didn't have the money to spare. I talked nice to the tooth and told her to behave till the price goes down to the old price, fifty cents, and then I will fix you. And she had to give up.

The most of the prices are reasonable for our stuff, so we don't have to send to Montgomery Ward or Roebuck's for our stuff. That's our poor people's duty to be true to the business man and build up our credit. We are the ones that spoil the credit, not them.

I think it isn't more than right that the doctors and the nurses and the hospitals and the undertaker, too, follow the times. I think a doctor can cut out a little chunk for less than $100.00. I think a nurse could work cheaper than $35 to $40 a week when she can buy a dress for 60 cents. I think the hospital could rent one small room cheaper than $30 a week when we can rent a four-room house for $10 a month.

And when we do business with the undertaker, we are always down hearted and when a father has been good and worked for his money in a life time and his children have to bury him in the potter's field because they can't stand the expenses.

I wish you all go together and talk it over. You know you can't take a dollar with you to Heaven and not in the other place either. And don't take this in a bad way. You and I am thankful to you all for what you answer.

Johannes Johnson

31.
Mister Republican
I see that the prohibition wants 50 men more to watch the moonshiners. To my ideas that would be the same as we would get 50 mosquitoes more next summer. Or that we pass a law that any cat couldn't have no kittens for a year. And up to the owner to watch the cat. If he filed, sixty days in jail.

I think that God wants wine, else He would never made it out of clear water; but we have got to have berries, sugar and yeast. If God wants to have liquor on the earth, don't try to take it away. He had all kinds of trees in the paradise, but there was one He told them not to touch, but Adam and Eve did and that's what we suffer for.

The meaning of our lives on this earth is to be brought up for Heaven. And He wants us there. But He gives us our free will. He don't want any there that don't want to go there. You can be a drunkard, moonshiner, bank robber, and thief and a sneak, but He has got plans for them too, with a fence so high you can never fly over it. And a drop of water can never reach you. Our daily song from pool to pool is "Hard Times". I lived in Red Wing for more than half of a hundred years and I never see any better times but our life is different. We act like we got a million dollars and we aint got it. I am old and nobody want me to work so I went and hunt for the hard times. I went to the factories, there was all four walls lined up with cars and kids' salaries from $14 to $45 a week. I couldn't call that hard times, so I went to the moonshiner and he seemed to be happy, plenty money and I couldn't call that hard times, so I went to the picture shows and there they was packed like Norwegian herring. I couldn't call that hard times. So I thought I had to see the poker player too, and they handled money so much they needed a pitchfork to pitch the paper dollars to the other side of the table.

Now I want to tell you rich or poor. Live according to what you got. Pay your bills that you know is right, thank God for all and God is good and He got lots of good people in Red Wing. They wouldn't see you starve, but step back where God and the people that can help you want to be. And now to all my friends no Christmas presents would be accepted, there's nothing that I need more than money to pay my debts with, because the interest eat more than a cow. And if I should die through the Christmas, not any flowers on my coffin, but if you want to chip together for a pair of over shoes for a poor child, I know my soul would like that better. And if my writing smells too ripe eggs to some of you, what can you do if it is the truth?

Johannes Johnson

32.
Monday, January 5, 1931
Mister Republican
The last letter I wrote in the paper two readers examined it and they said it was all right, but one said I should not put God's name in it. Now I want you all to know the reason. It's a habit from my mother, when my mother put the potatoes on the piano with the jackets on. They were grown in the country when we had such a short summer that they were small and the oats was froze and to save it all we chopped the straw and all, dry it, ground it and bake bread out of it. And the Norwegian herring, she cut in seven pieces and we got one each and we could never start to eat before we thanked God and talked good about Him. My mother counted 22 men one day that wanted to work for their board and better mechanics Red Wing can't show up today, some of them. My father drove on horse 75 miles to Christiana *(Oslo)* of Norway to buy flour and he couldn't get more than one sack, which held as much as a barrel, and when he came home, he sold five pounds to each, but I never seen any money and I never heard that my father asked for any. And now to some of you ladies, look and think before you fill the garbage can. You might live a day when more look in it than the rats. The way I learned through my life is a certain percent of poor people is careless and a certain percent is lazy and a certain percent got bad luck and poor work and half of the time, no work. Big family, big hospital bill and big doctor bill and they try to be right with everybody, but the more they try, the worse they get.
I think that's the people that God wants you rich people to help first. And there's the other kind that they call property poor, I am well acquainted with them, I think they have been hoggish so they wait for help. And there is a certain lot of ladies that expect so much. Let me tell you, you can't expect God to open the window in Heaven and shovel down gold money to you to buy silk stockings and small heel shoes. You wear them out at a dance and if you don't sit right in the show case *(car)* when you ride home, you tear the stockings too. Send the silk stockings with the ducks when they go south. We are satisfied to see your nice legs so long as the ducks are here. But when it gets below zero, we want them covered up.

And now to you my best friend, Republican. If you think my letter is too thick to go under your rollers, don't let it lie upon our hook in the corner, don't throw it in the waste basket, give it back to me and I will post my birch tree next to the park and let the jack rabbit read it. But if I got luck, I will put little salt on richer meat next time.

With love to you all,
Johannes Johnson

33.
Mister Republican
The world brings us always something new. For all the money I paid out in the courthouse for half a hundred years, I never had so much as a cup of coffee but when it was tore down, even to the first load, I was invited for coffee and Freeman's vault was used for a dining room and kitchen and bedroom.

I asked a Swede if he had something I could buy for an antique. He said he sold everything except the safe in the treasurer's office. I asked the price and I said the safe is mine if you can pull it out when the steam shovel and if Kosec's team can pull it and I can collect enough money to pay for it. That will be a chunk that won't be so easy to put in the pocket when I go.
I've been lucky enough not to have a cup of coffee in the next building and I'm glad so long as I ain't invited. But I'm sorry to see that mastodon come down from the city and grab hold with his four steele teeth. Them heavy walls would last for five generations to come.

If they would leave them small rooms in the basement to show the coming generations where the law breaker had to live, I think it would be wiser than to hire a half dozen extra policemen.
I don't think that the jail house had to be put in style. I for my part believe the Old Testament as well as in the New, and I believe a solid stone wall 'jug' is stronger than a common shell even if it is full of spider webs.

Johannes Johnson

34.
Dear Master Republikan
A 50 year old friend from Chicago came up from Chicago to see me. We used to play hiding go seek together and one time I pulled him through a window, when he been out too late, and I dropped the window over his back and he hollered like a pig, so he wake up the whole neighborhood. We had to explain to a jury of the neighbors and the first thing he asked if I remember that. The second thing he asked, "What do you see now days the most?" I told him, "Reckless drivers."
"What do you know that you are most sure about?" I told him "If they don't change the style to the ladies to be poor instead of fat, the sanitarium they had to double." "Do you know of any cure for them?" "Yes, but doubtful, take birch buds in the fall or in the spring before the life goes out of the blade and cook tea of that and drink all you want, and put birch bark next to your feet in your shoe and cut two inches off your heel on your shoe. Let your body down closer to the ground, your heart and liver would work better. And you will save money on corn cure and your nice toes will feel much better. But to be sure, ask any doctor if I am wrong." He said, "Do you know of any other cure?" "All the cure I know is to die." "Do you know of any way to get rid of moonshiners?" "Yes, I do, leave them right to sell it." "What shall we do with drunkards?" "Let them drink all they want. They will get enough, but the way we got it now, they never get enough." "What can we do to reduce our big expenses now days?" "Pay all the bills." These recipes is taken down as an old goob's example, but don't you know it anyway before you think about it?

Johannes Johnson
35.

Thursday, June 18, 1931
Mister Republican
I had my vacation the reason is that I rote two letters that was so thick that they couldn't go under the rollers, the most trooth and the best I ever rote, but that couldn't be helped. Ve vouldn't pinch no fingers. I stowed them away in Swede castle so when the time and business change, some that come after us can pick them up for a relic.

But what pains my heart now is to tell the public I lived in Red Wing of more than a half hundred years. And the first year I couldn't pay my taxes. I went to a good old friend, to the right one, he owned 900 acres of the best land in the county. I asked him if he could help me out. "No, Johnson, I couldn't do that. I paid min yesterday and that took over $1,000, but I will tell you what to do. You can take those 900 acres free, only keep up the expenses, that is more than I can do."

I feel kind of blue, but I pick up my nerve and went to a man that I think either him or the assessor know how much money he got. I told him I did not have enough money for my taxes and asked if he would help me out. He said we haven't got any money in cash. But go to the bank, that's vat we got the bank for, and they are nice to come to, yes, but they are hard to get away from, and he smiled and said that there is something in that. If you get stuck come back, but I didn't. I paid all I had and I wish people did that to me and if I get good luck with this letter, next time I will tell the reason we can't pay our taxes.

36.
Mister Republican
I vant to tel a story thet my fader tol me van I was a boy, and my fader never lie. And my muder always sed van she was mad, I was like my fader. Der vas a neighbor of my fader he vant to sell a pair ov oxen. He vent to a place thet was stablish by de government tri days a year to buy and sell. He vent der and sol de oxen. Van he com home, his wife ask, did you sell de oxen? "Yes." "Did you get de muney?" "No." "Vat vas his name?" "I didn't ask him, but he was going to meet me by de big stone next year and pay me." His wife sed, "Thet was to bad I didn't go vid you." "Oh, you don't need to vorry, he vas a man and he promise."

His vife feel mad and blue, but in de old time de man vas de boss and de voman vas de halper. Now it is different.

His vife vated for de next year and she vent vid him. And she vant to go to do big stone first, and look for then man. And van dey come der, de man vasn't der. His vife said, "Thet's vot I tol yu." "Oh, he might got late. Ve go down town and do our trading and cum back." And van dey cum back de man vas sitting side de big stone vid de money in his hand vid intres and all.

This is from de old time, van a man vas a man. My oder story is 75 years later. A old man that couldn't hear good came into a drug store and vanted a scripshun filled. The druggist tol him, "That kost 85 cents." De old man thought he said five cents, so he shoved five cents op to do druggist and said, "Her is your five cents." Dey stood der shoing de rag till de drugist got mad and said, "Go on, I made tri cents on you anyhow."

I yust vunder if de business man and de ded beet know do hint.

Vi lav to you al,
Johannes Johnson

37.

Editor the Republican

I promised in my last letter to try and explain the reason we can't pay our taxes. I will do that so plain that both bankers and woodchoppers-we ain't got woodchoppers, but we got wood sawyers-will understand. But I have to use both old and new figures. I start to figure out how many bosses the city and the county got now, and what salary they got now. And what machinery they got that never go before they spend money on. Then, when they get old they get both cancer and consumption, and some get lockjaw-and if we are going to do something for them the doctors charges so much-we bury them without flowers but that costs money anyhow.

I try to figure out how many licenses we have to pay. I went to a professor that we pay $3,000 salary, but he didn't know, but he said that it was plenty-and that must be 20 anyhow.

I went to the new courthouse and I discovered a boss on every corner. But I didn't ask what salary they had. I know the new courthouse ain't going to pay my taxes. I went to the swimming pool when that opened, and that was a great thing to see the people act like young trouts. But that ain't going to last longer than the German carp goes up in the weeds. I went home and sit down on the roof of the Swede castle to count the cars that come from the park, and they pulled so tight as the strings on a rope. I got headache and went to sleep and dreamed that the cars were still approaching on the road.

These is my new figures. Please readers, let me take a step back and take a look in the old figures. My mother and father brought up nine children. My mother never bought a pair of stockings for any one of us. She made them. She never bought a pound of wool, they never bought a ton of hay for the sheep.

We children helped to cut the leaves and dry enough of them for the winter. She spun and weaved the cloth. The tailor maybe get a bushel of potatoes for sewing us a nice suit. When the long Swedish winter come, we had thousand bushel of potatoes in our cellar, two barrels of Norwegian herring and ludefisk so much as one horse could pull over a stony road, a good sized pig, couple pigs dried hard as basswood, all kinds of wild berries and when we was through eating we couldn't see each other cause of the potato peelings.

I haven't seen a suit of underware before I come to this country. I did not use mittens or gloves on my hands after I lived here two years *(after his wore out)*. I am healthy. I have lived a long life, over seventy and what I am over-that's my business. And I believe I ain't got anybody in my relations that can lick me today. But I don't know anything for tomorrow. I chopped my road through the woods with tempered steele but not with sunshine and hot air.

With love to both bankers and woodsawers. You're both good help to me.

Johannes Johnson

38.
Coming to America
Mister Republican
I like to tell my trip as a newcomer to dis country. If you please correct my spelling. Deir might be some of de old folks that believe me and dose that don't believe me, we are yust as good frans. Kom de same night as de cyclone event over Vasa and took de children's home. Ve got so far as de Wacouta bridge ven de rain stop and de cowcatcher was over twenty feet of vater, and thank God, I didn't know before de next day. Ve back up de train to Lake City and de next day, dey took us on a steam boat to Red Wing.

Ven ve com up de river I see de tree vas laying one direction on de ground. I ask the reason why de tree lay one way. He told me dey had cyclone. Cyclone, vat is dat? I never heard de name before, and dey told me hard storm.

I said if it blows so hard in America, God help me back to my muder. Ve landed close to de mills on a nice sand bank dat was covered vid Swede, Norwegian, and German and a few Dane, all eating, not pie and kek, but vot de cooked in deir own kettle.

De vit *(wheat)* come in a bog hopper every ten minutes, loaded in open barges going down de Mississippi River. Red Wing looked batter to me than he do today. I tole de boys, let us go look over dat town. Ve vak East Main street till ve see a big bank building vid a sign, Svenska Hotel.
I said ve better go in there. Der might be some of our relations, so ve vent in and asked for de man, and a fat, clean and stylish man kom up-and answer my name is Patron Carlson.
Ve ask if ve could stay. Yes, and de price vas a dollar a day. Ve sit all down and look at de high long table-for legs all boxed in to the floor, and small tubs three feet apart and once used to a table for four and a nice girl holding her hand on our shoulder and ask vat ve vant. I said to de boys dis isn't de place for us. I got only six American dollar in my pocket and ven dat's gone I have to die. My belief it was de same as de vomen ven de prophet come to her, I vil go out and look for Swedes. I vakt a hundred feet and see de hotel Scandinavian-and I vent in and asked if dey could talk Swede. Dey answer yust as good as you can. I told him de story and he sed you can board here for tri dollars a veek, and I will set you to vork tomorrow morning on de section-one dollar a day and you're paid once a month. I vil send my bill in to de company so dat you don't need to have any bader.

Next morning we moved to our new place and started our work on de place below de training school bridging over a sink hole.

Ven ve vent home at night one of de boys seen a nice animal, black and white stripe. He yump off de handcar and grab it and vas going to take it home and the boss hollered skunk, so he couldn't ride vid us home-he had to valk and ven he kom he had to dig down his clothes in de back yard, and in de morning all vas all right. Dat wasn't half as bad as de holler.
Now two weeks is gone in de section and I find out dey offer tri dollars a day in de harvest, and I kom to dis country to be rich, and it vas my duty to look for de higher wages. I had a friend in Visconsin that had thirty acres of farm, and I vent to him and ask him if he vill learn me to bind, and he vas villing to learn me and he learn me the right way. So I bind thirty acres for nothing and I thought I made a good bargain. I vas a professor in the besnes, so I started off for de country, took de Vasa road var de Swedes lived. Ven I left town I vent to a place in the vest vat I found out afterwards dey called de Last Drink. Det stood in a fine line dish on de kounter,

tomatoes, and I thought it vas apples so I ask if I could get one. And I took a bite and spit, and I tought it was de same kind that Adam and Eve played vid. And ven I come up in Spring Creek I got hungry.

I see a white house vid green blinds and I tought dat here must be Swedes, so I vent in and asked for something to eat. But dey didn't understand me. So I saw a knife and fork in de sink and I got hold of dem and made motions and dey pointed to a chair and I took der hint and sit down. Two nice girls fixing de dinner and deir vas vatermellon and I never seen thet before and dey pass me first, and I took a chunk and I started on de outside. De girls started to laugh, so I feel blue. And I said in Swede, "Next time, you take first, so I can see how you do." And dey understand it. Ten years after I find out dey vas Swedes.

I tank for my dinner and start to valk de Spring Creek road till I come to Lasell. Deir come a man vid a nice team they vak more on de hind feet. I ask him if I could ride to Vasa church and I did and when I slipped off I ask him how much that cost. And he said $1.00. I as close to fainted. A big American dollar and de last one I had, and I could never find out who he vas. But if he live I feel to lick him. And if he is dead I feel to lay a black snake on his grave.
I stood and look at de church and nobody to talk to, so I said to do church, "Good day, you stand there like a bride vaiting for her lover, and I don't forget I'm one of dem." I vent into do next house below de church, and she vas a vidow and she had two nice girls and I vas valcom like I was relashuns.

Next morning dey vent to church and dey vant me to go vid dem. I said, "No, de next church on de hill." I said all churches is good and I am thankful to go vid. And here I had my best home next to my muder.

Johannes Johnson

39.
(Continued from my last letter)
Mister Republican
Next day came a neighbor in with name Andrew Peterson. He said he was going down town and hire harvest hands. The lady said, "We got a new-comer boy here. Can't you hire him?" "He don't know how to bind and if he can't keep up, it will cost me ten dollars to come to town to hire another man," he said. "Can't you try him out before you go?" she said. And he did.
When he come to the first corner, I took the last bindle and he looked back and said, "If you can keep up like that, you can bind my 160 acres. And I don't need to go down town." I said, "I think I can keep up as the third man." I run and bind and sing for a few days, but we sleeped in the granary and there came a windy cold night and I got cramp. I hollered to the boys, "Get me up. I am dying." I got up and get on my feet and when I come to I run for two miles down to Belle Creek and back and I was all right. And that's the cheapest doctor bill I had in this country.
Now I had 14 days at three dollars a day so I had that big American dollar back that I paid to ride up Lala Lie. Now comes the stacking and the threshing at $1.50 a day, so I was going to be rich fast. An old friend want me to go with him home and stay over night and ride with them to church next morning.
And that newcomer's place was on the bottom of the wagon box and the teem run away and the lady and the men was thrown in the brush pile side the road without getting hurt. I jumped

up to get hold of the line and stop the teem, when the teem run each side of a big oak tree I fell to the ground, broke my arm in two places. But they was good church members so they walked to the church and left me with my broken arm in the woods two miles from the church.
I carried my broken arm in my other arm and when my toe struck a root in the poor road, I thought she broke once more. But I come to the church later and went to doctor name Brynlidson. He fixed my arm and when he was thru he said, "You do as I tell you I ain't going to charge you a cent. You go up to the church door and watch him come out and give him a good blow with your good hand and I will stand back for all that comes after." But I couldn't do that. He was a Swede.

Now I had a vacation with my broken arm for two weeks in Mrs. Carl Johnson's home in west side of the church and my wish is that I could find her grave and put a flower on becus she is next to my mother. Now comes a Vasa farmer in to see how the newcomer come out with the broken arm. I told him I was lonesome. I couldn't do anything. He said, "I got a job for you that I know you can do. Plow my farm. You don't need two hands to steer the plow. Have the horses' lines over your back. That does good when you get used to it." I commenced to think about it.

I red about the king of Denmark when he captured a Swede he cut one leg off and one arm and he said the Swede can steer the plow with one hand and walk on a wooden leg. So I took the Vasa farmer up and I plowed for two weeks and when the plow struck the roots in the new land my arm hurted so bad. One time I fell down on my nees and prayed to God that I should find some gold so I could get back to my mother. I asked the farmer what he was going to pay me. He said, "Pay you? You can be glad you got a home and I will see so my oldest daughter is going to learn yu to read English and that's worth more to you than money." Here is one of my mistakes. I vent back of a strawbarn and cry like a baby and when I couldn't cry any more I went back into the house and start to pick up my dirty shirts to put in the sachel and started out on a round trip around Vasa and when the sun went down, I come into a man named Bengt Anderson, a big man and well-built man, religious man. I ask if he had any work for me. He said "If yu will work cheap nuf I got work." I said, "What you call cheap?" "8 dollars a month." I will take that but I have a broken arm that aint strong yet but I will see so yu don't lose eny on my poor arm." Now the bargain was made and we sitting talkin to bedtime. He tok down the Bible from the shelve and rode a chapter. And then he said, "Nobody can go to bed in my house without going down on nees and thank God for what He don for us." And for two months I was there they didn't fail one morning or nite without prayer. Religious life shud be started when you are yung. When yu get old yu stand like a half rotten tree and the wind from Heaven can't bend yu. But when yu get to old that can brek yu.

Johnannes Johnson

40.
Continued from my last letter)
Now I am through with this gud home and they didn't lose any money on my por arm. I made 20 days with the treshing rig with $1.25 a day the last month. Now he giv me a ofer for to work for the bord and go to skul. If I ben listened to him I wouldn't need The Republican to korrect my spelling but I had in my mind to be rich fast,, so I hired out to Wisconsin cutting cordwood for 60 cents a cord and for $3 for veek for the bord. And went good when we had moonlite I cud cut 3 cords.

I sleep in the upstairs and the outside wall had only thin boxwood siding on. The sun pulled the nails out so we cud put our hands through anywhere. Sum morning we wake up the quilt was covered with 3 inch of snow. Ve had to figure to kep the nose under the quilt. One time we had a big snow storn so nobody cud cum to town and the tresuri got low in the pantry for the lady. So she started to cry and I said don't you cry I no a way to git to Red Wing.

I vent out and cut out a nice hickory tree ad split it in to and made a pair of skiis and vent to Red Wing and ven I crost the san prair *(sandprarie)* I froze bot my big toes and I vent in to a plas named of Setterberg. I said hullo and he said, "Yu have froze yur nose I vill go and get snow to rub it with." I had a hot time for a while. But I crost Mud Lake and cum to town and loaded in a what sack about 50 pounds of grocery and started for home and the lady was glad to see me back.

But the old man had a tooth ache so he was half crazy and he holler ples help me to git that toot out. He cum with a pincer that was just rite to shoe horse wid. We culn't git it in moud. We tried, but then he find stove pipe wir and I help him the best I cud and he vent upon a chair and stood,, tied wire in the hickory tree that we used to dry ax handle on. He said, "Ven I jump yu jeark the chair." And I jerked the chair quik and ven he cum to the flor he groled but the toot hung to the wire in the ceiling and ve was all satisfied. Ve didn't no any beter. The vinter vent fast and I cut many cord of vood. But the farmer didn't have no muney to pay for the choping but he promised to pay ven he cud sell the wud. I dont no if the wud is sold yet. Ven I left I looked back from a high hill and that was the last I sen the place and the wud. My Swed close was wearing out and my muney was invested in wud and they are der yet and when 100 years is up that don't make any difference.

Now I left and started for Red Wing to friend that vorked for Sterling and Foot and I ask him if he couldn't get me a yob to be shu maker. Dat vas pretty gud in the old country and I given up all hope to be big rich and I cud make beter living as shu maker as cutting cordwud. One day my friend kam and tol mem he got a yob for me. Lasting gren lether boots for 40 cents dozen pair. I made $2.50 the first veek so I vas only 50 cents short to pay my bord but I picked up fast and master Foot was gud to me. He cud see that I want to go head in this world. In six months I was bos over six men and sum of dem was de best shoemaker in the country.

And my wages was $7.50 a veek so now I cud be wit the boys and see a girl hom once in while. One time I vas to Olson and Kempe paint shop cros from city hall and spose dey vant to have fun mit the newcumer. Dey gave me vat dey call cater snuf. I sneeze so long I cud stand up and down on my nees sneezing and lay down on flor sneezing til I bled throgh my nose and moth but I get over it and in my next letter I vil tel vat cum after.

41.
(Continued from my last letter)
Now is the sneezing party over and I am a sik boy. And I had to go and see a dokter. He pounding my chest and loked in my moth and he asked how old my muder and fader vas and my gret granfader. I tol him he vas 102 years ven he got to nu teeth but he died. The dokter gave me a quart botel of greese medicin. I loked at the botel and vent hom, set it on table vitout open it. Next day I vent to a Sved druggist and vant him to go vit to the dokter and tak to him. I vant to no vat sikness I had. The druggist told vat he vas cuming vit for. And dey talked together and dy vudn't tel me anithin. But I voudn't giv up befor the dokter tol me vat he tot so he got mad and told the druggist to tell me dat vun of my lungs was gone and other vas on god start.
I vent hom and lay down on the bed crying to I vent to sleep. Ven I wak up I member vat my fader holer to me ven I se him de last tim. Hold yur hed op over al sarrow dat you in a stranger country. I valked over de flor a few times and I open de vindo, tok dat grees botel, thru it out and it struk at ol vagon veel and vent to peces. And I tot to myself if I got consumsion I goin to die vitout any greef. I quit my shumaker yob and hired out as helper for carpenter and a contractor vit name Lauver and Hold Hagerstrom was the forman.

Al vent gud but I vas a sick boy for the hol summer, spit blod and week so I had to rest ven I valk to vurk in de morning. But I never said I vas sik, never tok a drop of medcin but I keep my chest and arms klen and rub dem wid a kol towel every day. The fall kum and de vurk was don and my vegt vas don to 130 pounds. I vent vit coupel boys to Eau Clair, Wiconsin, hire out as blacksmith and wod bucher for de wod. And we had to travel hundred mil up tru the wods and I vas tire out and a temster, A Norvegian step out from lod and said yu driv my team. Yu are tired out. And day vas the first tim I like Norvegian and I like them al sinc.

And in de log shanty ver ve stop overnit vas hole cut in dor so kat and dog cud go out and in ven dey vant to and no bed. Ve had to lay don on de flor. One morning ven I voke up, my hair vas froze to do flor, so I had to tak my jaknif and cut me loos. But I thik it was gud medcin for de consumsion. Ve cum to de kamp and the first I tok notic to were de stal ver dey sho de oxen. I ask my Norvegian fren vat dat vas for an he said, "If you don't know dat I tink you wudnt be old here." I said, "Yu help me to get here and yu can help to stay here and I vil sure be rite to you." And he drov dey oxen into stall, hoist it up and sho me al abot it. So dat vent gud and horses I use to shu in de old country. Dey first order vas to make a "gud devil." I didn't no vat dat vas so I had to hunt for de Norvegian an he said, "Cut don a croked birch tree, put croks together in the frunt and bolt thru, and a cross bem on the midel, dats all." Dats vat ve use to pul the logs to the rod on. And al vent gud for a hole munth and I sleep gud and eat gud. Sum times I eat 9 biscuit and beens, potato and big pece of pi and my consumsion vas dry and I vas a helthy man.
Now de bos giv me the bigest order to mak an ox yok. I tot anybody cud mak ox yok but I found out different. I cut down big birch tre and vork hard al day. And ven I tok it over, dat vasnt lik a ox yok so I no dat vud never go, so I hide it all under de sno and ven de box cum home I told him I ben sik so I cudn't vork, but now it was up to me to hunt my Norvegian frend and how dat turn out I will tell you in my next leter.

Johannes Johnson

42.
Mister Republican
And I tol my norvegian fren what happen dat I vork hard all day and I had to bery it under de sno. He said, "I vil show yu how to lay out a ox yok but dat vil cost you 1 pond of chewing tobacco." And I said, "I vil giv yu 5." So ve vent out in de shop and he laid it out on a pec of bord. And he tol me to not vork it clos. "Tomoro nit I vil help yu to finish it." So I kame out of the vurst pinch, but he tot he wud hav sum fun. He tol the boss all abot it so next nit the bos cum wid a smil on his face and ask hav yu ben sik today and de next nit he kum an asked, "Du yu feel any beter?" And sum tim he said, "How is yu helth?"

I looked don in the flor and said, "It sonds lik yu are after me for de lie but I vant yu to no dat my muder didn't lern me dat, but I codnt se no oder way out of it. And didnt lik to be shoved out on the rod and wak don to Eau Clair." And he said, "We Irish kal dat a wit lie and anyway to mak the logs rol, dats vat I am her for." And Norvegian and Irish been my best frens all since. If I got a Norvegian fren on one side and an Irish fren on the oder sid, I am satisfied.

Now the spring is her and I had 3 months in Eau Clair cuming at 60 dollars a mont and dat I had to tank the Norvegian and de Irish for. Now I rote the most ones lov leter I ever rote and tol my loving gurl to be ready if she like to married me and I tink ve didn't du any mistak either one of us, but der is now a time dats goin by and lots of yu Republican reders vil hav dat cuming and her is de end of mi nukumer lif. And now I am an old goob and dat didn't tak long.

With lov to yu al,
Johannes Johnson

43.
Mister Republican
Two men talked togeder de oder day. One asked de oder, who is dat Yohnson dat holer so much in De Republican? Now I vant to answer so day al no. I am a Yon dat started to holer in the desert where thistles vant to gro and my time is going to be short and if my hed is going to be carried on a plate tru de casel dor, dat mite be de only honor I get and tank yu al dat read my leters and tank yu al dat don't.

And we are yust as gud friends, only yu kep De Republican and pay for him. If yu don't, we al be kue off. And now I am readi to holer. De winter stay bak two monts. Sum gud friends to us told him we got so hard times and lots of por peepel and dose gud womens and mens that kan and vant to help us has been busy to take advis and figur out the best vay. Now I got my as a old man and dat got my advise as dat seem easy to me if you follow my advise.
Don't go to do poor peepel first. Go to de courthouse of Godhu county. Cut off 4 percent of de helpers. Go frum dere to de city hal and do de same dere and if half of dem quit, I think we got nuf anyway. And go to de factories and de big stores. Do de same thing and when yu get the muney, bring dat to de post office if yu are fraid de banks is going to bust. But be sure to bi ten acres timber land.

Now yu kan go to de por peepel and if yu find a lazi man siting in de corner playing cards, tel him yu kan kut wod fre of charge so yu don't ned to go to de kol deeler. Dey had deir harvest long nuf. And if yu don't get nuf vod kut go up to de county jail and tak de law breakers. Be sure to take a blacksnake *(whip)* long. Dat aint more sinh to lick a lazy man dan to lick a mule dat maybe cant pull de load. It aint no use to fil up de lawbreakers so dey are like broncos when de kum out. Any dey aint no use to holer if you cant kik. I luv y al yust de sam.

Johannes Johnson

44.
Mister Republican
As yu al no, my lovly hom had to be turned into a public plas with the nam Red Dragon and the tenant and customer work it to a blak nam. Now der is up to yu to kum and se if ve vant to better our self. De walls and de flors is klen and if yu order anyting to eat or drink, it is guarantee to be klen, but the tenant and de oner ned yer help to bild up to meet the expenses. Nex Saturday and Sunday ve vill hav a grand opening on the shed dat I bilt bak in de bluf dat our old mayor Pierce giv the name Swedish Castle. Kum and see bankers and vodsawers. Yu all be treted rite. And yu kan drink from kups of 1700 from Sweden, Norway and Germany and from Jerusalem and ve vill sho yu money big as a cofy kup and small as a fish skale and old since 300 yers befor Christ.

And if we got sumting yu want yu kan have it for de rite price.

Johannes Johnson

45.
Mister Republican
I am getting old and I seen lot in this world dat I don't like and lot what I do like. Dem small happy bird dat yump from lim to lim and sem to satisfied wid vat day can find, but I never se dem yump down in de vater and try to play with the small fish and de fish is yust as happy. De small bird no better and the small fish no ver de belong.
But I hav seen ven sum of de church members have played with law-breakers and sinners and the law-breakers seem to no better ver dey belong dan de church members. But of all people church members are de best people, so ven yu look for company, look in de church. Yur best company is der. And always look for one better dan yourself. Religion and church members have civilized de world and stood in de wurst batel the hold world tru.
Now a frend kum in spoil my leter. He said I was the wurst kiker he ever herd. I said vad du you tinking bout? Don't yu remember ven Betcher run de sawmill? He had a kiker dat kiked a three fot log like it was matches, and he kiked till the log lay de way he vant it to lay. I kud kik more but Mr. Grondahl will duble me up and put me in de wastebasket and in the bail I go and maybe he sel me. I am thankful to the reeders of de Republican dat yu let me kik so long as yu have, but if yu let me, I will kik some more and if yur sho pinch, giv the feet mor rum. Yu no the Swede licked the sled and mean the hors. With love to yu al.

Johannes Johnson.

46.
Mister Republican
As yu all know I am a kiker and I bin dfat al sence I was born. Van ve had our vater carnival I vent der yust to find something to kik about. But I couldn't find noting. That vas the nicest I seen tru my long life. And I vill tank yu al dat had yur hand in it. You made dat so complete so it couldn't bin batter. I stood side of a ledi vith tri kids. She said, "Here y ain't got bread for my kids now and the sitty burn up thousand dollars." Y said, "Ledi, ve shouldn't kik long as dey don't burn up do vater in de Mississippi River." Some day a man like Kaiser might come in a flyin machine and dump a barrel of medicine in de river and burn up do river and dat vil be a drier spell than ve got now. But der is one ting kings and vunder men can't do, and dat's to live forever. And ven Mr. Ford die, his bodi vont be worth more than mine – I mean de flesh, but dat might be a better time all around. Respek my age vit forgiveness.

Johannes Johnson

47.

Mister Republican

De oder day I meet a young man on de street. He said, "Yu shudnt' rite so much bout yourself. Rite sumting abot somting else." I said, "Ven I rite bout fools I hav to rite abot myself, because I am de biggest. And dat tok me more dan 50 yers to no dat was so. But I don't tink dat vud take yu so long. Yu got better education dan I have." Dats a hard ting to rite bout, tings people don't know. Ve got dat tatle tail vat de call radio and ve got morning papers and ve got thousands of nite hawks dat kum hom in de morning and tel all about it.

I tink dats a good ting to remind pople of vat so many hav forgot now days. Dat ve had a good muder and if ve aint git it now ve had it vunce. Yu kan hear ven yur kar mises but yu cant hear ven yur muder missing bred in her home. Yu kan bi a hole gallon moonshine but yu kant bi a botel medicine ven yur muder is sik. Yu kan se ven yur clothese aint maid up so nice as yu vant dem, but yu cant se ven yur muder's toes stiks out thru her shues. Yu can hear ven your lovers car stop outside de dor but you cant hear ven yur muder beg yu to go vit her to church. Yu no lots bout all kinds of things and playgrouns but yu no litel bout hospital and sik people.

Yu curl yur hair and yu brush yur teeth but yu let yur Bible lay disty on the closet shelves. I no dis is de live for de most of yu reeders, but if der is only one dat tink about it, my leters aint gud for nothing. And if der is any Republican reedrs dat vants to reed my letters any longer, invest a sent and let dem no, yes or no. And if no got it, ve vil al be beried in de bluf and let de roks reed it. Dar mit cum a day ven edikation goes out of stile and somebody is goin to scratch in de bluf after common sand.

De vaves on de ocean are going up so hi, but de aint going to strike Heaven. A tre goes up so hi, but de got to fal. I growed up in 25 yers and I stod still in 25 yers and I got old in 25 yers.

Now I am redy to fal and the reck of the fal aint goin to disturb many of yu and we all got a place to rest in-robers and minister, president and pope. Ve rest in the sam hight from de surface, but remember ve are al to be kaled on have to go ver God tel us to go. Mak a stop in your livs and tink it over. God aint goin to tak hold of yur hair and pull yu into Heaven.

Johannes Johnson

48.
Mister Republican
I am here agin and I vish to tel yu vat I see dat I think is de prettiest I see in 15 years. Two stone drays kuming down frum de bluf. Dey vent slow but shure. I tot der vas sumting for me to figure out and I did and der is up to yu readers to do de same. I no der is sumbody who vil lose muney on dat deal but de por peple make muney on it. Dis country are in a pinch dat yu got to let the por people make sum. Els you kant mak anyting. And yu officers of Goodhue County and Red Wing, you are all good, but yu have to se so the laboring man kan pay de taxes. Else ve have to cut yur salary and dat has to be don quik. Ve lik dat yu are gud to the por people. Dats yu duti, but yu kankt bi dem a car and a radio and ve taxpayers kant tak hold of our bodies and karry ourselves. And if ve lose the middelman so ve kant pay our taxes, ver vil yur salary be? Ve better start to lern frum the bit city's fal. Ve preciate wat yu done for us poor people of Red Wing, but don't yu put too big burdens on de one dat is villing to carry it. Ve kan carry the kros for a while, but ven it gets uphil ve vil kave in.

With luv to you al.
Johannes Johnson

49.
Mister Republican
Believe me or not, I got $30,000 wurth of property and I kant feed my 2 pets. I had to give dem bod away. When yu are gud to de por pepel, tink of us. Al ve vant is merci. Don't chop de tree off, scratch round de roots and it mit kum to and be a hom for bod burd and squrrels. Wid luv to de one dat got de sharpest axes.

Johannes Johnson

50.
Mister Republican
I bin a helthy man thru my life, but the last day in last munth I was sik and I can yust as wel tel you de reason. I kudn't pay my taxes. And de reason vas I didn't have the muney. I had both value and muney, but oder people used it up and sum kudn't pay and sum wouldn't pay. Dose that kud not pay was easy to forgive, but dose dat kud pay, dat was the wurst batel I had since I bekum a property owner of Red Wing. I vent to bed three times and started to read the Lord's prayer and I had to quit and I kudn't go to slep eider.
And my tought vent so low dat I wanted to blame the ded beat if I had to go to_____. No slep dat nite and not the next nite, but now I slep gud and I am shure of 2 tings, my taxes is goin to be paied and I am goin to dy. And den I wouldn't need to vury about taxes or ded beats and neider for dat big American dolar. He has been a big load to me and I getting too old to handel anyhow. He has ben like a bronco ven I handel him. I like de pennies beter. Dey stay hom in de Irish jug. De truth sonds funy ven de president tells us. But sometime dat goes a long vay.

Wid love to all,
Johannes Johnson

51.

Mister Republican
Yu don't kare if I tel yu of vat I think and vish. Ve al no der aint much to listen to a fool but sumtime it take a professor to figur out vat he meens. Every word got a meening. I am glad dat the wages is quit on us por peepel. Ve commence to talk to each oder. Ve kan let the kar stand in de shed and go to de neebor if dey vant any help to vash stormvindows and always can split litel kindlewod for our wives.

And ve don't tink it a shame to go to de rummage sale and luk for shoos for our kids and a varm coat for our wife and ve kan make it gud for de low wages if ve get sumting to do. Der is lots ve kan do ven we have to. And ve kan pay our bills beter with the smal wages. Ve got to figur more in a busines way. Yu no the chain store alvays figur in de cent. Ve got de same chance.

And here is my vish. Dat de officers of the state and Gudhu county and all towns follo us and kut their wages in half and my believ vud be der wouldn't be one dat quit dir yob. And dey kud get long just as gud as ve kan and my next vish are only men dat sels a kar on time he shud serve one year in prison and any gas deeler det sells gallon gas on time he shud serve six months and any garage man dat grind a valve on time, he shud have ten days in the county jail and anyone dat don't like my wishes I wil take it al back. I vant to be friends to you al. But on the rate ve are goin ve mite hav a chance like other countries and to yu dat don't like my wishes give me an answer thru The Republican so I kan feel proud a few minutes of my old age.

With luv to you al.
Johannes Johnson

52.
Johannes Says (*Column head sometime before the end of 1931)*
Mister Republian
I seen in a dreem a big tre with 48 big limbs and the hole world was proud over the crown it had, and the leaves was shade for about 90 million white, brown and black skwirrels. The kings kum from south, north and west and east and stud with their hats in their hands to give the tre the honor.

Then I seen lots of elephants that kum around the tre, rubing their hed so to rub the bark off. And they al had a sign on their backs, but I don't remember al of dem, but der was "iron trust", "lumber trust" and Rockefeller, and Ford had a hole lots of wulves behind dat bit his legs but he didn't put much atenshun to it. He rub al he kud.

Den a masterdom kum and shake de tre so hard that al de nuts and half of de leaves fel off so de swirrels didn't have nuting to eat. And den I lok at de sign and dat stood "Wall street." And den I se thousands of wite wurms wid black heds dat made a hole down to de roots and cut de small roots off. I kudn't see de sign good, but I tink dat stood de "Post Department."
Den I seen tre kinds of ants dat kum from al direction, crawl down in de small holes and suk de sap from de small roots. I kud se de sign on de old one dat stood "Soldier," but I tink he oders taught dey vas. Now dat tre is sick and de swirrels is hungry. Wat kan ve do? We got masterdom and elefant and cut wurms and solders ants. Soldiers ants are de wurst of dem al. Dey don't leave a fresh flower in a leter dat goes tru de mails. I tink we need a good gang to take karte of de tre and de swirrels.

Wid love and gud luk to you al.
Johannes Johnson

53.
Mister Republican
I like to tel you a story about Christmas when I was a boy. Nine days before Christmas was the day that we called Lusota. Then we was up 3 o'clock to butcher for Christmas. My fader tied the four legs of the criter wid a wonderful snare. In one yerk de criter laid on a foot high bench. My muder grabbed de nife and she said, "Not for we don't like you, but for our food. God bless you."

The day befor Christmas we all had to take a bath. Our bathroom was a block frum de house, about 18 feet square. We had a rough granite oven in de korner and a balcony for de family and not any windows. But a dozen three inch sticks the length of the rum to hanger de clothes on. When all was ready and we was on the balcony my mother took water and throwed on the hot oven. The best bath I ever had. The hole family was kleen at once and the clothes to. There wouldn't be any flees that bite us for a munth after.

And my fader had his place next to de wall on de balcony, sitting dere in de dark, shaved himself with a homemaid razor after his grandfader. I spose de barber don't like if I said he made a gud yob, but he did. The next yob was to have de light for Christmas morning. My fader went into de bathroom and took one of dem sticks, split it up fine and tied it around on every foot. Now dat was Ma's yob to feed the kows Christmas eve. When she was thru the feeding she had mixed salt and flour. She opened the mouth on the kow and put little in de mouth and she said, "Eat and feel gud do hole year round. Tonite is de Christmas Eve."

Now is de Christmas in de house. We was 8 children round de table and I kan see de colr on the tablecloth and de dishes on de table. I kan here my fader's prayer. I kan se my muder's teers running down the cheeks when she was wundering what wud be next Christmas.

I ben de owner of more dan 25 homes in Red Wing, but altogether they aint wurth my first home. Here I sitting alone like in a forgotten town. Also the moss start to grow on my bak and wondering how it will be next Christmas. I got lots to tel about old Christmas, but de teers runing too fast and I see a day is cuming in de future when de teer is going to run down de cheek of sum of you reeders. If der is welkum to de reeders, I will rite about de old church befor Christmas is over.

With luv to you al.
Johannes Johnson

54.
Mister Republican
Now it is Christmas morning 3 o'clock. An al de family is dressed. The brown horses stand outside de door, pounding deir feet and want to go. Wid a brass beau over de bak wid a dozen bels dat no country can imitate. Two home-made candels in every window in de house and de stik my father lit up for the bathroom was in full blaze, more than 100 kandel power.

Now down the hil to what we kal do King's Road. Frum al direction of de hills, dat look like an ocen of fire. When ve kum a half a mile from de church we heard the pipe organ and when ve cum to de dor, they was 20 feet high, made of double planks nailed with home-made coper nails, in de hall was a log to each side split in two wid a hole big enuf to put a leg in. Deir was de place for de law breaker and when de people went into de church they used to spit on dem. De church had a 40 feet high arch ceiling wid a rainbow with angels sitting on it and wherever you sit in de church, dey al look on you. Dat was the biggest gift that any artist had. And now de tourists from al directions in the world cum to se de church. The walls is 6 feet thick made out of 2 and 3 inch flat stone and common clay for the mortar. De bells hang in lether straps on 12 inch squar timber 100 feet up in de tower. And dey was ringing with so gud time that Nickie *(Johannes' son, a fiddle player in a band)* cant kep better time with his fidel.

The balcony was cross over the church in the back and the pipe organ in the front In the center and In holidays der was two dat play and on de pump was 3 six by six timer that a man could step with his weight and couldn't be stil of vibration and the floor was made of three feet thick logs smoothed with the ax. And on the left side of the balcony was Hel painted. And I ben scared of dat place al since. That wuld not hurt de yung peepel to se dat picture and dat's of more need to us old peepel. We mite be closer to it. The church was repaired in 1726 and how old that was before I don't know. The saying is that when they bilt her the first time, they lod up a pair of oxen and let them go widout de driver and they even vent as far as dey kud go on a point in the lake and deir de church stands today and der is where is 400 year old relations rest.
Johannes Johnson
55.
December of 1931

Mister Republican
Would you plees let me tel my wish for the kuming year? I wish my helth wud be so good in the kuming year as it was in the years that went by. I kut wud on the mountain enuf to last me three years. I don't need to bet the kol dealers for fuel. I always get sumthing to eat. And I like to live to see what is going on. I wish that the por peepel wud be brot bak where they belong, honest and thankful to God and the one what helped them.

I wish that the rich peepel wud open their pocketbooks more for God and the por peepel. I wish that the government start to sel liquor and kut out al the moonshine. It aint any gud anyhow. I wish to see the wages kut on al the officers from the president down to the game warden. The game aint wurth more than what we pay them. The game belongs to the poor peepel anyhow. I wish that peepel wud pay me. Then I kud pay my taxes next spring. I wish that the yung girls wud quit drinking alcohol and smoking cigarets. They kud save muney and make their mothers happy.

I wish that al poker players wud lose muney and I wish that the swimming pool and the big snow plow wud be a big income from the city. But I hate to see the new stylish courthouse be be turned over to Montgomery Ward to pay so much a week. But I wish that you quit al papers and read only The Republican and if you got any time to spare, read the Bible. That's the book I read if I got any trouble with anybody. What you need is there and what you wish for is there.
I wish that the ladies quit talking in the radio and stay home voting days and don't bother with any jury. They got a gud hearts and the lawyers is so gud to preach they kan send a gud angel to Hel by mistake. And now don't get jealous for my wishes. I wuld not get the muney anyway.

With luv to you all.
Johannes Johnson

56.
January 6, 1932
Mister Republican
I tok me a walk on the top of the bluf to se the new charity work and God bles all that give the muney and dose dat do the work. But I want yu al to know that I, in a way, have giv to much now. For a half hundred yers I never bin so por.

But when we Svedes pushed the wheelbarrows up to make those piles so high, our wages was 90 cents a day and we never no of any hard time. Nobody told us either. Now yur peepel level it down for four dollars a day and now there is hard times. And the reson you kan figure out yourself beter than I kan. To many bosses. One wants the pile down and the other wants it up. If you kant agree, give the yob to Hay Creek farmer and be satisfied.
If al the officrs in the county and the city shud desire where I had to go when I die, I think I wud never get a place. We got a nice gud road to the Memorial Park. We want to lok at yu when yu go up and we want to see how you look when yu kum down. We don't like any sneeks and our muder told us there is only one small road to Heaven and we shud be satisfied with one road to the park when we got so many parks.

The parks wouldn't help to feed us but our backyward wud if we tok gud care of them. I wish that yu boys would not be sore at me for al the hints I threw, but I think that's gud for yu. Yu never lern any more if al the peepel holer, yes, yes, to everything you do. And to yu gud klas of peepel that done need to look for any help, keep yur mouth shut and don't talk about hard times. Al the gud that do is giv peepel a gud excuse to not pay their bills and before you no, yu will be on the same side.

With luv to yu al.
Johannes Johnson

57.
Dear Mister Republican
One yung smart man told me the oder day when a man gets so old that he has to use glasses, he kant see things rite. I no we don't se the same. When yu luk in a luking glas yu se a smart yung man that know when both God and the kings do mistakes. When I luk I se only one big fool. And the difference, you se like sum one hapen to se on Wakuta prairie sum times, and I se the truth. We all luk different and we all se different. Maybe I kan se without glases a crook thru a cast iron crak, when you with $20 dollar glases think he is a minister. I kan se without glases moonshiners and sum that get help from the county riding in swell kars when the taxpayer have to walk. They aint got muney enuf for gas. And I kan remember when prohibition preached out al the policemen and al the jails and al the taxes and promise us Heaven on erth. Now put on two pair of $20 glasses and find out if they told us the truth.

Go and talk to the policemen and the judges and ask de sheriff how many boardrs he got more this year that the county have to pay for. Der is about time for both minister and gud church members to se what they kan do.

If I had the right as a profet, I wud like to tel yu what I think is kumming in the future. But I am put bak as far bak. My office are where my kow use to eet her hay and my life is onli old fashion lamp and the blame I give to prohibition and the moonshiners. Rome had to giv up when the measure was ful of sin, so have we. We shud never get into our heds that God don't know what we are doing. He's got a radio just as gud as we got.

With luv to the readers if you lik it or not.
Johannes Johnson

58.
Tuesday, January 12, 1932
Mister Republican
I don't mean to seed any wild oats in yur field, but I like to study on how to get out what we do got. How much have yu and me got kuming that we got rite to ask for? Warm clothes and gud food and a gud drink once in a while if we need it. If we dont we dont got no rite to ask for it. What more rite have the president and the congressman and the man that work in a sewer in Red Wing? Pay the same wages to congressman as the man working in the sewer. The congressman got the beter yob than him anyhow, and there is thousands that wud take the yob yust for de honor der is in it.

Der aint any use to put a big load on a horse that is to weak to cary his harness. Be gud to him, feed him, don't let the rats and soldier ants eat up his feed. Dey aint no use to try to bild up the business in Red Wing with only gas stations and tire shops and moonshine joint. De farmers and de citizens have stepped bak. Now der is up to yu officers to take a long step bak. Yu have made us kum to time.

We have puled together so we are ful of rheumatism to meet yur high salaries. I maybe are the first grashooper that tok a yunp for yu and I want to giv yu advise, follow us. And I want to tel my riting, but I kant stand the price the officers set, so I have to sneek dem in the same vay as the moonshiner. A man that ben helthy al his life, never been cross-eyed or sneek-eyed, he kan tel what he kan so best with or without to pay the doctor a 5 dolar bill.

We had to step bak yust as fast as we went ahead. Our food has grown frum the grund and frum the water. Al kan not live frum being sneaky. My belief is if we kut out al the officers that we dont need, and pay the rest what they need, just a gud living salary, that wouldn't be a por *(person)* in our country. I don't like to go to any long plan about it. Yu al get mad. And I dont want that for the hole world.

With the same luv for yu all.
Johannes Johnson

59.
Mister Reppublican
One that sposed to be my fren toll me that he was fraid I losing lots of frens for getting so much on the officers. I said that must be a mistak for they always treet me right and they are al kleen and gud-looking to me. Why shud I kik on them? But I said they kud get along with a smaller salri yust as wel as we kan. And so far as frens, if I lose 25 per cent of my frens 25 years ago I wuld be wurth 25 per cent more today. But yu mite be surprised befor long see yump on crutches and put a flower on my coffin. We aint al dead.

They excuse those funni ideas I got. I goin to tel yu one now. I wish that sum of yu that got power to go Wisconsin and hire the governor for the state of Minnesota. Maybe we kan get the taxes down to half like Wisconsin got. That luks to me that the land is wurth more across the river in the swamp eith feet below the hi-water mark than in the fire limits of Red Wing.
That must be sum reason. We dont want to let Wisconsin muv Red Wing cros in the mudhole. I rent my homested for les than the taxes and if I vant to muv it cros the river I bin oferred $50 a munth. That must be magnet sum kind that draw the valuation kros. If we let Wisconsin do as they plees, it wont be long befor we have the owl sitting on our front porch and I lik to no how yu feel that giv away the bridge. I wil tel you how I feel. That is forgiven but not forgotten.

With luv to both side of the river.
Johannes Johnson

60.
Wednesday, January 20, 1932
Mister Republican
My fader was a smart man. That was the saying among the peepel. It is always the case that the smartest fader brings up the biggest fool and it is a gud thing there is a limit set. If the boys shud keep on being smarter than their fathers, they wud do as they plees with both Heven and Hel. And what wud they do with the world if they got mad? I heerd that they fool Uncle Sam by taking a bite of a piece of soap before they got examined and I have heard when they fooled their father to sign the farm over to them, and send the old man to the por farm. There is lots of boys that got a big brain in the back of their hed that never sleeps and with the educasion the country give them, the fader beter luk out.

A mean boy I blame on the muder and a spoiled girl I put on the blame on the fader. But there is lots of boys that been beter off if they had been sold as slaves than to go through the high school.

A boy shud lern to reed and rite and before he lerns any more, he shud be examined. And find out if that wud do him any gud. And a girl shud be lerned to kook just as quick as to reed. The woman is maid to help them and the man to be gud to the woman. And the man that is mean to the woman, he is not wurth a home. And the school teacher shud study for the hie wages she draws. She is in school to lern the kids to live a decent life when they are through with school. The Minister isn't in the church to soot the congregasion. He is there to tel the peepel what God wants him to tel them, if it hurt ever so bad. A president isn't in the White House to pik up a row *(fight)* with the hole world. He is there to keep peece with the world and se so we git our daily bred. Por fellow. We shudn't expect so much of him. He got tousands dat van to bos him. I have live a long life already, worked hard and save my muney. And sum millonares and ded-beets got it al. Por and onest peepel hasnt got much to tank me for.

Johannes Johnson

61.
Mister Republican
We living in a time when it is us old peepel's duti to check up our officers and our own familes and see what they are doing. What wud we do when our country and city and home tresuri got empty? Holer and expect God to kum down and feed us with a spoon? He set us to run this world, to be onest to each other and live a life like sisters and brothers. And He gave us plenty for a gud living and if we dont hande it rite, He mite laugh at us when we starve.

When the measures of sin were ful were we no want he used to do. The young generation always holer, if they cut my wages I wouldn't work. You mite be glad to sneak a living like a lion and a kat. The king couldnt talk to his son, Upsala, but God hung him up in an oak tree and yu know how that turned out. We no that we got a good God, but we kant fool with Him the hole life time. We no that yu boys got a gud muder, but yu kant buy cigarets with all yu earn and expect yur muder to feed yu when she gets old. If the hole world were onest there wuldnt be a hungry person on the erth.

Ther warehouses are ful and the rats and the soldier ants got a gud time. When children are suffering we are looking for one beter than Musolini to teach us to live a rite life for God and give us rest for a thousand yers. I for myself have nothing to kik for. I never missed a meal yet, but sumtime that mite be long between meals.

We shuldnt holer so loud when we kom home and super don't wait for us on the table. That wil kum a time when yu have to holer to yourself. When I kum home and holer the one that answers me is the kat. Maybe she stole my super. That aint no use to kik the kat. She be just as hungri as I was. That aint any muney in starving a kat.

With luv to yu all.
Johannes Johnson

62.
Mister Republican
I bijn kiking and throw hints in yur teritori for a long time, but I always let the bankers out, but now they are going to git it. But the first I want yu por and rich peepel to do, take yur hat in the rite hand for the bankers of Red Wing. They have put up a record that we shud be proud over. Since the first house in Red Wing was bilt, a bank here never busted. Rap on wud.

The robbers have been scared and the sneeks and crooks have been held outside the fence. I aint much acquainte with the bankers, but got gud wurd to say about them. For more than half a hundred years they never cheat me out of a sent. And al the gud I did I told the truth.

And if the times turned so bad that I lose what I worked for my lifetime for ten cents on the dolar the bankers are more welkum to it than crooks and sneeks. So my advice to my friends is, quit yur bisness with crooks and sneeks and with the moonshiners til yu get stumich ache. If yu git hold of a dolar, bring it to the bank. Yu shur will git it when yu need it.

With luv to the bankers and the muney they handel.
Johannes Johnson
63.

Mister Republican
Now I got anuder talking spel and I want to talk to the best muder with the softest hart. For mor than a half a hundred years I have study the muder's luv to the children, but I never happen to se regular meen muder with exception of sum time stepmuder. But I seen thousand gud.
Hav yu ever stop and think that we got lots of peepel to gud and they have to sufer for it themselves. Yu shud never give yur boy muney for cigarets and gas for his kar. Do like muder rabit do. If yur boy got as big eyes as yu got, tel him to help himself. Yu shud never give yur dater muney for red paint to put on her cheks. We no yur dater is beter loking fourout that. But if she ern the muney herself, let her paint her check with red paint or pine tar. She will soon find what she like the best.

I kan never be to gud to a paper boy. He grew up like a kornstalk in Juli, when I grew like a cowstall in the winter. If I shud buy newspaper boys, I shud be wiling to pay tousand dollars apiece, but I dasn't offer ten cents a dozen for high skul boys.

It happens that newsboys grow up to be president when a high skul boy grows down to a bank rober and yu al no that I aint got any high skul word in my letters. But I don't tink that wil hurt either yu or yur kids to reed them.

With luv to both newspaper boys and high skul boys.
Johannes Johnson

64.
Mister Republican
I find out the other day that al the muney for license and for gas taxes goes back to the county so near a 8 percent. There is no wunder the big check is gud when the officers receive them. I for my part wud sooner have the scavenger yob in Red Wing than a 100 acre farm in Hay Creek and I wud sooner have the office to be yanitor in the town hal in Hay Creek than to be owner of $30,000 properti in Red Wing.
This sonds bad but what kan yu do if there is some truth in it? Yu kan do the same as they do in our state schools with what they kant eat up in one meal, throw it away. But remember if yu are a minister or a moonshiner, God ses yu when yu go to the garbage can and he know where those liv who wud be glad to get it *(the leftover food)*.

Have yu ever stop to think that yur children am maybe sum day will sneak around like the old bachelor's *(Johannes')* kat for a livin? Maybe yu are the one to blaim.

Punishment for sins goes to 3rd and 4th generations. With luv to yu al as long as yu let me kik. That feels beter when I got kramp in my legs. We feel beter when we kan pay the interest on our mortgag in our homes and if we got lots of rats in our granary, we feel beter if we can kil one and we got the house ful of small kids we feel beter if the muder kan button up the koat on one of them. If we have to go to the por hous we feel beter if we kan see we are welcome.

Johannes Johnson

65.
Mister Republican

I sitting here alone to tri to figur out the reason that kost more to liv when everything is so cheep. 50 years ago we bot a bushel of beens in the fal for dolar, a bushel of pees for a dolar, rutabegas and potatoes we had in the bak yard. Wheat we brot to the mil and brot home enough flour for a hole winter. Now we have to have a millionair to bak our bred. Yu no they wuldn't work for a small salari. Where we used to raise our potatoes and vegetables we got a tousand dolar kar and the house *(garage)* we keep it in cost maybe $400 or $500 and we have to pay so much a munth. The boxes we had the beans and pees in we cud burn up in the spring. Now we have to pay ten dollars a day to hal it away. If we don't they put us in the yailhouse. Now when we got dri, we used to go into Remmeir and cal for scop of beer. Now we sneek in the ale and pay a quarter of a dolar and that tast like wash water with salaratus in it. When we want to have fun we went together and maiD the fun ourself. Now we hav to go to the piktur show and giv them another half dolar.

When we want a smok we put the tobako in the pipe and we blow the smok out. Now the tobako hav to go in papir tubes and the smok down in the lungs so that the flesh on yung gurls lok liked smoked German karp.

This kan be enuf to kut down the figures for hi kost – a sinful life – but I lik yu al just the saim.

Johannes Johnson

66.
Mister Republican
Years ago the minister used to co me down to mi hous. We had always a gud time, so I told him, "I dont want yu to wer out yur shues to kum down and see me. Yu go down town and get a pair of the best shues and charge them to me." Next time he kum down he show me the shues. I said, "They look gud." "Yes, but I took a pair for mi wife, they luk better."
I said, "Yu were smart. I never thot of that." But I keep that up for three generation of ministers. I kud even lay the foundation for the church. So long as I went to church I had muney, but when I slacked off going to church, the money slacked off kuming in. Church and religion keeps the crooks and sneeks out of yur busines and if the busines had the foundation from religion, we al wud be siting prety. So long as we kan keep peepel going to church we kan keep starvation away frum our dors.
But if the religion is taken away frum our country we aint got no country. We got a Hel and if yu minister preech so that the plaster shake off the wals that don't du yu any gud if yu aint there. Maybe yu feel the same as I do – shamd – because I aint bin to church for a long time.
If I start, wud yu start? Let us surprise sum of the old peepel.

With luv to you al.
Johannes Johnson

67.
Mister Republican
I like to giv little advis with frosting on. Take gud care of the kow that milks the most if yu are seling grain, be gud to the chickens that lay the most eggs and play with the one of yur children first up in the morning. And don't forget to be gud to yur wife. If she wash yur overhalls and keeps the stov klen. If she waits on the breakfast table dont yu forgit to wait on the super tabel. And if yu help her washing the dishes yu will look ten years younger and yu will get 10 steps closer to Heven and maybe the children wud follow the fader's example and befor yu know it yu are al in Heven and yu got al the luv with yu inside Heven and no gangstger or underworld is going to bother yu.

With luv to yu al.
Johannes Johnson

68.
Mister Republican
Im glad so long as yu let me throw out the plank to the thousands of taxpayers that is drowning. Let go of everything and hold to the plank. Let that three ton tractor go that pul yu down the bottom so yur children cant afford to buri yu. Let yur tousand dolar kar go befor it tips over the bank and kils both you and yur good-looking wife.

Buy yu a teem and do the repair with oats and the price of oats will go up to the ful value. Have yur children to milk yur kows and send yur milking machine bak to the gret inventor. Ty yur wheat bundle with straw and then yu would not hav any twine bil to pay. Hawl yur pigs to market in the lumber wagon and then yu aint got no gas bil to pay. Send yur county agent to Washington. Maybe he kan lern the congressman something I know he kant lern yu anything. Dont spend yur moni on the countri roads. Yu kant ride to Heaven that way anyway and if you in town, dont think you got so much moni as Mr. Ford and if yu got lots of properti dont feel proud over yur big taxes. And if you got lots of frens dont expect them to pay your bils, but if yu want to lose a frend, borrow him a dolar. I had good many frens in my days, but they all kost me some muni.

I bin a gret man and had my pleasur in helping peepel, but they are few that what bin satisfied. If we aint got work for a common shoful in Red Wing, I dont think we hav to use the steam shoful and if the rats are going to eet up what we are going to eet, it aint no use to fed the kat and if the Mississippi River is going to dry, the German carp have to sufer first.

With luv to you all,
Johannes Johnson

69.
Monday, March 7, 1932
Mister Republican
I want peepel to no I am bak in my homestead where I live in peece and happiness. I thot I beter stik to the ship til it sunk and I invit my frens to kum and see the broken mast and the torn sail that the last three storms did. And when I get the barnacles swept off, I am going to steer it into softer water and I will then look for a man to have hold of the ruder.

With luv to the one that broke the mast and the one that turned the lites off.
Johannes Johnson

70.
Mister Republican
Der is a thot with peepel that if a man lie he will steel to but not always, so I never stole a peney in my life that I no of, but I lied gut many times. And I feel shamed for it to, but there is one that I like to tel that aint so bad but it is a lie just the same. Bout 35 years ago, when I kum from town late I seen a boy siting on a stone by the gas hous and crying. I stoped and ask what was the reason, when he was out so late crying. He said, my fader threw me out and he told me I kan never kum home any more. I said that mite be a mistake. I wil go with yu home and see so everything be all right and he said I never go home. I goin to yump the train tonite. Dont do that, go home with me and I will pay yu al yu are wurth and yu kan lern my trade and play with my boys and neebors got boys and yu wil have a gud time. So he went with me home and I holer to my wife, kum and see what I found down the line that beets what we got.

And the boy stayed about a year and he never said a cros wurd to me and I didn't to him, but he commenced to feel like home and my boys wants to be the bos and he wuldnt stand for it. So I got order to quiten down the family. So I went to his fader and told him that I didn't have suitable rum for him any longer. If yu wud take him home, I will pay as much more as the board. "No I wil not. I giv him up and you kan keep him," he said. I see the mother wipe the teers with her apron and I said, "Yur boy has bin in my house so long, but I never herd him said a bad wurt bout yu. But I always herd him talk gut bout yu and today he said he wud like to see them home."

I liked that and more to. So the fader giv in and told me to send him home for a trial. I see I kaim out gud with that lie, but had to start to plan and say not more. I went home and I said, "I bin to yur home and they are both sik and they want yu to kum home." He said, "Me goin home, I shud say not." "Yes, but yur fader cry and told me he know he didn't treet yu right and he said he think he wud be beter if yu kum home and I pay yu so much more. Do as I want yu to do, try it out and my home will be open for yu any time yu wil kum bak." So he gav in and went home and the next day I asked him how it was home and he said he was glad he went home because he was needed there. "But I shud like to bring a load of koal home," he said. "Yu go and order a load and charge that to me. We wil fax that," I said. Couple of days later he said, "I wud like to bring a pig home." "Yu go down to the bucher and charge the pig to me and we wil fix that," I said. And the boy staid home and was a gud boy so long as his fader lived and I think he dont know anything bout the lie, but I do. That the only lie of mine that I wil tel, but I wish now that I never told one lie.
With luv to yu al, Johannes Johnson
71.

Mister Republican
There is a awful shok to the hold world bout Lindbergh's stolen child. And the reason are that he had gud luk and flew over the ocean first and then happened to marry the rich gurl, but his child aint got more than one soul and if he is ded we al know that his soul has gon to God and he is out of risky world. Maybe 20 yers from now he mite drop frum the air and brek his nek and his soul have to go to Hel. Then there is something for the hole world to cry for.
There is wonderful how big sympathy there is for the man that get hold of those big American dollars. And how litel sympathy a man get if he happen to lose that. When he have to go to the por house yu hear them holer that's gud nuf for him and they mention that nasty name.

With luv to both the reeders and Lindbergh's baby.
Johannes Johnson

72.
Mister Repulican
I always vant to talk to yu al, but this time I vant to talk to one and that the one that vent into my hous and opened the lock kover and took an imitation 50 dolar gold piece and a big silver dolar, Dane and Norvegian combined since 1600 two 50 sens gold peeces and one eith-kroner, one California gold dolar and one 2 ½ and oder gold coins. Now to the one dat took it, I wud advise yu to bring it bak. There isn't one dolar like it in this country and yu kant show him to nobody and yu kant take it with you to Heven. And Peter vil vant to know how yu get him. If yu bring him bak, we are just as good frens and yu can keep the rest of the muney, but if you dont, yu shal never have a hapy day in yur life. And yu shal never look at the sun forout you see the silver dollar between. I know who yu are and I means to be gud to yu, but if you dont listen, yu wil harvest yur seed.

With luv to yu al,
Johannes Johnson

73.
Mister Republican
I vant to lern yu sumting that kost me many tousand dollars. A man that rent houses and pay his rent regulari and never kiks. Yu kan trust him with yur yewlry box if yu got it ful of yewlry, but the man that never pays and dont vant to pay, dont wet yur feet to save him from drowning.
I man that alvays expected help frum yu and never return ani, don't let him kum to klose so he bite yu. Yu vil sure die from ratelsnak poison. And if you got a doctor in yur relation thats gud, but yu kan get gangrene in yur toes anyhow. And if yur next neebor is a lawyer thats gud, but you mite pay biger fine ethan if he liv in Jerusalem. Thats a gud ting that our officers of Red Wing and Gudhu kounty keep trak of us, but there wil be a time when we vil luk up them too. And when the treasury is empty, we wil luk up the boks too. And now we got plenty rum. If the bumblebee got a nest in one room, we kan go to the other and we dont know how mani there is in an oversized cigarbox before we open it. But there used to be a picture of a nice lady on the top of the box. Now to folks that dont like mi letters, I certainly will take it al bak. Yu al know it don't take a smart man to giv peepel hel, but when it koms to get a sun to go up in the east and down in the west, then it takes a gud man to figure. I for my part believe that the sun goes up on the best side and down on the best place.

With luv to yu al,
Johannes Johnson

74.
Mister Republican
Der is alvays a case that old peepel wury more than yung peepel. I vas told the oder day that the highway department have 175 kars and truks and now I wury for that. I wury that I kant pay my taxes so I kan help them out. I got $1200 rent kuming from one house at last three years and now I wury kaus I got nine mor. And I'm afraid those that owe me muney wury bekaus they kant pay me and then I wury for the kounty have to spen more on the county yail to get that to correspond with new courthouse.

And then I wury for the kolor that I have to be like a jersey kow and then I wury why we got 2 banstans in one park. That mite be fite between Hay Creek and Spring Creek and we might have to put up one on the shor of Mud Lak and then I wury for hole yer how Red Wing are kuming out with the swimming pool.

And then I wury how the mushrats getin along underneath and then I wury how the por peepel and moonshiners are goin to get along next winter. The busness getin por for both of us and my last wury is if I rote this letter so yu reeders understand what I meen. I meen wel for the state and the kounty. I dont kare much for myself.

Johannes Johnson

75.
Mister Republican
I vant to tel to me smallest pay thru my life for what I bin doing. There is for to being gud and the wurst I cud tel peepel is the truth. Now yu kan figur out how I feelin the evening of my life. If I didnt hav life after this, haven't I bin a fool? But my belief is that my return is kumming and the bad in me is scratched out. So I am thankful for my life and so long as I kan stay.

Today I bin and luked at the new bandstand. I try to figur out how many corners and circles that had, but I kudn't, but that dont maik any figurs. I kud see that hadn't bin any old fool that maid out the plans and as an old settler of Red Wing, I wish that the boys wud let me maik the first speech.

I wud pik out the old settlers of Spring Creek and Belle Creek and set them on the big circle and maik ladys and gentlemen take off their hats and giv them the honor for saving the money so yu boys kud pay for many corners. It luked to me that the old peepel's silver and gold dolar turned into paper and yu no paper is getting cheep nowdays.

We old peepel hav to get long, but when the city hall and the courhosue and the white house be without muney I tink yu boys hav to go to work and yur most important tool wil be the gun. Yu have to do like the bee, kil those that we ain't got no use for. We mite get chance to play hiding go seek in our own kuntry so we don't need to go to France and the bonus wouldn't be so big eether. And we mite talk to eech other more friendly than we do now.

I tink I throw hints to you young folks nuff. I beter smoth it over. I will giv yu a receipt for a luv kak that is many hundred years old, if you plees kal it square. One pond of luv, two rosey cheecks, two lips well pressed, four hands clasped, one shady tre, one narrow bench, stir gud and serve it after dark.

With luv to yu al,
Johannes Johnson

76.
Mister Republican
I is a old man and a haf hundert yers setler of Red Wing and wud like to see a klear book akount on the Auditorium *(Sheldon Auditorium)*. Frum a gift of that gud herted man *(Mr. T. B. Sheldon)* that I know ment the well of the city of Red Wing. We hav men that hav bin gud to this town and let us not forget them. We al no they getting les everi yer. Nothing better than a business than kan show the public a cler book.

We citizens of Red Wing is now kuming to the time so we need to see the books clear from both the sheriff and the scavenger. Our treasury for the por is getin low and our taxpayers getin tire out and hav to stop at the cultivator in the korn field. What are yu officers gon to do with the land? There is now time for yu to stop and help us to figure the rite way. If yu officers of al kinds think that we por peepel kan make a living off concrete rods and swell diring, yu wil see the mistak and the time is soon here to yu wil feel it to. But there is gud money in it for yu yet, but there is starvation for us. When we help eech oder to pul out a lode frum a mud pool, we had a gud livin. Now we got nothing. When we used straw stead of twine, we had 3 dolars a day and the farmer had no twine bil. Now we got nothing but farmer got so big twine bil that they have to leeve their farm. When we had to much oats we kud give it to the horses but the steam shovel and the katapilar had to hav their feed *(petroleum products)* haf way from hel and that kost money. Dont the truth stand bad. I beter quit. With luv to both the one that ownes and the one that feeds the steam shuvl.
Eskuse my adition to the leter. My long life is ful of mistakes and I want to tel yu three of the bigest before lection day. I kut a house in two for a friend. That kost me $2,500 and I married a sekund time and that kost me bout the saim, but the bigest I maid over more than 50 times and that I maid the voting days. That tok al I work for my long life.

With duble luv if yu don't throw me in the waist basket.
Johannes Johnson

77.
Mister Republican
Sum of my frens tol me I didn't hav no rite to menshun ani relgion in mi leters. I wil giv the anser to yu al. I tink I hav yust as much rite as anyone. I beleev al relgion is gud but I dont no wich are the best. But when I sue to sit on mi muther's nee she said I could talk al I wanted about God, but that al had to be gud.

God is gud and we cant talk ani thing but gud about Him, but the Devil is a crook and a sneak and a lier and a theif. We didn't talk ani gud about him. I tink we shal tel our children about thos tings. He had no vakation when the world war broke out. He had one link of the chain dragging frum each country. What did he do? He killed millions, he maid crippels and sik peepel of their millions. He maid millionaires of theeves and crooks and sneeks and tok al the muney away from onest peepel and what he didn't taik then he taik now.

He was here in Red Wing and tol the milers to ship the best flour to England for a gud price and give us the red dog flour for a higher price. He had 2 karloads of sugar on side traks in Red Wing for six weeks and told the merchant to giv us a snufboxful for 25 cents but not ani more. He told the butcher to pres a little with their hands when they way us the meets and maik the baloney ring 2 inches shorter. He changed his nairn and kal himself Temperance and Probition and he was going to maik the hole wurld dri. He maid it dri for muney and wurk, but alcohol and moon shine this country used in 24 hours wud be nuf for a whal to swim in.

Don't yu understand now he is a lier? And he bin loose long nuf. Let us tie him up. When he kum to us and want us to buy alcohol with red peper and drink so we get crazi and go home and lik our wives and trow out our children, let us bi rok candi and go home and giv the children a peece eech. But dont forget to giv the muther the bigest peece. She is wurth that. Let us spin al kinds of string and maik a rope and he can not break it. Ladies shud help to. Yu kant expect yur men to do it al. I meen if we al liv an onest life and do what God wants us to do the Devil wil get so week that we can tie him up with a grocery string.

With luv to you al.
Johnannes Johnson

78.
Mister Republican
I wish yu wil put mi letter in the front pge but I tank yu where ever yu put it. I am mor interested in mi life than I ever was. I always thank God wen I wake up in the morning for letting me see what yu folks do and what is goin on.

I bin working hard and tru for 50 yers in yur city. I bilt hundreds of home for por peepel. The rich peepel cud afford to have a beter man. I always had my pay and I increase up to $30,000 properti in our town. I never losed a dolar in ani corporation or company and al the bankers respect me and are willing to giv me a lift whenever I need. For 50 years I never fail to pay my taxes, but I do now and I want the publik to know where I put the blame to.

I put the blame to peepel that I bin gud to and now I have to kal them deadbeats and krooks. I cud look out for smallpox and lepresy, but I could not look out for deadbeats and krooks. But I don't want anybody to wury. If I kan sel for 25 cents on the dolar before the sale for tax yu al wil be alright. There is hard to see so mani por peeple in our hom town. But there is just so hard to se mani Christian women that goes from hous to hous beging clothes for poor peepel and see them in the rag bag and sold to the ragman. And see the county pay for steaks a dolar and a half and see it set down on the flor for a dog. Dont the truth sound bad when the old man tel it to the yung folks? Yu wouldn't work when they ofer yu 50 cents an hour. Now yu kant get work for 15 cents an hour. Yu wouldn't sel yur kow when yu was offered hundred dollars. Now yu hav to sel it for ten.

That feels gud to sit in a nice kar and ride over the country, but that dont feel so gud to sit in a nice home and se it sold for taxes.

We maid a big mistak when we bot a swell kar to ride over the county when we shud be home and plant and hoe up our potatoes in the bak yard. We turn our muni over to the milyonire and they gave a hole lot to probation and the probation giv it over to officers by the holesale and they giv it to judges and sheriffs and polismen and skul teachers get litel of it for to educate peeple to be foolish. My idea is to keep yur boy hom so long as yu kan and let him play in the backyard with his own playthings. Thats more natural than to lern him to say the hardes wurd in the Amerikan language. Nowdays they bi glases big as a plait and put on the boy and send to the hi skul and tink he wil goin to be a presedent sum day and maybe he wouldn't be fit to drive a mule and yu hav to send him to the training skul to be a burden to the state and yur muder wud sit there under a tree, talk nice to him and maik him give yu gud promise and later on yu se him go to the prison. Yur hair wil turn grey and yur frends will turn kold and now yu no who tok the rose of yur life.

With love to yu al but most to the muders.
Johannes Johnson

79.
Mister Republican
One of mi frend that I tink got jelous tol me he was goin to se Jins K *(Jens Grundahl, editor of The Republican)* and giv him h___ for letting me print those kiking letters. I tol him to giv me h____ and leave him alone, for he's got h___ enuf already. He got big burd with long wings and hevy spurs on the legs to fite with and he to hold out for so many years and al I kan se is mater with him that his hair turned grey, but he isn't licked and the hair is all there so the burd didn't get much for kiking al those yers. And if our president had ben so gud fiter as Jens we wuldn't hav so big war debts we now got and I never found that he threw mi leters in the waste basket for not being stylish and speled rite. But if I shal try him with the lie but I wuldn't, I got so much truth to tel so I kant tel half before I have to leeve.

Canada thisels dont feel shamed to grow in our beautiful city. I see the brush and rough elm tre, and wont to kil them new planted evergreens in the park. I started to kik and that helped rite away. I am glad to kik to officers that dont tel me to go to h___ and that aint no use for us to tel our officers to go to h___ either. I found that beter to kik in a nice way, but there is a relief when we got a nice mayor if we kan holer.

And sum is born only to kik and they git expert when they git old and sum is born to say yes, yes if they put the pig in the parlor. They holer, that's rite, and they know beter, but al newspapers need a kiker and Republican has me so long as they let me. I am thankful to the reeders of the yob. That helps my wurries. But work hard al mi life, save al I kud and 75 years old and use to be rich and have to sufer and have to wury for living and my busness is best on a false promis.

With luv to yu al.
Johannes Johnson

80.
Mister Republican
I am glad that yu and the reeders wud let me slip in a peece in the paper once in a while and the reason is al pleesur I got out of half a hundert yers life in Red Wing is to tel peepel the truth and that sound bad lots of times.

Now I want to explain my asking of the council and bord of public works on their last meetings. When the city paved 7th street, they grade down the stree two feet in front of my driveway and they made a horseshu turn in the park road so al the snow that kum on east 7th lay rite in my driveway. That kosts me five dollars for one snowfall to pen it up, so I give the city ofer if they give me right to a strip 10 feet wide and 20 feet long to get in the park road for the winter I wil giv the city right to my road to the east bluff of the park, which wil kost a city $3,000 to bild a road to, but that didnt sound gud to sum of the boys becaus I mentioned the swimming pool in my leters.

I bin a builder for more than half a hundert yers and I kan tel or wurk forout figures; I did lots of it myself and yu know the Swedes pay for everyting they lern and thats becaus dey are stubourn like sum of the other nations. But I wish tat eiter me or my children wud ofer Red Wing 10 dolars for one and I want you al to know that the park wil never be complete befor you get the easterly point. That would not be so easy to get as it was and now I want nobody to get sore. Yu al got to know if I have to post it in the parkway and go to yail.

With luv to yu al,
Johannes Johnson

81.
Mister Republican
A butcher ask me the oder day if I no what lov was. "I kan tel what I tink it is. To be gud and onest to peepel. That meens if I kum in yur shop and ask for a spring chicken and if yu luv me yu wuld't giv me a old krow." He gave me a funy laff and said, "What are life?" "The life is hard wurk for us that want to go uphill at the time, but it is easy for you that follow the river and the railroad tracks." He got mad and said, "What have yu got for yur long life?" "Old and yur body ful of rumatism." "What can yu fal bak on?" "I got six tousand dollars kuming for hous rent, that is now seeded out in Minesota and Wiskonsin and cler up to Winpeg and that turned al into Kanada thistle." "Hav you lived so long a life and hav yu get ani beter?" "Yes, I brot up a big healthy, gud luking family." He said, "That's gud, but mani told me that yur children's bred tastes biter. Haven't yu got ani of those big American dollars? They kum handi for old peepel."
"Yes, I use to have lots of them, but there ar so mani smart peepel in this town that they fooled them away frum me." But I wil tel both the butcher and the reeders that mi wife and me was gud to the sherf and the one that runs the por farm when they was small and if I get the return that is gud nuf for a man that wated along life to help dedbeats and krooks. We al get an extra plesur in sumting. Sum got the plesur in fishing and sum in hunting and sum in lying and sum in telling the truth and if I got that habit that don't sond ani beter than the oder

With luv to al that don't owe me ani money and plees read my leters slow. There is a hint to yu al.
Johannes Johnson

82.
Mister Republican
Ven I vas in the brite al my life and my children was growing up and I believed the wurst bout them, I was klosest in my thoughts. Dont that sound bad? But if we Amwerikans beleev the same about our officers dont you think we getting klose? If yu readers are gud citizens it is yur duti to studi those things to the welfair of the town and kuntry. The times have changed so crooked seem to be strait and there is easier for the rich man to maik a million than for the por man to maik an ax handel or milk a kow. Fifty yers ago a gurl wud get sik if they maik her smok a cigarette. Now she wil get sik if she kant smoke it. That kant be the climate has changes.
Fifty years ago the government maid whiskey and the salon dor next to the church and we kud go freely to ether Heven or Hel. Now they want us to go to Hel, but dont you do it.

Fifty years ago wen we kum up in the morning and we didnt feel gud, we kud go to the cupboard and taik a gud drink. Now we hav to wait til the doctor kum up to giv him two dollars or sneek out in the brush pile and we are both mad and skared so we always taik to much of the bottle and we mite go bak and lik both the muder and the children.

Fifty years ago we used to maik our living in sunshine. Now the most have to maik it in moonshine. In moonshine the darkness is when the seed maik roots, but it takes sunshine to maik it bloom. Stop, luk and listen. We got al the state prisons ful of moonshiners and crazyhouses to, and we got a hole lot of our churches. What kan we do if we dont get ani sunshine?

With luv to yu al. Yu are al gud that let me stay with yu yet for a while.
Johannes Johnson

83.
Mister Republikan
Deres lots of tings dat ve old gobs cant see into. I cant see how a minister can make a sermon and hav a radio in his house and listen to all dat scrap and dum and childish tak dat goes on over de world. De radio have take bred and butter away from many tousand minister. And radio hav spoiled de most der is left. And de radio has spoiled de church member.

Fifty year ago ven a church member vould sit and luk de minister rite in de face dey help de minister mak a gud sermon. I tink dats enuf dat de electric got a power in de hole world. Let de minister pray for de power to de One dat promis to giv him de power. Eder radio or prohibishun vil open de dor to Heven but dat look to me dat dey got de road open to Hel.

How smart and educated yu folks are. Yu can never maik me beleev dat moonshine is better than sunshine. How nice flowers yu folks can maik out of a paper an wax, dey aint got de life. How nice yu trim up a ded person, he is ded and he vil stay ded til de One cal on him dat give him de life. I cant see how a world ful of educated people have start to run de world to hire officers by de tousands and buy shovels and snow plows ven de soldiers, paper flowers, rode scrappers, steem ant can valk on top of de snow. I tink de time is soon here ven de big cedar on Lebonons mountin are going to get de tops broken off in a hard vind storm. Stop, luk and listen. I can heer ven de fiddle is out of tune but I cant fix it but I got a boy dat know how.

With lov to all dat God give two eyes and two ears.
Johannes Johnson

84.
Mister Republican
Yeers ago when I was a gud man, ful of religion and ment wel and see the Heven and Hel two feet away, that was a better life. Now I am like a red sedar fence post standing in the crack of the rocks side of Belle Creek, but the time is not forgotten. Our church was too small and the dirt from the bluffs filled up the church whenever it rained. I got up a way to beter ourselves. I tol two of the members I'd bild a foundation and yu muv the church and you paint the church and we three maik a gud yob and lev the congration free for expenses. That sounds gud to the most. Next day I had teems and filled up the street with stones and sum got yealous and want to bak out. But al went thru with changing new windos.

The one that giv the windows, he got his name in them with colored glas. I thot I'd get my name in the cornerstone but they didn't want no cornerstone that year, but the next yer they laid it outside the wal. I commenced to be blue. I kudn't sleep at night. When I got so tired that I had to sleep I drem a man kum up and ask me, "Do you remember that curl haired boy that fed yur teem with leves and gras when yu hauled the stone to the church?" "Yes, I do."
"That boy did mor for the church than yu did. His name is roted down in Heven." We got a wonderful God. He kan put yur name down if you give a kat milk when she is hungry, but he wuldnt put yur name down if yu put a tower on the church.

When we giv anything we shouldn't let the right hand no what the left hand do and we got such a man in our town and God bless yu. Yu will hav gut intrest for yur money. A glas of water that's given wil be wel paid for if that's given right.
With luv to yu al.
Johannes Johnson

85.
Mister Republican
There hapin to me sum things in mi life that kant be forgotten. When I was a newcomer to this town ful of religion and luv and I had a sweet heart like lots of boys got nowdays and one of mi boy friends tri to kut me out and I tri to forgiv that boy that maid me that sorrow. I was shingling a hous when I had that luv spel. I had a pece of blu chalk in my poket and I rote the Lord's Prayer on the rough bords and shingel it over and rote again so one side of the rof was covered with Lord's Prayer. But a few smiles and sunshine blow that sorrow away and al was forgotten.

That roof dekayed and a new roof was put on and I hapin to get the yob to put the third roof and now I am a old gub and married the second time and when I started tering the old shingel off I see the blu chalk riting and I was in the same fix, and a man kan luv if he is old.

Luv is a funy thing. It never get old, never rust and it's the only think we kan take with us into Heaven and we kannot get in without luv. Our teeth get old, but we kan by new nice ones, but we kant by no luv. But I wil send sum to Republican readers.

With luv to yu al.
Johannes Johnson
86.

Mister Republican
Hav yu ever thot of that beer is no gud befor they put bak what they took out of it? Hav yu ever thot of we are foolish that spend so mani millions on a scaffold to the moon when we al no we kant git there? What is the shining of the moon gud for if it never strikes the erth? What gud would it do to put a padlock on a por widow's home when a six or seven story building are occupied in the saim business? And our paved roads are open from kost to kost and our factories are making machin guns and sel them frum right to left and our officers if they got the rite mind are afraid of them when they aint afraid of the old widows?

Why shud you kil a two week old litel pig when yu got pigs ten yers old with teeth in the sides of their mouth like an elephant? There is not time for us peepel to wake up and talk it over with our ministers and if he is lazi and careless like we are the time is soon here when the last grasshopper is here and goes for him and gives us a beter chance. The time aint goin to stay the way they is long. If we got the power over the wurld above there wil be a kleening up. The moon is beginning to show buld now and he was set in the sky to silver up the nite and maik it beautiful for rabbits when they have their super. Now he is used for kidnapping and bank robbers and that luks so the whole wurld like beter to do their business in moonshine than sunshine. Our children used to sleep and rest in the nite and git their education in the sunshine. Now they want to sleep in sunshine and want to git their education in the moonshine. Don't the truth sound bad? But I wish there is sum chiken that piks up the kernels and that chickens and grasshoppers wurk together. They kan eat up both millionaires and chain stores. This is what I tink, but if yu dont tink the same we are yust as gud friends.

Eat what yu kan and I will do the same and I will send my luv to yu al.
Johannes Johnson

87.
Mister Republican
We know al that there is hard time al over the hole wurld. There is what we kal the wurld panic and we al got a idea how to get over it. Mi beleev is furst to make us beleev ther is a God, a Heven and a Hel. We start with our children to lern them like we used to do in the olden time. I as a old citizen want to tel yu, yu kant get far without beleev in religion. I don't kare what religion yu beleev in. They are al gud.

That takes a harness and a hors to pul and that takes a gud man to drive the hors. Yu kant drive the hors yust for the big Amerikan dolar. Yu got to luv the hors. Yu kan not put a big load on him and yu kant do like the farmers do nowdays, drive the hors farout shus. You kant cheet yur landlord on hous rent. Yu kant cheet yu groceri man on groceri and yu k nt cheet yu lawbreekers forout to suffer for it.

Mi beleev is if we al turn onest to eech other an the hard times wud disappear at once. We aint got no reason for hard times. The warehouses is full, but we turn into krooks and now there is up to yu minister to preach the gospel and do yu duti. God sure wil be with yu. And dont forget that Baal's preechers got killed. And the rain soften up the ground al over the land and dont git sore if I mention religion. That's al old man's duti. Mi mother did that with me and that's al she had to giv me when she send me to this new wurld.

With luv to yu al.
Johannes Johnson

88.
Mister Republican
We old Peepel want to talk over our long life. I never thot we was so foolish as we hav bin. I know I dont deserv no flowers when I'm thru. Wurk hard the long life, saved penies and the dime, invest in farms and property yust like we kud live so long as we wanted to. Now in the evening of our life we luk bak and take the length of our life. We take a peece of chalk on our rite hands, cross over the left. There is the lingth of our life. What are the life? Nothing more that to be brot up for the next life. I don't think that God gives us ani credit for savin nickels and dimes and when we get old giv it to lazy peepel, dedbeats and krooks. If I bin as God wanted us to, I wud be wel off now. But to late are the siners gong to wake up. The world gets so lazi and stylish that our minister sent to Chicago for the sermon for Sunday morning, and our rabit hound we have to chase to the wuds.

The fish and the birds got protection but the sheep have got no herders.
With luv to both the sheep and the rabit hound and the only advis we kan giv each other is to be satisfied-say nothing. If the yung generation tel us the karp is white we beter nick on our hed and said, is that so?

Johannes Johnson

89.
We bisnis men are going to hav a meeting for ourselves so al of the reeders dont need to listen and I am going to be the alderman at large and I want to ask yu, when is the morning star for our bisnis going to show in the east? And nobody ansers so its mi duti to anser myself. When we kan invest our muney in bilbords and horses' shoes and grub hoes and wiskey barrels and beer kegs and giv the por peepel freedom and we al go to the funeral and bury al steem shovels and caterpillars and buses, trucks and flying machine. That kost muney for us to fli in the air and it kost the burd nothing. We wud be beter off if we stay where we belong-on the ground with a shofel in our hands. That was the order we got when we were driven out of paradise, but the Devil is smart mechanic. If we start another Amerika on the other side of the north pol he kud git up machinery to it wud be lik that *(like it is)* in this Amerika in 5 or 10 yers.

And the Devil wil hire al the ladies he kan for officer. He no they are master in his wurk than the men. There was a man in olden times so strong that he licked 7,000 and the sord he had was only the yawbon of a mule. But the Devil hired a smart ladi and she licked him so bad that he lost his eyesite for life. So be kerful boys that lady yu hire. I hire one for 7 munths and that kost me $2,000 and the best bargain I ever maid was when I paid her off and got rid of her. And now to yu al, where is our liberti? I want to find it and kis it before I die. Wud yu al help me to find it and only way to do that is that we live a honest life. We kant let ourselves into Heven. We kant cry ourselves in. We hav to live a life on this erth for Heven. We have to be redy for Heven before we kum to the dor.

With luv to yu al, but I wuldn't hire yu al.
Johannes Johnson

90.
Mister Republican
I'm giting so mani new naims in mi old age. Sum holer, "helo Republican" and sum holer "helo, Johnson says" and I proud over those naims and I tank yu al. I taik it is a friendship. But plees dont kal me the eagle. I wasn't born with wings and I don't clim hi. I got mi nose in the mud like a pig and turn the sod over to show you the rots of wild oats and Canada tistle.

Plees dont put no ring in mi nose. I aint goin to stay long with yu. Al $10,000 a yer is Canada tistle and $3,000 salari for a gaim warden is wild oats. Why shudnt we old settlers hav the right to go and git a few sunfish for supper? Yust as wel as those Indians? Giv us peepel of Amerika freedom. If you officers think yu will be mistake – the saim as the officer that tried it and drown half million peepel.

We had lots of them big officers in olden times, but when God put them on the skale they was lighter than nothing. So I think of Hoover gets weighed on the saim skale we wil see him like Absolam hangin in the oak tree. And that's the right place for the feler who sends his nice boys to another country to kil just as nice boys.

And then sit home and drink wine and smok a pipe and then expect the hole wurld to thank him for it al.

We had oficer in the north when Norway was split up in 27 countries and there was nothing but fites. And he said, "If you boys wil folo me I aint goin to kut mi hair and shave miself befor I maik it al one country." And they started out. He was always in the frunt. One time they kut his lower jaw off and he stuck a biscit in his mouth and bite his teeth to hold the jaw up and he won 28 fites. That's' officer I like and they are easy to pay off and they are satisfied and they maik muney for us and we liv a happi life.

With luv to yu al.
Johannes Johnson

91.
Mister Republican
A smart yung frend of mine asked me if I know how much mi leters I write in the Republican amount to. Yes, I no, they don't amount to much, but one mesketo that flips its wings over the see dont amount to much eether, but he do his duti. If he dont flop the wings he wil fel down and dron, but both of us want to live as long as we kan. And so long as the Republican reeders want to reed mi letters and ask for mor I will write if I grow so old that the moss grows on mi bak. Kan yu tel me how much the swimin pool and the junk pile side of it kost Red Wing in muney? He said that wasnt in his business. I no yu are mani steps higher, but kan you tel me how mani peepel Uncle Same hav to pay off everi day in a munth? He said he didnt kare about that so long as he gits his muney.

I no litel more than yu do then I told him. He's got round 7 millyun to pay off and I commence to feel sorri for Uncle Sam. If I was him I wud quit them all and hire a new crew. They wudnt need to be so highly educated from Germani and England, yust so they was onest.

One cinch bug dont hurt the kornstalk much but when there gits half a millyun the kornstalk wil dri up forout of the kob. And if you and me and al that God and Uncle Sam is sposed to be boss over wuld liv the life that they want us to do the hard times wud not last 24 hours.

But Lucifer, the one that fooled the first ladi to take a bit of the appel, he is yust as smart today. He wants a man to wer wite and green pants with a bottle of moon in the hip pocket and ladys dresses so short that they need a dentist pincher to pul them over the knee. The lips got to be red and the eyebrow like soot and the fingernails polished with lucky strike and the feet like a mountain goat and the hair have to be burned with lectric. And al in the homes hav to be run with lectric machin.

How do this leter suit sum of yu? Or what kan yu do if theer is truth in it? I wil advis yu to tink it over and turn in the krek before you kum to the flood. The old Roman time is here and the fal is going to be yust as big, but when we fal let us fal into the hands of God. He got lots of forgivnes.

With luv to yu al.
Johanneson Johnson

92.
Mister Republican
I rote so mani letter to yu so I havent rote so mani to al the sweethearts I had in my life. And I always want to tel yu the truth and the news. Dis time I no yu wil laff, but I wish yu wuldnt git the lockjaw.

I invented a machine to pik bluberrys isn the north. The machine is maid of hogwire like lady's hairpins with a blower to blow the leaves and leev the berys to the one that push the machin.
I was al set to go for to tri it out but find out that my breaks was wear out on mi kar when I tried to sneek in on the paving. And when I lok in mi pocketbook I couldn't afford to fix my break, so I had to stay home and al become a failure.

I spose mi children don't like that I tel the truth so plain, but if they lie that ain't mi fault. I don't brot no muney to Red Wing when I kum and I ain't going to taik any with me when I go. I luk yu in the face when I kum and I wil do the saim when I go and I wish yu al kud look back and said, "Im glad I don't owe him anithing."

Yu wud feel beter and mi children wud feel beter to.

With luv to yu al.
Johannes Johnson

93.
Business Men
I vant to giv in mi standing report a a citizen of our butiful city. I got property that was wurth $30,000 not long ago. But to be tru to yu, dont giv me ani credit. I dont see ani way to pay yu. I need everi dolar that kuming in to pay mi taxes and I giting old and peepel dont tink I need ani muney. And I was born with a rabit heart and in mi old age I sufer for it and grow like the cows tale.

The gud times teech us to spend muney and the hard times teech us to be krooks. Who are yu going to blame? We started on a wide concrete rod in a swell kar and landed in a mud hole and crutches are gud enuf for us the rest of our life. We brot home books from both library and book stor and studied to get rich fast. We send our children to hi school to lern to read Greek and Latin and we let our Bible lay on the shelves covered with dust.

We let our children go to the picture show wen we shud hav them home and teech them bout Heven and Hel. There is the only thing that civilizes the wurld and brings up peepel that don't land in prisons. The Bible is the string that leads us to Heven and the Republican tells us whats goin on in our kuntri and that's al we need to look both God and our nabors in the face.

That hard time we preaching about and use for tool to beat eech other with. It aint goin to be ani betr for a time yet. I beleev the Devil is loose and he works on al the officers in the wurld. A haf a million salri aint enouf for sum of them and I think he dont leev the ministers alone eether. But ther is a time in our futur when one is goin to be our king and do al the office wurk free and he is going to burn up the krooks and sneeks like straw before he start in. No professors for hundred dollars a wek are needed in our town, not no public wurks that spend our money for swimming pool and snow plows, no judges, no ladies on the jury election day. He is goin to do it al and free and rite. I will advis yu al to live a life and be prepared so he dont have to burn yu up when he kums. Ther wil be lots of officers that lose ther yobs, but that wil be sum that wil have a beter yob to be with Him. And He wil rest his feet on those that tink the wurld cant get long forout them.

When the officer get so far that he tinks the wurld kant get long forout him there is sumting rong, when Red Wing manufactori and wurk hav to turn into log shanties and fish pond so our officers are more satisfied with moonshine than sunshine. That mite be mor in it for them. I know this is hard to swallow for sum of yu, but what wil you do if the truth protects me.

With luv to yu al.
Johannes Johnson

94.
Mister Republican
Hav yu ever thot of that a profet is not recognized in his home town? That's mi last studi. I practically spent mi life for kurios and mi pleesur hav ben in old tings. Where I seen them, not for millions, but for muney I kud spair I have bot them. I never did kare for what mi neebor had, but for what he kudn't get. That's what I feel proud over. I bin asking different parties of musikans in dis town if they wudn't kum down and play a few peeces, but they al no my treasuri is empty, so I told a coupel girls if they wud ask Salvation Armi if they wud cum down and they kum yust as quick as Amerikan soldiers and play so the hole blok shake, but mi children didn't her it in the saim blok. But peepel frum Kanada heerd it and kum visit with us al evening. And they gave the Salvation Armi a dolar. One old ladi said, "I never feel so happi since I vent to Sunday skul." And now with this heer I hav to tel a stori frum a Sunday skul. The teacher know that they maid moon in the neeborhud but she kud never find out who, so she asked if there were sum of the children who kud tel who maid the sun and a little boy raised his hand and said, "God maid the sun."

"Yes, that is rite, but kan sum of yu tel me who maid the moon?" she asked and a small boy raised his hand and said, "I know. Larson and his father maid the moon." Out of lunartiks and children yu kan find out the truth and yu kan kal me either one. I like to see all Republican reeders happi. Play and hav a gud time if you see me go to the poor hous. Do the saim when I am buried. I know God don't want ani cri-babies. My muder told me so. Mi life have bin in the hands of God and I want mi deth to be the saim. I know He wudn't maik no mistak where ever he sends me.

With luv to yu al.
Johannes Johnson

95.
Mister Republican
Our muney of Red Wing has bin spent freely for neccessari wurk and a hole lot of luxury. Now they want to save the kost of the man to xamine the boks. They want to do it themselves, and maybe call it free. Now there is up to yu taxpayers if you are satisfied. I no I am not and on mi rod to the porhous I shal kik and if I git mi last home there the taxes of Red Wing and the dishonest peepel are the cause of it.

But I vant to no befor I go if the boks of the city hal is kler to meet the judg that reeds our minds and who wants to be mi helper. I am like a rat in the trap. Al I no is to holler.

With luv to all that cudn't.
Johannes Johnson

96.
November 18, 1932
Mister Republican
I rote so mani leter to yu and onli 2 got rejected. I tink I wil rite one to our new president but I want yu Republican reeders to luk it over and see if that's fit to send. If they ain't we wil say nothing bout it.

"Our hi king president and fater, Roosevelt.

"Yu can not git on to the highest step befor the dors of heven open up for yu. One of the 2 powers that we believe in brot yu where yu are now. Lucifer, later named devil, that is one power, and our God are the oder power. Yu got yu ful rite to serve eder one, but we wish and believe that yu re goin to wurk for God and yu shal not be a failure. Yu are like a fader over one hundert millions. Yu got boys that got billions and yu got boys that git anything they wish for but yu got boys that got nothing and al ther wish is wurk so that they can support a luving wife and small children. Talk it over with them boys that got millions and millions if they kudn't do sumting. We wil wurk onest for a small salari.

We kan get long with littel, but we kant liv on nothing. If we happen to send to mani krooks to Washington, pay them off and send them home. We got sum left that we kan tri out and if yu hav to raise the taxes dont forgit the milionaires and the steem shufel.

And we wish yu kud chase the railroads off our streets. Them big trucks giv us hert trubel. We have to be scared al the time. I got lots to tel yu bout, but I will wait til we git more quainted. This is the feeling of sum of yur boys that got no edukatshun and we meens wel. But I am fraid this leter are going to stay home, but mi best luv are going to both to the president and reeders.

Johannes Johnson

97.
November 30, 1932
Mister Republican
An old frend was to mi hous the oder nite and we figure on what we have done thru our long life and he told me what yu have done dont mount to much. So both me and the kat feel hert. So I tuk my pencil and said I am going to tel the Republican and find out if yu think the saim. I hav worked for 8 dolars a month in the harvest fields and kut kord wud for 60 cents a kord and 3 dolars a week for mi bord. And I worked on the section for 90 cents a day and when we bilt wit the white ston blok I tended to 7 stone masons for a dolar a day and when I straiten mi back, the ston barrow kaved in and when they had fixed they raised me a quarter.

I bilt hunderts of houses for por peepel and lots that aint paid for. I level off a hole lot of southside Barm bluff and the north side of Sorin's bluff. I sold to the Milwaukee railroad tons and tons of ston until I quit the yob. And I treated a quart of blue ribbon to the engineer that maid the figurs. I was the first champeen on skis in Red Wing going down Green street forout to fal.

I bilt a viking boat with a viking hed and fish tale and seined in Mud lake when he had water in Mississippi valley. I bilt 2 Swede castles and filled them up with guns and the older the gun was the mor I paid, old drinking cups from German sellars and ash trays from Rome, first miller ston from Belle Creek and a fence post from Spring Creek. I bilt rok gardens like Jacob's, but I didn't dreem on them and the last hous I bilt stands on wheels and that mitc meen a long trip for me. This is only a small part of what I do in Red Wing and if sum of yu reeders shal ask me what its wurth to anser yu truthful, I hav to say – nothing. But if I am brot up in this wurld so God kan use me for beer in the next wurld mi hard labor is wel paid for and wil be in mi glory when I get across, and dedbeets and krooks talk what I bin working hard for life time.

With luv to the reeders.
Johannes Johnson

98.
Mister Republican
I met a kupel of friends one day that thanked me for mi leters in The Republican and they want me to keep on telling the truth. But that sounds bad, but I am glad ther are sum who like it.

I walked round nother bloc and met nother man and he said, "If yu dont stop to rite bout relief peepel sumbudi wil kil yu." So ther is for me to pologize to yu if I expect to liv ani longer. And bleeve there is yust as gud luking peepel in them as Victoria of England or the King of Spain and yust as gud herted as President Roosevelt. They eat what they git and if they git ani they are thankful for all.

But ther is nother kind there is no bottom in, and they inkreese everi day and nobody knows it beter than I. They ate up 22 houses that I owned and paid for with hard labor. I sold my rite eye and they ate that up to. And if yu wish to know how that hapined I had a hert like Roosevelt, but I did not have the muney he got.

If yu hav got a gud hert yu will liv long, but yu wil die por. And if yu don't kolekt yur bils ther wil sure kum a day when yu cant pay yurs. It is no shaim to be por and beg, but ther is a shaim to steel and lie. Mi grandfader tol me bout relief once when I was a boy. The government had sections of timberland here and ther in the kuntri. And they let the por peepel go ther and taik the bark on one side of the tree and they dryed that and maid it to flour and baiked ther bred out of it. That was all the relief they had. And the government taxed the smok that kaim out of the chimneys. If a farmer had 2 chimneys he had to pay dubel of that tax. They mortgaged the church bels except 3. Where Gustaf Vasa stud on the ston wal and tried to gather the peepel to chais the Daines out of the kuntri, but Sweden has got beter footing now. It is the only kuntri on erth that doesn't owe a dolar to any other kuntri. And Milwaukee are the only city in our kuntri that doesn't own ani and they have got a mulyun in the treasuri.

Releef peepel didn't do that, but onest and gud koncil men and officer. That is wat bilt that city. That dont bild up and maik a city when one officer raise the salari for the oder and keep on until they got 4 mor times more than they are wurth and to hang swimin pools on stilts and maik parks out of grub piles and pump up the mud frum the river to lay the winter kole on. That aint goin to make Red Wing rich.

And to yu now that dont like mi leter. I expect yu to know that when a man is 80 yers he aint responsible for what he says, but if yu want to go to heven I wil advis yu al to forgiv me, but dont forgit I luv yu al.

Johannes Johnson

99.
Mister Republican
I rote so mani letters and I always kik. Now I wil giv yu rest and yump bak to mi fader's neebor 75 years ago. The neebor had the smallest hors in the kuntri and when they went to church al drov by and the ladi of the hous played in a loteri in Germani. And she said "If I win ani muney I wil bi anoder hors" and she happen to win 3,000 krowns. And wanted to stik to her promis and they bot a swel hors. Ther oder horse had to be sold.

And when the oder hors kum to the top of the hil bi the barn he turn round and ran and he went bak to the stable before they kud git him to his new home. And they went to church the next Sunday, but they had to hold hard on the lines, but he kud go bi everybody. They had 2 children, a boy and a gurl. They began to fail. The boy wudn't eet anything and the gurl wud not help muther. They yust thot bout the small hors. So two months went bi and the farmer went to the hors man and asked him, "Hav yu got that hors yet?" And he said nobody want him. And the farmer said he wanted to bi it bak and pay yu 25 krowns for feeding. When the hors seen the farmer he pretty nerly yumped over the stals. He follow the master hom and he wud never pul them to the church anymore. He went like a king round the plais til he was 32 yers old.

I am gitting old and loose mi gud luks and lots of frends, but I got a big tom kat that likes me yet. He kan tel the sond of mi kar for a blok and meets me down the street and he kan tel if I brot meet. That's mor than the neebors kan tel. I kant tel why the kat dont eet pork, but I spose the kat knows.

I dont know why a dog maiks a yerk on his nek for every step he taiks, but the dog mite know. We aint so smart as we thinks we are. If nature wants to fil up the Mississippi valle I dont tink the engineers can hold it bak with a led pencil.
England kud not help that the king luv a ladi and if I like sum of yu ladi reeders, nobody kan help it, neether me, not they and nobodi else. The luv is the onli thing we can taik with us to heven, but I send sum to al of yu.

Johannes Johnson

100.
Mister Republican
Hav yu study up the north part of our wurld – Iceland, Greenland, Norway, Sweden and Finland? Do yu know that everything that grows on the land near the see is better than on the oder parts of the erth? So yu know that they got a longer life? A krow kan liv up to 200 yers and a northern wale they think never dies if they dont kil him. Lots of Icelanders got diamond wedding and they celebrate by polkas and kiking the ceeling. And if yu go bak thousands of yers when ther was heathen yu find out that their character and luv was kleen as in the south and they didnt took a step bak for the rong thing. The farmers wives was just as wel dressed as the kings and the king had to listen to her wurd and if he didn't the hole relashum had to stik together. That was a shim to steel but there was a honor to tail it. Ther we was a honor to fite, but ther was a shaim to be the loser.

They had mani gud times and they got that yet. This northern men found our kuntri and they gav big gud to our kuntri since 400 yers before Kolumbus and they are gud yet.

Their blud may be giting thiner, but they are proud nuf yet and if I shud be licked, I shud sooner be licked of a Norwegian than a klear Yankee. That wil be a prouder and beter yob and I wud not need to pay the fine, but if a Yankee do it, I have to pay a fine on both the Yankee and the government.

Be proud over the Swedes and Norwegians. They are the ones that got the stump out of yur fields so yu got free sailing and take gud kare of the big Merican Dolar. That wil soon cum a time when oil stashuns and old kars kant feed yu. Kum bak to the older time when yur wurd is gud or die. And stay more home with yur wife and children. If I had a wife now I wud put her in a glass kage and walk around and holler Peek-a-boo. And mi luv I send to you al, but most of the ladies. They are the krown of what al God maid.

And I don't like to leeve this wurld and hav the ladies to be mi enemies.
Johannes

101.
Mister Republican
To al of yu that works for The Republican and even the boys that kari the paper round, yu al hav treeted me like I was the king of Spain and I wil not forgit the most of the reeders. I tol so much truth so if it wasn't for yur protecshun I wud go the saim way as the Salvation Army went 40 years ago-inside the bars.

I know a good gub who had to pound stones like sugar lumps befor they gaiv him brekfast. That is a bad report to tel our yung generashun, but that got to be told if I hav to ride the saim way and in the saim conektion I want to tel you mi wish. I wish to see the family kut in haf for all the officers frum the President's chair to cities like Hager and Wakuta and they al wud be yust as satisfy.

Klose to 60 years ago when we didnt hav no sewer in our city the street commissioner had to go to the midel of the nite and see small churches flot in the midel of the streets and cows droned in haler that was fastened to the manger and his salari was $40 a munth and he kud afort to taik of his own muney and buy a keg of berr to treet his krew.

Now we got sewers so we kan let Hay Creek, Belle Creek and Spring Creek go thru our town if we dont git a cloudburst. Fifty-five years ago I kud notice if ther kum a strainger into our town. Now I kant kount the oficers. I hav to luk for even step so I dont step on one and I do know we got oficers that got over $2,000 a yer, but to tel them peepel that is waiting to git 2 or 3 hours snowshufling and they are sent with the noder bos for 55 cents an hour to luk at them when they wurk and see so ther is charged up to the taxpayers.

And this is a smal truth, but I reed bout a biger the oder day. A gurl between 20 and 30 yers got a salary of $330,000 a yer in movies to akt silly to fool away the nikels away frum the por peepel. How do yu think Roosevelt wil kum out. Borrow bilyn and pay pit out to salari and relief. One that is use to relief will never be satisfied. He wants the hole wurld and heven forout to die. I hope I aint hurt nobodi's feelings. If I hav taik it as a yoke and be mi gud frend and yu know we talk so much when our town is ful of bock beer and the last time I talked to Roosevelt he had 1,300,000 officers to pay. So I kudn't see him. They hung a big canvas between us the saim as when Moses talked to God and now this is done, but dont forgit mi luv to yu al.

Johannes Johnson

102.
Mr. Republican
Out of al the leters I sent in three slipped in that tub yu got side of yu tabel and I expect this to go the saim way, but if yu do, remember God sees yu. And do as He want yu to do. But I want to tel yu what I bin reeding in the book that is spose to tel the truth. Germany sent a profesor to our kuntri to examine America's peepels brains and when he kum bak his report ten was normal, was one out of nine was phools and they want to know what kind of phools and he said yu kan kal them edukated phools.

Dont sum of yu reeders think he is right? We are a mixed up mess redy to put the yeest in. We had a free kuntri but we had a limit to all. Now there is no limit. We are al slaives with the exception of the millionaires and the relief peepel. We had saloons, but we had a limit. We got churches left, but they are empti. We had dance hals, but ther was always a limit. We had oficers to run our kuntri, but ther was a limit. We paid them gud, but we had a limit. We had gud laws, but we always had a limit. Al we got left that runs the saim is the sun, moon and stars.

But they got a new glass soon reedy to luk the sun and moon and stars over to tri to maik them go the oder way. We got al kinds of machinery in this kuntri so we kan level it up. Fil up the ravines and we got explosions to throw the mountains in the sea, but we aint got blacksmith that kan maik a lok. We aint got a shoemaker that kan taik the measure and maik a pair of shoes to fir our feets. We aint got a carpenter that kan fraim up a old-fashund barn. We aint got mani tailors that kan maik a suit to fit our bodies, but they kan kut off our pants if they are to long.

What hav improve the most in our kuntri is taxes and oficers and that isnt much to liv off for a man that wants to pay his bils and liv forout releef. But we got a gud kuntri for lazi peepel and thos that we kal dedbeats, but they are goin to eet up our kuntri the saim as the grasshoppers did with Pharoh's kuntri when he wud not let the Jews go home. I spose I maid mani mor enemies in this leter, but do as I do, forgiv and let yur rolers go over mi leter. I wil stan bak of what I rote. I got only one life and that is short. But befor I lose it, I wud like to see a itemized bil of our swimming pool and the rode that goes to the esterly point of Memorial park. That wud keep me busi til mi time kums.

With luv to yu al.
Johannes Johnson

103.
Mister Republican
Mi edukashun and skulling was 60 days, but I read for the minister once a week a hole summer and when I was 14, I was reedy to fais a big wurld. And so I went north so far that I kud see the sun at 12 o'klok at nite and south so far that I kud see the katel taik their feed in the pastures on Christmas day and east so I kud see the icebergs in Russia and west so they had goats insted of kows and they feed them brush and moss.

And I seen mor. I seen a 12 year old boy who went into his fathers shed and where he had the summer oats and tuk a few bundles and pounded them on the flor with a stick and shook up the loose straw and put it in a big basket and threw the grain frum one wal to the oder and the gud grain fel down by the wal the lite stuff was stranded on the midel of the flor. And he filed it in a sak and walked about two miles where they had a handmil maid of two flat stones with a handel on the top to put it like a coffy grinder. He brot it home to his mother and they were al wel satisfied.

And his father was out in the sea fishing and a storm kaim up and he was carried to land on the ruff and stormy shor, but finally they seen him kum and when he struk the shor the boat was smashed to pieces, but the father was saived. And that was the happiest family I have seen in a long life. The kisses that soaked man got from the mother and the children was sweeter than what we pik up in the kalf stals in beer parlors in Red Wing. And I seen one mother that rigged out three small kids with a sack on her bak, but no shoes on their feet to go frum hous to hous begging. And she patted them on the shoulder and said "Whatever yu git-ever so little-don't forgit to say thank yu and God bless yu."

And I want to tel yu that I seen in later yers. I seen boxes of appels and oranges, shipped mani miles carried into the frunt rum and nice shoes and clothes so yu kud not open the door in the kloset. And in a few days yu kud not walk around the hous for appel and orange peelings. And when the pay day kaim the children got to be sond asleep and the mother sitting with kurly hair waiting for her man to kum hom with a swell kar that isn't paid for, so they both kan spend the releef check when the kids is sleeping. Don't the truth son bad when we tel it? I expekt sum ladi to be so mad that she wud wish to kari Johannes' hed on a plait to show her best friends.
But when God lets the rain fall he lets it fall on bad as well as gud. And so does Roosevelt. And all of you kan reed this leter, but I don't meen all of it.

With luv to yu al,
Johannes Johnson

104.
Mister Republican
Fifty seven yers ago I did sum work on a Milwaukee bridge cros the krek and one man sliped and felled down so we mesure and that was 14 feet to the water. And I told the boys that 15 yers frum now that wud not be 15 inches and they al thot I was krazi. Now a coupel yers ago befor they raised the trak we kum in disput bout it so we went out 11 klok at nite and mesure and I loosed out only 2 inches. That was 13 inches frum the ice to the beem of the bridge.

When they bilt the Red Wing bridge between Frontenac and Lake City, I kum bi and yu know the swede is always nosey. I told the boss that this bridge shud be 10 feet higher and he roared like a bul and asked me what I knowed bout it. And I said I studi natur and yu studi the big Merican dolar. And I had to run to not git liked. Fifteen yers ther wasn't rum under the bridge for the water so they had to dig a hole for the water, but nature filled lit up so they had to bild a new bridge and giv the water rum.

How bout the dams in the Mississippi? The government gav theme lots of rum, but the waters maid their own bed and that wil stay on the top and that wil go down hil like a man that seen his 50 yers. I used to be proud as the king of Spain, but I aint proud now. When I speek to peepel they feel proud to anser, so I hav to luk with the only eye I got left and rite with both hands and send it to The Republican. And when that bin in the vault for half hundert yers that mite be wurth to reed.

But when natur dig a hole in ground, when he gits reedy he wil fil it up. And if the natur maiks a krak in the west point of Barn Bluf that meens that wil kum down and Rokefeeler kant hold it bak. And if Rokefeller steels gas frum natur four miles square everi yer there is no wunder that sum farms disappear.

We got wonderful rich and gud Merica, but we got lots of lazi and por Mericans. We got a sekund paridis, but we let the thistles grow. We got wonderful churches but we lern our yung generashum to turn them over to dance hals. We got lots of gold and silver, but we hide it the saim as Jerusalem. Sum Romans will hav it sum day. The higher we klimb, the biger fal we goin to git.

With luv to yu all.
Johannes Johnson

105.
Mister Republican
When we kumed to this wurld we didn't know much but we kum here to lern and we are brout up for a komon wurld. But sum of you reeder think we kant lern when we could. I tel yu that I lerned in this wurld.

I was 77 then I lerned if this keeps on much longer I will be a gud fortun teller.

Yust think, I can walk along Red Wing and tel you where releef peepel liv and if I see yur clothesline after the washing is hung out I kan tel yu what kind of a wife yu got. And if I open the dor and luk at the kitchen stov I kan tel yu sure.

I only got one eye I kan see with and my hering getting por, but I kan hear and see that the Ford kar maid a billionaire of its fader.

The Wisconsin farmers when they use to bring wud to our town didn't hav no bal bearings in their wagons, but they had blacksnaiks and we kud depend on both the man and the hors. Now we kan depend on Roosevelt's life guard or his gaim warden. Roosevelt and the mothers are alike. They both spoil lots of boys. Nothing else beter for the boys than what the farmers use to feed their broncos. If they feed mor of that down to the Training school, they would not hav so much troubel.

I thank mi father today for everi liking I got. I thot I got it for al seven children and I thot I was the best of the seven. But now I am at the end of the rope and waiting for mi bigest surprise ever.

And if yu reeders wants to know what that is, it is to see myself in heven.

With luv to yu all.
Johannes Johnson

106.
Mister Republican
Put atenshun to the time that goes by and yu wil know sumthing but that aint goin to bring yu eether to heven or to hel, but yu aint her to sleep yur time away. Yu are here to better herself and yu got right to luk into both churches and dance hals and the saloons to. And yu got ful right to taik yur choice. But I advis yu to ask God where to go.

And if you are goin kros the Ded sea taik advis of the one that went kros and not of the one that staid in the harbor. We are left in this wurld with free wil. God aint goin to taik hold of yur hair and pul yu into heven. And the devil kant taik yu, but he kan fool yu to walk rite in. We got wiskey and beer in our town by carloads. But yu don't hav to drink it al, but yu got free wil. We got gambling machines by carloads, but yu dont have to play one.

Dont try to maik mules of American peepel. Yu kant git the bridal on. Yu kan fence in a town and keep the sheep out, but the goats wil yump over. When yu maik a law and taik our free wil away, think two times and yu wil find out that what we kant git is just what we want. And yu wil find out yu wil grow like a cows tail and the dog yu chais into the wuds aint goin to bring yu mani foxes.
But if yu maik a law that brings bak the muney to the midel man we wil say Amen. And if yu kan maik a law that fils the churches ful Thanksgiving day and the saloon empty we will say Amen. We shud taik one day off to be thankful to the one that lets both the weeds and the Thistels grow.

With luv to yu al.
Johannes Johnson

107.
Mister Republican
I want to tel yu the reason I didnt rote to yu when I was yung, gud-luking and know sumthing. The reason was I was to busy. I left mi faderland when I was a yung boy and I went to the new wurld-that's what the Swedes kaled America. And I went here to be rich. I then intend to go bak and be a big man and I tel the Swedes that I seen the new wurld. And I started on the south side of Barn bluf and put mi bak against the bluf and I had the sunshine in mi fais and mi bluf, but the mouth was open nuf to swalow the hole Barm. The man that owns it giv it to the city for nothing and he wud not sel it to me for a thousand dollars. But in 15 yers I had 18 houses lined up under the bluf. I graded mi own streets, laid out mi own lots and had mi own waterworks. And I was busy in both sunshine and moonshine and when I went to church I kum in right like King Solomon, but then mi frens started in to be yelous and I got the saim siknes as Lucifer when they throwed him out of heven.

I got proud so I started and figgered where the kuming street was going to be and I piked out East 7th street. Nobodi kan kum frum the east without kuming on that street where the sun rises in the morning.

So I stoped with a big burch tree where ther was nailed 2 signs on it. One said "Go to Clausen's for Groceries and Carpets" and the oder said to "Enseth for Fly Powder" and I sit down under the tree and thinking big and I tel yu what I thinked bout. Here I am going to bild a kastel for me and mi family and I did. And to be sure that is shud be recognized I put 32 korners on the roof, but I put one dor to much in the hosue where death sneeked in and tuk the best frend I ever had and ever wil hav.

Andn I kount that the end of mi business. I had lots of frends since but the best one is the big Tom kat. He stays home, but when I turn mi back to her, she steel the saim as the rest of them. But I dont blaim the kat. He is here for to sneek and steel his livin, but we are here to maik on onest living and we got a tousand chances.

With luv to yu al.
Johannes Johnson

108.
Mister Republican
A old fren kum up to me and he said, “Spose yu liv gud on old age penshun?” And I til him I was to old for a pension. When they giv penshuns, they giv them when is the best man they got and he had done sumthing gret in what is wise and gud. If I shud hav penshun I wud hav it for keeping roofs over heds of the wurst dedbeats in Red Wing. “The government dont giv penshuns to phools,” I said, “but they giv help to the poor. We had big silver dollars-both yu and me-nuf to taik us thru the old aig, if we aint bin a phool. If yu shud hav penshuns yu shal hav it for trying to drink up all the whiskey and beer in Red Wing, but yu kud not do it. Ther is plenti left and yu are yust as bad off as I.”

And he got so mad he said that if it wasn’t for mi aig he wud nock me down and he said, “If I ask yu a questun wily u answer decent?” I told him I wud.

“What is the reason yu cant talk or rite without kicking? Answer me now.”

“Mi aig is to the higher limit now.” I said, “and I dont like to lie. Ther is one reason for mi kicking and we got thousands in our kuntri today that pat eech oder on the sholder and steel our kuntri blind. That it haint so bad when rich and educated peepel steel, but when the por peepel start in that is the saim as the cinch bugs and grasshoppers. They taik it al and they taik the litel man furst.

“And a kuntri cannot git long forout to have a parti that tries to help themselves and we kal them the midelman. Taik the harness off the por peepel. Giv them freedom, foler them out in the pastures and show them how. That is beter than to giv them $2 or $2 an akr for to let the land like idel for the weeds to grow. Bi them a grub hoe, instead of oranges and bi them a dubel bit axe instead of apels.

“What tols did Adam git when he was chaised out of the paradise when Eve ate that apel? And who lerneed Eve to maik pie and caik? Now we got forout to plant them. Rosevelt passed them rond. Who going to peel them. If we dont git them peeled we wud eet them with the peeling on. Ther is to much wurk to peel them.

“What is cuming to our kuntri to bring us bak where we belong and maik us satisfy with our government and ourselfs? That wud not be a cinch bug, but we played with the fire hundert yers. But when they git the bos they wil be awful. He kan hide and bery a city like Red Wing for 2000 yrs.”

Plees don’t throw this leter in the basket. There mite be sumbudi that want to reed it. And dont forgit we got two kinds of peepl so yu dont git al mad.

With luv to yu al.
Johannes Johnson

109.
Mister Republican
I find out ther is a parti who dont like mi kar and I dont blaim him, for I dont like it eether. But instead of puting water in after taiking out the gas, go after the kar with a grub hoe. And if yu hav not got one, I wil borrow yu one. That wud be mor muney in it for me. But when yu put water in, it wil taik the last dolar I got so ther wont be anything left for the krooks and dedbeets. Taik it eesy, for it wil not be long befor Johannes and the kar is covered over in the "forgotten sea".
And al I kan giv yu is mi luv and forgivness. And I wud luk for beter business. To trade water for gas wud not feed you thru the wurld and taik yu to heven.

With luv to you al.
Johannes Johnson

110.
Mister Republican
And yu ladi reeders; if yu stay with the man that show yu nothing but luv, yu stay with the rite man. Do al yu kan for him and always keep in yur mind yu kant do nuff. But if yu stay with one that kiks frum the time the sun kums up to when he goes down, yu know that God dont want yu to stay with him. He took a rib out of Adams side and maid him a helper. And if yur man didnt preciate the help, let him stay alone. He wil kum to time.

Yu know that Eve brot the hole wurld into sin, but Adam sticked rite with her. He maid the bigest mistake ever was maid, but I giv him the kredit-he sticked with his wife. And to yu men that reed the Republican, hav yu seen aniting prettier in this wurld than a ladi with a smile on her lips? I seen the wurld from Lapland to South America, but I aint seen ani prettier so I think that wil pay us to be gud to the ladies.

If yu put a blue mark on a ladi, that wil taik the blud of God to wash it off. And she always pays for her mistaiks. Even times she bring a child in this wurld she pays, but yu dont. She got the pain, wurri and trubel for a long life. Hav yu notice that the homliest man got the prettiest wife? And the meenest man got the best wife? Natur knows how to pair up rite if we wot to behav.

I am so homly as a man kan be, but I had the best and pertiest wife that ever lived, but that big thief what we kal deth steel her away. Deth shud never be brot into this wurld. I wud like to be maried yet, but that wud not pay no ladi to mary me. I wud not liv long nuf, but I kan luv them al. I tried to git mad at a ladi, but the mader I try to git the mor I luved her. So the most truth in my leters is when it stands I luv yu al. And if yu want to be a old man, be gud to the ladies and watch mi last trip. Yu wil see mor ladies that use their handkerchiefs than men.

Johannes Johnson

111.

Mister Republican

When we git old we ask to mani questions and we want to anser them to. What is the matter with the old wurld when so mani peepel are kiking? The wurld is the saim. She giv us both gud hard wheat and thisels. Sum klaim that thistles kum from Canada, but I think we had thistles befor we knowed where Canada was. When the devil phooled the furst ladi he droped the seed on the ground and thistles hav bin growing ever since. Therefor boy don't phool with the ladies. If a ladi tells yu that blak is white, anser her, "is that so? Isn't that fine?" A ladi is given to this wurld yust to be gud to and not for a slaiv. And if you aint gud to them that wil grow thistles in everi korner of yur home. And to the last they wil grow in yur bed and then yu will hav to sleep in h___.

We phooled the ladies to go into the saloons and than, "Oh, they don't belong ther," so they tri to hide in the caf stals and sum times they wish they had a kover on. Ther ladies know where they belong, but lots of men dont. But I shud know to quit befor they al git mad at me.

What is those blak posts with the hed on both sides of the highway? They are a warning and protecshun for al and the most for drunkards and sneeks and phools. A drunkard he want to git fast to the next plais to git a drink, and a sneek wil be the furst ther to git a dolar mor, and a phool-you all hav to sho him where to go. And wherever yu see a accident, yu see one of them in the gang.

What maid so mani milyonaires in our kuntri? War and new kars and oil stashuns. What maid so mani releef peepel? Old kars and oil stashuns. What is the deerest ground in our city? The graivyard and the swimming pool. What is the heaviest our city carries? A lazi man that is meen to his famili. What is the prettiest we got in our city? A silver-grey ladi that lived a onest life. Where is the best plais to go when we leev Red Wing? To heaven and don't forgit mi luv to yu al.

Johannes Johnson

112.
Mister Republican
A other yer has moved on our bak and to al Republican reeders that lived in the blooming of their lives and think they no it al-skratch out the wurd al. I want to tel yu what I had to lern when I kum to the river of death and readi to put one foot in. I had to lern to be left-handed and see with one eye. And I kan see with one eye now what I kudn't see with two before.
And if you wish to know what I kan see with one eye, I wil tel yu. I kan see mi best frends in the river of the death and I can't help them. I kan see with one eye mi best frends having auction on mi friendship and they sel it for a glas of beer. And I can see hunderts that owes me muney, but those that want to pay I hav to use the spi-glas and they luk small like blackbirds even then.

Yu mite went to skul til yu were 30 yers old, but yu got the experience of yur life left to lern and that wil kum just as shur as yur birthday, and yur death wil be anoder shur thing that yu must meet. Yust think how much yu have to meet if yu live a half hundert yers mor. I as an old man wil advis you to be kerful with yur step. They goes eether to heven or hel and I want to tel yu as a frend if I kud walk mi life over I wud be mor kerful. I dont meen that yu shud sit down and tri to cri yourself into heven, but I meen that yu and me shud live the lives God wants us to live. If you dont like thes leters, let yur children reed them.

With luv to yu al.
Johannes Johnson

113.
Mister Republican
I did not kik in mi last leter, but I tol the truth. Now I want to tel yu that I driv the menest kar that ever went thru our town. If I git him to stop when he gits to the stop sign and I want him to go again he shaiks his bodi like a big new-foundland dog and taiks a scoot like a jak rabit. And if ther wasnt for the police using their judgment I wud be in the jail everi oder day.
I use to let him rest in the bak side of the city hal blok and when I kum bak the rats had chewed the veins off that goes to the spark plugs. And the fox got under the hood and hang a bone on the hert so when I start up he sonds like a Milwaukee engine when he goes by Swede hill with hundert freight kars.

But I want to tel yu if I katch the fox in mi kar I am goin to do like the old Norwegian Vikings. I'l kil him. If the sheriff stands on one side and the chief of police on the oder. But I wud not put a cros over mi hert when I tel yu this.

But I want to tel yu the oder side of mi kar. He has bin a frend to our city and neebors. If a frend want to go to the next state for a drink he always bin reedy and if they want to go to the church Sunday morning he always bin reedy. And if the ice got melted in the ice box Sunday afternoon for the neebors he always went to the west end and bot ten cents wurth of ice. And they want to baik Munday morning he goes to town and gits a pakage of yeest.

But the kar and me are goin to part. Our days is numbered and then the rats and the fox kan hav a farewel parit and I send mi best luv to yu al, but the rats and the fox can use their own luv.

Johannes Johnson
114.

Mister Republican
I want to talk to yu bout friendship and luv. A frend tol me the oder day yu rite in The Republican that yu losed al the frends yu got and al mi frends is al weared out the saim as I. I meet three the oder day that owes me over $200.00 apeese and two didnt know me and the thurd one laffed at me.

When I got old I started to luk into friendship and I find out I had only two left that I kud depend on and if yu yung folks want to know ther is God and the big American dolar and I hav got two of them in silver. One I got frum a banker for teling the truth in The Republican and the oder I got frum a wash-woman from being gud to her. That is her statment.

I had al kinds of frends and kumpani in mi long life, but the best is God and the big American dolar. If I bin knowing 30 yers ago what I know now I wud serv both beter. If we erne a dolar we shudnt bi perls for it and throw the perls in the pig pen. If we got an enemi we are natural born to luk out for him, but if we got a fals frend we wil be fools like Eve. I think the devil akted like a frend to her and one fals frend maid the hol wurld to die. I had frends that I bleeved wud follo me to the river of death and never had a dolar to gud for them.

But I didnt have no mor dollars to giv they was redy to stab me in the bak. I had frends that I thot was wurth milyhuns that tuk the nektie off mi kolar and giv it to one that they thot was beter luking. This leter is for old peeple to say amen to. And for yung peepel to find out if ther is the truth. And now I want yu al to know I dont liv forout frends. I got hunderts of them that reed the Republican that I never seen and I wil trust them and the reason is they dont owe me ani muney.

But I wil send mi luv to yu al.
Johannes Johnson

115.
Mister Republican
I want to ask yur posted reeders if yu kan tel me why God piked out yu for His peepel yust to be gud to yu. Why didnt He pik out the Norwegians and the Swedes and I think He kud yust as wel pik out the Irish. Yu reeders shud stop and think what God did for yu for the last 4,500 years.

One time He let them walk on the bottom of the see and when they kum cros the see closed and both the king and the army git drownded. And one time He moved the sun bak 3 hours for to giv them chance to lik the enemies. And if He forgav them al they had to do was to pik up the meal on the plait and eat. And one time He sent His only son to them and He walked together with them, kured al kind of sikness and waiked up the ded and He ofer them to be their king, but then they killed Him. They must be meen peepel. Now He started to bild up the old Jerusalem for them. What do that meens?

I bleev frum where the sun kums up and end when the sun lays down, the Bethlehem star kums frum the east and it went west for to show the wise peepel where to go. She is soon here the sekund time. I wish that yu al wish her welkum and be like the wise ladies and be on yur watch and hav yur light in order. I know litel bout God, but the older I git the mor respekt I have for both God and the Jews.

And to the gud and to yu wise peepel of our city, giv me an anser. I am not to old to lern.

With luv to yu al.
Johannes Johnson

116.
Mister Republican
I am now home frum mi vakashun and this time I didnt kum no further than the hospital-a wonderful plais to go to git into frum the storm in the desert and a gud plais to check up yur frends. Ther dont kum mani that owes us muney, but thos that do kum luks like angels. I tel yu reeders what I wished and tink I wud do if I kud liv over mi life. I wud in the blooming of mi life buy me a nice lot in the graivyard and invest mi furst muney in mi home town. And then I wud taik that I kud saiv in the morning of mi life and instead to go to the shows and beer parlors I wud put them in mi inside vest poket and I wud keep on put them ther so mi frens kud see a bump in mi vest frum the outside.

And when I wud hav nuff I wud buy me a small farm and I wud paint the barn red and the corner white and I wud build a nice fence around the farm and I wud be both a king and a hired man so long as I kud taik kare of it gud and then I wud giv it away to the one that bin best to me in mi olden dais.

That is wurth a farm to bring a child into this wurld and taik kare of him and bring him up so he will be ani gud for the wurld, and that is wirth a farm to taik a old goob over the last river and kover him up gud. If a man got a gud helth and a gud yob and gud pay and the quilt is to short to pul over his fais when he gits old that hav bin sumthing rong in his life.
If I have don what God wants me to do-help the one who try to help himself and kodent of them that kud pay I wud not lay here with a bair fais and feel shaimed for yu al. The wurld is to big and to mani kinds of peepel liv in it to let them al owe yu muney. Kolekshun is the hart in bisness and a onest life is a key to heven and if sum of yu reders find a kernel of wheat in this leter do like a chicken-pik it up and let the rest lay.

And one thing that I kant forgit-to thank yu al that bin so gud to me when I bin sik. I wish I had a farm to giv yu al.

With luv to yu al.
Johannes Johnson

117.
Mister Republican
I want yu reeders to know I had mi vacashun.
I went to Vasa on Midsummer's day and so far as I bin traveling Vasa is the most wonderful plais on the wurld. I bin out so I seen the most northern parts of the wurld and south so far as the granite bolder stones clung to the ice in the glacier period and wherever I bin in a big krowd I always see sumbudy that luks homely, but in Vasa I kudn't find one. They was al gud luking.
And if I want to see a nice gurl I don't hav to stair sideways into a kaf stal to see them. I kan see them in frunt seet in the church. And if her father said he wud whip yu. Yu kan depend on him. They are related to the old Vikings. They don't say one thing and meen the oder. And but if it wasn't for the naim Gustaf Vasa ther wudn't be a Swede today. But ther was a time that both England, Russia and even the Germans tuk off their hats to the Swedes.

But yu reeders kan do as yu pleas. I wil always taik off mi hat to the Vasa farmer. And to you boys that luking for gurls, luk furst in Vasa if they ani to spair and let the oder gurls git more sense. I fond the best gurl in the wurld more than a half hundert yers ago and I wish I kud leev a milyun dollars to Vasa in return for her.

And the way home we tuk to the left and that was down hil so I thought we landed in a salt mine, but it was the new city what they kaled Welch. A glas of beer cooled us off and a nice luking ladi served it. Welch got sumting to be proud over, and they got their own lectric plant. That more as Red Wing got.

And to al that gaiv their time for that midsummer fest I thank yu al frum the bottom of mi hart and send mi luv in return.

Johannes Johnson

118.
Mister Republican
The longer I liv the mor valuable the wurld lukes to mi eyes. I had 2 blue eyes-two gud blue eyes-and I used them in both Lapland and Meiko. Now I got onli one, but I kan see mistaiks that the city council maid more than a half hundert yers ago. And frum mi kradel to the graiv it is only mistaiks that I maid myself. What do yu reeders think God is goin to do to me in the kumin wurld? That wil be up to Him and I wil say "Amen". Our kuntri improved so fast so that it taiks edukated peepel to folo the rode to hel. We improved the rode to hel and spend milyn dollars to maik it strait. We even hav given them free bridge and kut down expenses. I think that if the city council kut off the rode to sum plaises at 11 o'klok at nite the ministers wil see more faces in church Sunday morning. Yu got to put a bridal in the mouth of a hors to maik him go where yu wants and yu city council got por horses if they kant cary their harness.

And if the poleecemen of Red Wing kum and arest me I wil say "amen". The less I talk to them the beter for me. If the judge said 60 days I wil say "amen". The power is in his hands and he kan say 90. If God tells me to go to hel I wil say "amen". His power is over al that got a life. When that kums to fais God with truth we are al smal King of Spain and Roosevelt and Republican and Johannes Johnson. They hav to be washed kleen frum sin to step in the kumin wurld.

With luv to yu al.
Johannes Johnson

119.
Mister Republican
When I was 21 years old I was sik and I went to the doctor and he ponded with his finger tips over mi chest and bak and gaiv me a quarter botel of medicine. I didn't like that big botel so I went bak the next day and asked him what was mi trubel and he ansered "Yu wud be smart if yu knew." And I said "That is what I caim for." And I said I aint goin to pay yu befor yu tel me what yu think.

And the doctor thot mor of the big American dolar 60 yers ago than he does now, so he said, "Yu hav consumshun-one lung is gone and the oder is on a start." So now I started to fite. I thot I had a brite and long life in mi futur and I seen lots of nice gurls that I wanted to be quainted with. Now I went hom krying and I laid down in mi bed krying and praying til I went to sleep and I wished that I kud see 30 years of mi life. And when I kum to, the furst mi eyes struk was that big medicine botel and it kaim to mi mind the last wurds mi fader told me when I luked bak and seen his fais for the last time. "Don't giv up mi boy, whatever meets you in the new wurld." And I tol myself, "I aint goin to feed concumpshum and cancer with cod liver oil." I opened the window and threw out the botel so far as I kud and it struk an old wagon. Too bad for the wagon-that didn't git hurt. I didn't taik a drop of medicine, but washed mi arms frum the shoulders and rubbed them with a ruf towel for munths and when the fal kumm I went up north to the wulf and ox teems and mi dinner was frozen beans and mi best frends was Irish and mi bed partner was awfl smal, but al was gud for mi helth.

And when I kum bak in the spring I stepped on the skails and I was 182 ponds and kud not git ani hevier for 30 yers. And I hapin to git acquainted with the nicest and best gurl in the whole wurld and I asked her if she wanted to mary a Swede and she said, "That is al right." She was a Swede herself.

So we raised a big and gud-luking family and a few days ago I kounted my birthdays and they are 80 and it was to bad that Eve tuk the bite of that apel so we al have to die. Both Roosevelt and Mussolini hav to folow us. And if this leter shud hapin to be the last I want yu to know I wish yur man to be gud to your wife and children and pay yur bils and don't forgit to kolect yurs.

And to the ladies-I kant say nothing. The nature taik kair of that. If yu aint gud to the children yu aint a gud mother. But don't lift yur child up on the saloon counter when yu drink yur beer. Lift them up in the front seet of the church. And always remember that religun civilized the wurld and ther is yur key fur heven. And if yu want to go to h___ you don't need no key. It is open al the time.

With luv to yu al.
Johannes Johnson

120.
Mister Republican
I met a frend the oder day that said he reed al mi leters and he thot I wud do beter if I never menshun the saloons and the calf stals. I tink I beter excuse myself to al of yu.

The Swede is fraid to run through the brush so they sneek round. I tink that saloons shud hav protekshun under laws our kuntri gives them, just as wel as the churches. It is now the bigest business in our kuntri. This saiv us frum both starvashun and revolution and Roosevelt is the best man that put his feet on American soil. He kud see what was goin on and what six dollars tax on a barel of beer and six cents on a pack of cigarets wud bring. How much do we use of them both minds? The taxes on them feeds thousands of peepel that want to wurk and is luking for wurk and kant find ani. And that feeds thousands that don't want to wurk and thousands that don't need to wurk. One Saturday evening I thot to luk over so mani I kud. I was to al in Red Wing, on the Island and Hager City and kum bak thru Frontenac and Lake City and on sum I tuk a glas of beer and in sum I ask for Pete Monson and on sum for Ole Olsen, but I didnt tuk a hard drink al evening, but I luk and size up the buseness so gud as I kud with the eye I got left and I report it gud to yu al.

And I didnt see one moonshine parlor and that was bak of the wuds and they didnt hav mor than one haf pint, but I got a other excuse for to go to the saloon. I always bin a lady's frend and I kant help it and I don't tink you kan eether. The best luking ladies kan be in the saloon and I got a pleasure to luk at them.

They smile nicer Saturday nite than they do Monday morning when they bend over the washtub, but I wish you al the old times bak when yu go to the church to pik yur kumpani and when wherever yu go to be sure to pik a beter kumpuni as yourself. Dont do as I do, but do as I tel yu. And I wish to meet yu al in the land where we never grow old.

With luv to yu al.
Johannes Johnson

121.
Mister Republican
I never rote a leter that suits yu al, but I gained lots of frends and I wil be proud to stay with yu so long as I kan. Yers ago they use to kal me the "king of Swede Hill", but I tangled up with so mani krooks so the bisiness men scratched mi naim off. Now if I shal hapin to be elected for king in our kuntri I wil tel yu what I wil do the furst thing. I wud hav the saim law on both sides of the Mississippi river and in al states in our kuntri akording to the climate. The second thing I wud do to run the steem shufel and caterpillar and kotton piker into the Mississippi valley to help natur to fil it up. And I wud put a limit to the doctors and lawyers prices. We shud pay the doctor when we is strong and helthy and not when we is sik. A lawyers shud hav gud pay to defend a onest person, but he shud be fined to defend a krook and the minister shud hav a route the saim as the mail karier to see his congregashun bring up the children beter for the komon wurld.

The next thing I wud do, I wud put the wiskey bak in barrels and I wud maik kindling wud out to the calf stals in the beer parlors and if a man asks kredit for a glas of beer I wud giv him 6 munths and 2 months to the one that puled the beer out of the keg. I wud quit out al gaim wardens and giv them a beter job. I wud pay a skunk's price for everi pair of small heels that he noked out of the ladies' slippers. I wud hire a expert welder to burn al the links in the chain stores. Ther wud be one king in Washington for the hole kuntri and one in Red Wing. Thos boys that we send from al direcshuns of our kuntri in a sheepskin koat when them kum bak they trade it way for a dogskin koat. And they git so smart that they tells us they kan run the batelships on the highways thru our kuntri and they kan put wings on the mountains and konekt the radio with heven and hel. Now I beter quit my leter. That taiks a smarter person to read it than the one that rote it. And I am glad that wuldn't be so much for me to answer for sum day.

With luv to yu al.
Johannes Johnson

122.
Mister Republican
I wish to talk to thos gurls that want to be the furst with the common stiles. Throw yur cigarets away and if yu hav to smok, smok a pipe. Let yur hair grow-braid it and throw one braid over eech sholder. That wud be beter for us old folks to drive yu thru the best rode thru the wurld. Set yur paint buket in the wud shed. God put the rite kolor on both yur finger nales and lips. Tak gud kair of the ketel which yu kook the potatoes in and the spider wher yu baik the pankaiks for brekfast.

The times is changing. Seventy-five yers ago it was a shaim to see a lady's feet, but now it is a shaim if we dont see her knees.

And to yu boys that goes to skul and tells their faders and mothers how to run their home. It is to bad when a kuntri gets a child for king. And it aint no beter if a lady gits that for a man. It never grows komon sense in a man befor he gits 30 yers old. And 7 yers later his hair komences to git grey and he isn't ani gud. And seven more yers he is in the way for both kins and the mous traps. And the time goes so fast when yu luk bak-the life is like a drem that it aint wurth to be born.

The best for a man to do-pay their bills and be gud to their wife. And we shal never forgit when we got a wife we got the best God had. And I feel sorri for al men that haint got one. It is beter to have a gud wife than a gud kar. And dont traid her away for an airship eether. And hold what yu got so nobody taiks yur kron *(wife)*.

With luv to yu al.
Johannes Johnson

123.
Mister Republican
I had king's orders to polgize for mi last leter. One reeder tol me I put a blak spot on church members. I hav to taik that bak, but I want yu al to no that the blak spot I tol bout was ther befor I rote the leter.

When I luk up mi life frum the kradel up to now ther is al blak spots. Like the katel they reech at the way down to the Training skul. I got only 3 things to be proud of. I never bin a kidnaper and I never robed a bank and I never stole. Mi father fixed me for that when I was a boy, but mi muther wasnt so particular. She said mor than one hundert times she was goin to lik me, but she never did.

And that I had to sufer for for a long life. And that meens I kan not steel, but I kan lie, and I hav to fite wit myself lots of times when I rite yu the leters. I know they wud sond beter if ther is a litel lie in once and a while, but it taiks a smart man to lie and not git caught. And ther is a hard yob to keep the lie out when yu talk bout neebors.

The furst one that lied was the devil and he mixed it with truth and that is the reason our furst ladi got phooled. But ther was one with the naim of Johannes. He seen al that was perfect and they was al washed in blood and their was 114 so I yust wunder if ther was ani frum Red Wing. Red Wing was known for a church town 50 yers ago and I was one of the members and I wish I was now, but ther is only one that kan sav me and whatever He does I wil say Amen.

With luv in the wurld,
Johannes Johnson

124.

Mister Republican:

Hav yu reeders notice how we old peepel wurri for the new life and the new impruvents that kums fast? A man tol me the oder day that the city has signed up for power and lite for 99 yers. Maybe the lite gits so high that we may hav to go bak to the kandel and sit in the dark. I kudnt sleep for two nites.

Anoder man tol me that they tuk out the hevy machinery out of the pump stashun. They shud hav left that for the yung generashun to see what the old peepel kud do when they had to. I thot that was yust as dumb as when they remodeled the Auditorium and grubbed up the big evergreen on Broadway park and then we wurri that the office burn down up to the dam. Yust think how mani maps they had rowed up, both with ink and led pencil to show Roosevelt what they did with the muney. Now he hav to taik their wurd for it.

Then we wurri for the old penshiun. Peepel git old so fast ther won't be ani yung peepel left. And then we wurri for releef that maid so mani proud oficers and mani lazi men and sum turn over to the naim what we use to kal dedbeets. And we wurri how ministers are going to maik their living when we aint goin to church.

And then we wurri because we kant tel the truth to peepel unless we caig it in a joke.

And then we wurri bekaus we spoil the land so the Indians refus to taik it bak. And haf a hundert yers ago I started to raise a family to be rich and liv a gud life and now we are al por.

And the last I wurri is this leter is goin to be pushed down in the waist basket side of the desk, but I tel yu the only thing to do with the Swedes is to forgiv them. And if yu know ani beter I wil send mi luv in return.

Johannes Johnson

125.
Mister Republican
We know that God maid al ther is on this erth and what is abov and below and I wants to tel yu reeders what I think is the best luking and the best what I think He maid in this wurld and that is the ladies.

And I seen lots of what I think is homely, but I never seen a home and I never seen a meen mother, but I heer bout them. I never seend a dumb lady, but I seen thousands smarter than a fox. What the devil kud not do he hired a lady to do. He did that when He brot the sin to the wurld and Godo had to send an angel (Mary) to saiv the wurld frum sin. That seems to me that the devil and God used the ladies for helpers. That tuk a lady to put a snare on the strongest man in the wurld so that they kud put out his both eyes. That was for two lady frends that Jesus told Lazurus to kum out of the graiv and that was for two ladi frends that He showed Himself when He went out of the graiv. I had one lady for 35 yers that maid mi life as brite as a heven and I had one for six months that kosts me thousand dollars to git rid of, but I lik her anyhow and kant help it. Ladies is the krown of what God maid, even if he maid her of a rib. But luk out for how yu treet them. If yu dont, the ribs yu got left wil stick out thru yur own vests. Ladies bilt the churches and gud mothers bilt the reform skuls and if ther wasnt for the ladies how much wud the wurld be wurth?

And I got ful rite to send mi lov to them al, even if they sit in calf stals.
Johannes Johnson

126.
Mister Republican
What does those church towers meen that stands up al over the wurld, one biger than the oder? Dont that meen that our faders and muders hav bin teached bak for thousands of yers that ther is a land abov us? It was given the naim of heven.

For tousand of yers we hav bin teeched ther is a land under the wurld that was given naim of hel and we were brot into this wurld to be teeched for one of them and we are left her with a free wil. Which skul are yu and me in?

When we git the stem shuffle and the radio we dont know what skull we are in. And if I had a steem shuffle I wud run him into the Mississipp river.

The divil is smart. The steem shuffle he used to taik the bred away frum the poor peepel so we giv them a new naim-releef. That sounds beter and that givs him a beter chance to teech them to be crooked and hav them liv on soup that is mixed up of truth and lies. That is what he giv our furst ladi.

I spose sum reeders git sore I mix religun in mi leters. But so long as I talk onli gud bout religion I got yust as much rite as yur own minister. And I wish to se the time kum bak when the churches are ful and the beer parlors are empty. When we was busy bilding churches in Red Wing ther wasnt ani por peepel. We never herd bout releef peepel and not bout kidnapers. And not bout forging cheks.

That big Merican silver dolar was busi squaring up the dets and the smallest muney we had was five center. The cents now has bin piled up so high on the side of our kuntri so it commences to tip over.

I bleeve that are goin to bring the peepel bak to what they used to be-thankful and satisfied-wil be starvashun and that wil bring them bak to religun. And religun is what keeps our kuntri civilized. Yu taik food and water away frum a wild bronco you kan drive him with a line.

With luv to yu al.
Johannes Johnson

127.
Mister Republican
I want to tel you what I fond is the hardest to go thru. If yu have a gud-luking onest ladi frend and she goes bak on yu that wil taik the teers out of a tiger's eyes. I wil also tel yu what I think is the prettiest in this wurld-a silver-grey haired lady that lived an onest life so her hair turned from golden to silver grey.

And I want to tel yu what is mor dangerous than a ratelsnaik-a lady that pretends to luv al men. Samson fond that out; he lost both his eyes. And he was the strongest man the wurld ever had and the furst lady brot sin in to the wurld and the oder kut the hed off the bigest profet the wurld ever had. And one brot the forgivness of al sins, so we beter thank the ladies for all-even the steemshovels and caterpillars.

Ladies hav brot lots of smart men into the wurld and don't forget they have to sufer for them al. Ladies are the smartest in both gud and bad. But it is an awful job to git sum of them to behaiv. And they got wurse since we got penshuns. The heels ar so small that they hav to stay out of office buildings. And sum of them smok so many cigarets that their fingers turn everi kolor of the rainbow and their lungs luk like a rok-garden.
But ther is no home without a lady. But ther is hel to hav sum of them home. I expekt ther is sum of yu ladies that don't like mi leters, but I stay here on Sweed Hill to tel yu the truth. And if I tel yu I lie it is yur duti to kal on the law. And its beter men hav bin in jail than I. And if I git ther I don't want antibody to shed a teer.

Luv to yu al.
Johannes Johnson

128.
Mister Republican
I rite now what I dont like, but mi relashuns way bak was thos kind of peoples who did not say yes, yes to everything. They tol the truth to both the king and the beggers. And mi time is short with yu reeders.

Roosevelt and Johannes are now alike. Johannes now taiks the furst step to the por farm and Roosevelt kums after with the hole kuntari. And if yu reeders want to no the reason, we have bin to gud and the man with the best hert maiks the bigest mistaiks. He didn't like to see a hungri muther with a hungri child in this kuntri. I for mi part is mor skared of releef peepel than the Wakuta ratelsnaiks. They rattle.

But befor I go ani further, I want yu al to no that ther is two peepel in releef. Ther is peepel in releef yust as onest as peepel who sit next to the president's chair and in the front seet in church. But ther is a big feeld for the devil to wurk in. And he is now busi and hiring al kinds and we kant git a day's work if we haven't got a releef mark on our foreheds. Giv us freedom. If we dont ther wil sum time kum a time when the rats wil starv in our big wheat bins.

I asked a man the oder day, "Why don't you wurk?" and he said, "No if I wurk I am ten dollars a munth out." And he told me what he gits thru the month and his figures cam out rite.

This leter is to sum of yu, but yu can al reed it. We fil our kuntri with machinery and we handel the lazi fellows with silk gloves and that bilds aditions to our penetenshuries and por houses and that shows ruining our kuntri. But dont forgit mi luv to yu al.

Johannes Johnson

129.

Mister Republican

Hav yu reeders notice what difference ther kan be in a man's long life? I wil tel it, but the truth sounds to yu yung folks like a lie. But I wil forgiv yu. When I was a kid in Sweden the old peepel and children forout support were sold to the lowest bidder, but the katel was sold to the highest. And the small kids was sitin in rags and didnt know wher they was goin and when the hamer hit the tabel they was sold for a yer and that was to eether gud or bad plais, but not a change for a yer. And that was in a hous next to the church, big as a kastel. Mi mother counted to 22 one day that beg for sumting to eat and when she giv them a hard pees of bred gron cours out of frozen oats they said "Thanks, ladi, God bles yu."

I remember one neebor kid that had a big bras buton that I wud like to hav and I tol him I wil giv yu so mani tabelspons of sour milk for it and we went to the cubord and he tuk hold with one hand in the cupbord and the spoon in the oder and when the time was up, I want him to quit, but he keept on and I kiked him and I puled his hair, but nothing doing so long as ther was a drop in the dish and the dish was 18 inches cros and three inches deep and when he walked frum the kubpord he walked on his toes. This giv yu an idea how it is to be hungry.

Now we luk at the new times. Since the furst cupel was chaised out of Paradise they never bin so gud to the old and por peepel as yust now and ther is al over the wurld. If a man has spent in gambeling or drinking a haf a hundert yers he wil git his penshun and liv like a king and not a word is said to eether the minister or the policeman.

If a hand-painted and kurley-haired ladi kum into the saloon with her child, lift him up on the konter and ask for a drink neether the minister or the oficers said a wurd. Fifti yers ago the ladies use to be home siting in the kitchen patching cloths fore the children and had a warm super on for the man. If yu expekt to keep the saloon git the kids off the conters and if yu want the ladies, keep them in the bak rum. Taik out the boxes with 4 stilts on with the bals in that sneeks around the nails to git yur nikel *(slot machines)*. Giv a free license to the one that noks down the caf stals and let the kalf go mor freely. I am sur the kow wud like it.

Johannes Johnson

130.
Mister Republican
I wish we kud stop and talk it over. What is the reason we has got so mani por peepel in our kuntri? Peepel are por that never use to be poor and it luks on their actions they want to be por. And I want yu to know mi bleef. We put religun to the side and religun is what civilize the wurld. When we go bak 60 yers in our time when we worked for one dolar a day and the church was filed to the frunt and they had to taik hold of both hands to kari the kolekshun box. Ther wasn't ani por in Red Wing and ther wasn't ani sik peepel eether and only three doctors in town and no hospital. And it kost only $5 for be born and $15 or $20 to die. Religun and muney works gud together if they is handled rite.

I luk bak haf a hundert yers and I know a time when I kud giv a $5 bil in kolekshun and if it was needed I bild a foundashon for a church 8 feet high forout ani charge. Now I kudn't bild foundashon for a dog hous. I had time to go to church 3 times on Sunday and I didn't own ani bils that I kud not pay in the midel of the nite if they ask me for it. I think the best al kan do is to go bak to church. I mite feel ashaimed the furst few times but that aint more than right.

I feel bad to walk down and meet so mani that owes me muney and never say helo. I think it wud be yust as eesy to maik releef peepel go to church and git their kard as to go to the korthous. But the sum of them a taik out the kard from the beer parlors when they cash their check.

If we kud move our kuntri bak where it was 60 yers ago I wud like to liv 60 yers longer, but if it keeps on goin like it does now I think I beter follow the old bugs up the hil and ther is plenty fools to taik mi plais.
And mi kar is tired out. She is bin running like a shutel in a weving machine between Swede Hil and Dutch Town for 11 yers. Now he wants to be neebor with the simin pool and I don't got a bad wurd to say bout him. The only thing the ox teems I use to drive with a stik and point out and tel them where to go. But I had to drive them with arm greese. But the feed and the drinks and the doctor bils and the roaming-so when he goes he goes with five tousand dollars of mi hard ernt muney.

That's more fun these days to tel the truth than to lie.

And don't forgit I luv yu al, if yu believe it or not.
Johannes Johnson

131.
Mister Republican
I wish to talk to yu reeders bout thos parties that the government is so very gud to. One parti has bin lazi a long life and spent everi nikel they ern and cheet both the minister and the salon keeper. And that seems they arc token kair of furst.

We hire oficers to buy them gud things to eet, both from Kalifornia and Australia. And what they drink they select from Kentuky if we is foolish nuf to pay for it.

The oder part aint in that gang. They draw bak and tri to help themselves. But they hav got bad luk, so wurk and a sikly wife that they tri to fix their kloths and keep half dozens kleen so they kan go to Sunday skul. Dont yu reedrs think we shud help them furst? God helps the one that tri to help themselves. Why shud we not do the saim?

We are a parti that dont bleev in to bild adishun to peneitenaries everi-oder yer and keep murderers and bank robers and kidnapers for 30 yers. I bleev it wud be beter to put a rope round their neks a few days after their krimes.

I dont bleev to hav a drunkard up in the swell corthous and giv him a new dek of kards and lectric lites so they kan see the Klover King gud. And thos that dont drink a drop hav to chip together and pay a dolar a day for siting ther and playing kards.

I wish to tel yu mi advis that isnt goin to kost yu anything and yu dont hav to bleev it if yu dont want to. After yu hav warned a drunkard and he be ashaimed in their hom and public, chain him to a log on the best bisines korner, set a haf barel of whiskey side of him, hang a diper on the side of the barel and giv him his free wil and if he gits drunk, yu shud use the saim tools as we use in the bronco 50 yers ago. Too bad that took is out of market. That is the reason we hav got so mani boys in the Trainking skul. Nuthing like a muthers hart when the children are small. Be we kant run our kuntri with that. And we see that now everi day.

This leter are goin to hurt sum of yu reeders, but I dont want to rid hiding under the seet when I hav git the tiket.

With luv to yu al.
Johannes Johnson

132.
Mister Republican
A high edukated wel-like man meet me the oder day and he said that I shud rite a leter wher we was going when we was ded. And I wil anser al reeders of The Republican wher I want to go. I want to go to heaven and yu al got yur free wil with me to go to eether plais, but I hav not talked to anibodi that hav kum bak for at the frends that left me.

But if I ever git ther I wil be saved thru fire and will see a wonderful God if he opens the dor for me. But I dont think that God put in in this wurld to wurk a long life hard and giv it to dishonest peepel so that wud not be so much left when I am thru for mi children to put a flower on mi coffin forout to ask the neebors.

And I wil tel yu reeders mi beleef. I think that the devil is loose for a short time and he sneeks around both the White House and the courthouse and he can hire lots of 30 big silver dollars and if he is short of muney he kan talk nice to Ford and Rokefeller and if he needs more he kan be a frend to the United States Treasury and tax the citgarets ten cents apiece and wil be lots of nice luking ladies that wil help him long.

Dont the truth sond bad when yu tel it? I think it is bad I kant stay with yu long. I am to the limit now and I see in the future a beter life for the hole wurld when the devil are going to be tied for a tousand yers and Moses' laws are going to kum bak and al penitentiaries are going to be tered down and peepel are going to do rite or die. And we got a promis frum the beinning of the wurld that the Father and the Son are gon to run the wurld with rite.

And when yu and me are gon ther wil be a beter man to taik our places. And dont expect ani beter of me now. I hav seen a beter time. Now when I rite I luk with one eye and rite with both hands and if yu liv long nuf yur time wil kum yust as sure as mine. Mi advis to yu al thru yur life-yu dont need to luk out for bank robbers, but luk out for yur best frens and peepel that yu help.

This leter are goin to hurt sum of yu, but dont forgit I send mi luv to yu al.
Johannes Johnson

133.
Mister Republican
When I was 21 years old I was sik and no show for recovering. I was 6,000 miles away frum hom and the wurld luked brite and I had alredy bilt me a few kastels out of wind and shadows and Red Wing luk like a flower garden ful of gurls piking the flowers and I had alredy piked out one of them and here deth luked me rite in the fais and al I kud do was to kri.

So I find the buk mi mother used to reed in so much and I reed about the man thousands of yers ago that had blud poison and that haiant no better as kunsumption and he didnt want to di neether, so he started to pray to God to giv him longer life to liv.

And God herd his prayer so he sent a man to him with a remedy for his poison and extended his life seven yers. Now I had a sparkel of hope. We got the saim God and if He wills, He kan. And I started to pray for ten yers of life and so far as I have gone He extends mi life 60 yers and yust think, I wud not die yet. If it wasnt a shaim I wud pray for 60 yers mor, but that goes with His rule.

But when He taiks mi life I wish He wud taik it like a hunter taiks a rabit-quik. Sum time ago the pope and me was sik on the saim time and the best man in the wurld had to die and I is living.

I spose sum of yu reeders think mi letters is gitting childish, but dont forgit we got to be lik a child to git into heven. We kant go there in an airplain and with kanan or maik saluts when we kum. Sum holer bout having a long life and never git ther, but He opened the dor for the rober when He hung on the kross. Now I wunder wil He open for me and I wish He wil open for yu.

With luv to yu al,
Johannes Johnson

134.
Mister Republican
I wish to talk to sum of yung reeders who is going to select what yur bissiness wil be thru life. Do not do as I did, but as I tel yu to do.

I built houses so I got rich, but I rent them out so I am now one of the porest men in town.

Now I luk bak over 60 yeers in Red Wing. Luk at what I hav done. Now if I see haf of the peepel sleep in the street with a ston for pillow. I wud not bild a hous to rent out. If I got a nikel I got over $10,000 kuming in hous rent. And that wil giv me about 40 chances to lose mi life if I ask for the muni and it shud hapin like did a few yers ago. I had a hard batel a few yers ago. I was fraid they were going to frees the heeting plant and that wud kost me $800. So I went to the sheriff and asked if I had a rite to taik kare of that and he said I certainly had.

So I went hom, tuk wud in mi arms, and was going down in the basement to build a fire and a man grab me, one hand on mi throt and got me bakways thru the dor and the wud I had luked like the burds tuk it. And when I luk the man up he had only one arm, but he was a lawyer from anoder state. So I went down and asked him if he wud find a poleesman watching when they mov out. And they hire an extra one and that kost me a dolar. But I was 30 curtains short in the hous anyhow.

A yung man shud not git a license to mari if he didn't hav a hom for a gurl or had the hous rent paid 6 months. Roosevelt shud pay the hous rent befor he buys apels or oranges.

Now to al of yu that rent houses frum me and don't owe me anything-yu are the most onest peepel on the erth and yu that want to pay and cant-step in line and folo us-we wil talk it over in the next wurld.

With luv to yu al.
Johannes Johnson

135. (copy of original article w/o picture; missing last part of letter)
Mister Republican
Sum days ago a man kum running after me on the sidewalk and patted me on the sholder and said "Johannes, don't write no mor in the Republican. Peepel laff at yu." "Oh is that so?" I said. "Peepel laffed at Noah when he bilt the ark for 100 yeers, but they wont hav the chans to laff at me so long."

And he said, "Yu go into saloons as well as I do and sum times yu put religun in yur leters and yu know that ain't rite."

Mi anser was I was 60 yers old before I tuk a drink of liquor. But yu know we want to ern and tri everything while we are here and I know mor bout saloons than ani minister in Red Wing. I know a man that stands bak of a hard liquor bar 15 hours a day sober as a judge. He hav beter character than both you and me and I dont owe him a cent and he dont owe me nothing.

Johannes Johnson
136.

Mister Republican
Fifty yers ago when we wanted to see a nice gurl we went to church and ther they was siting rite up in the frunt. Now we hav to luk in kalf stals and in mud ponds in saloons and in the wuds. What is the reason? Religun is taken out of the skuls and they trim the skuls with Yale Locks in stead of teech kids to maik locks that nobody kan open cept themselves.

The father of the furst lock was the devil and he was the teecher to the furst bank rober and kidnaper and now he tries to be bos over both our churches and skuls. I giv the old Swedes credit. When I went to skul I never herd of a skul children that sole or lied and I never herd of a bank rober and a kidnaper in Sweden yet. If they want kids they know a beter way then to steel them.

Al I lerned in the skul was bout God and the devil. If we kud not lern so much bout them we kudnt git maried when we got big, and yu know the Swedes like a maried life.

But be kerful boys. Dont' be like a mud turtle and snap at al yu see. Ther is one rode to heven and one to hel and wherever yu go, go arm in arm with yur wife. Th onli thing ther is gud bout me, I was gud to mi wife and that is the reason al ladies are so gud to me now. Yu kan fool a fox but yu kant fool a ladi. That taiks the devil to do that. Bur for a ladi to fool a man, that goes quick. But the nicest I ever seen in a long life is the smile on a ladies' lips that lives an onest life.

Luv to yu al.
Johannes Johnson

137.
Mister Republican
What is the use to hav a king in our city if they aint got anithing to say? What is the use to have a dozen prince siting around a long table and none wants to show off he is smarten than the oders? What is the use to hav a dozen men to tel where to buri the old dead horses when we aint got any?
What is the use to driv a football in a truk and spend $3,000 a yer when we does'nt giv him a kik? What is the use to hav churches when peepel stay at hom? What is the use to send sum to jail when they got beter ther than hom? What is the use to tri to maik a paridis of our city and let the thistels grow? What is the use to bi a silk dres for the wife if she wers the front out over the saloon bar?

The biggest mistaik I maid in long time is I bin to gud to peepel that God wants me to use the blaksnaik on, so mi advis to yu that figure yu got a long life in yur future-sel yur silk gloves and bi yu a blaksnaik and if yu money enuf forout to charg it, send one to Rossevelt to. What is the reason we have to bild aditions to our prison everi oder yer and chase yung boys into the reform skul like grasshoppers so when they walk over Swede Hil that luks like when the Swedes chased the Danes out of their kuntri?

Silk gloves and muthers' harts brot them ther. Mi fader brot up one and a half dozen and I tuk the likings for them al and I am the only one that's got brains and never nu to tel the truth.
The devil is now to the top of the hil for the sekund time to ofer us the hole world if we bekum his subjects, but he got new orders to turn bak and be tied up for thousand yers. And the time is kuming when we are al goin to liv a onest life or die and the hole world wil be nothing but luv and rite.

With luv to yu al.
Johannes Johnson

138.
Mister Republican
One day I fond a note on the frunt steps. On one side that stud "Who is the devil and where did he kum from?" And on the oder side it stud "Seven women after one man." It kud not be me. Ther hasn't bin a woman in the hous for months. And here is where they wud be needed. And I am willing to giv them a pair of overalls if they help me a kupel of hours to straiten up the hous. The older a man gits, the better the woman luks to him and ther is seven to one. But Johannes has got to mop the flor himself. When we git old the gud days are gone by.

And who is the devil? That's the wurst we has got in this world. And where did he kum frum? He was thron out of heven. He got proud and wanted to be boss. And now he tries to be boss over the hold world. But we are promise he is to be tied up for a tousand years, but what rope is goin to hold him? He is strong and he is smart.

I hav bin figuring how to get out of trafic on Sunday so I luk up the Island and Hager and Bay City, Frontenac and kler down to Lake City.

And I want to tel yu reeders the best and the surest plais is to go to church. Ther are not mani ther, but tri to git as mani as yuk an with yu. Jerusalem wasn't built in a day, but what yu kant do maybe yur children kan. And Sunday afternoon we kan go to the graivyard and we kan go alone and we kan sit down and think over how we treeted our frends that lie ther and waiting for us to kum after.

And if we got ani or time left of Sunday we can go to the hospital. We got two big ones in Red Wing and mani that lie ther that are glad to see yu in the dor.

I am a por example for yu al-but don't luk at me-we are both tryin to be beter. And the more we visit them plaises the beter for us and for the world.

With luv to yu al.
Johannes Johnson

139.
Mister Republican
I want to tel yu how peepel talk. Mi fader had 2 windmils on the plais, one for muther and one for himself, but he tuk one down and mi muther asked him why he tuk it down for. And he answered that it was not wind for 2 so next time she hung her dres on one end of the line and his pants on the oder and then she yerked his pants off the line and fader asked whey she throwed them on the ground and she answered ther wasn't wind nuff to dry both.

A few days after she told him that our hired gurl Mary was goin to mary and he said "What bed bug is she going to marry?" And my muther said, "One that don't bite," and he said, "That's to bad u didn't git him." A few days after she giv away the kat and mi fader asked why she did it and she said, "Yu got so stingi so not rats wud stay on the plais, I was afraid the rats was goin to starv.

"The oder day I meet a feler and he said, "Are yu the feller that they use to kal King of Swede Hill?" I said, "Not anymore, I dealed with to mani dedbeats."

Then he asked me why Roosevelt feeds the flies so gud. "Yes, I tel nothing but truth, the elephants don't need to flap their ears so much, but I mean yu."

Milyuns hav bin sent to kil weeks in the wuds that never did ani harm, but the pantry is locked from the nurses. I bin sik 3 times in soon 80 years and the doctor did nothing, but the nurses kari me thru with gud kare and a smile on their lips. And if I git to heven I wil tel Peter to hav the dor open when he kan see them with a spy glas and if 2 nurses sta side of mi coffin I will like that beter than 2 lods of flowers.

And if I liv I wil saw wud for a box of kandi for them everi time the Christmas tree is lighted and if ther is ani of yu ladies tha feels jealous I kan't help it if I like the nurses more than oder ladies I kan't help that eether.

With luv to yu al.
Johannes Johnson

140.
Mister Republican
To drink beer is gud when we is thursti and wiskey when we is sik, sum say, but to fil up the Mississippi river with old kars and empty whisky botels I dont think wil improve our kuntri veri much and to pay lazi boys to lern to be carpenters at $1.25 an hour and let the old man go idel that know mor than the boy ever wil lern, that kant improve our kuntri. And to maik the fingernails red and put on the dres the rong way and show crocked they are in the bak-that it aint goin to improve our kuntri or the gurls.

If Johannes Johnson keeps a roof over dedbeats and Roosevelt feeds-that aint goin to boost our kuntri. Investigashun shud be maid both with Roosevelt and Johannes Johnson then. Johannes spend his muni and Roosevelt spend our muni. The treasury is empty both in Swede Hill and Washington. And I kan tel our kredit when I meet a banker on the street. The smile aint the saim as ther was yers ago. We wil be put bak and Roosevelt wil roll out of the chair and Johannes Johnson will be taiken to the fox farm.

But eether one of us is no dumbhed. I dont know what edukashun Roosevelt got, but I went in one term 75 years and I aint thru yet and I had the best teacher in the world and the last yer I lerned what I know is the truth. Roosevelt and me is too gud to hav anything to do with the ones that runs the world now.

But I like to giv advis to yu that are goin to stay awhile befor they lode me up and I want to giv it to the yung ladies. I always like them. If yu want to liv long dont wear high heels on yur shoes til yu git 50 yers old. After that yu kan walk on stilts. If yu want to selekt a gud man dont show him red fingernales. Ther is a wulf in Afrika that got that and the gud man mite git skared. If yu want to be rich, if yu got a dolar kep it and try to git another one. Yers ago I kud send a handful of them. Now I kant send more than mi luv. The harm I hav to keep and the harm and luvmever agree.

Johannes Johnson

141.
Mister Republican
Hav yu readers notice how perfekt God put al this on erth? I luked at that for mor than 80 yers and I never seen ani mistaik-even a snaik that got dedly poison. He got a ratel to let us know befor he strike so we kan luk out.

A kow haint got ani horns when she is born, but when they are growed up and bekum a muther she got horns and they are kroked too. She need them to protect her baby. When yu farmers kut the horns off yur kows yu hav to taik the kow's plais.

But the sheep aint got ani protektun-onli to run and wher one go they al go. A Wisconsin farmer fond that out when he tuk a dozen sheep over the ferrie. One yumped in the river and they al yumped in yu know sheep ar poor swimmers. And they kant walk on the island in the mud for their feet is to small. They are in the world to be as high as they kan climb so they git a chance to see the herder.

Dogs I don't know so much bout, but I know ther is 2 kinds-hunting dogs and one what they cal "one man's dog." I had one of them and I tuk sik and I had to go to the hospital and the dog he stay hom and was kryin everi day. Afer two weeks-the day I kummed hom-the dog was on the hospital porch waiting for me.
Now reeders, who tol the dog? We got the most educated peepel of ani kuntri on the erth, but sumtimes we don't know so much as a dog. But we kan see forout education that the church seets are empty and the seets in the beerparlor is ful and we see peepel who got muney for both beer and wiskey, but the aint got muney to pay their neebors for sugar and south.

One that we kal a frend tol me the oder day that mi letter were not wurth reedin by him-they was to dum and to childish and I tol him, "Yu must lern quik." It took me a haf hundert yers to lern the saim thing and I am thankful for what I lerned and seen in the world and I wil tel yu sum of it.

I seen Norway, Sweden and Denmark, England and Germany, and Lapland. I seen the sun 12 klok at nite in Lapland and I seen the water run up stream in Mississippi river by Red Wing and I remember when we had several weeks gud sleying in the munth of March.

Don't this sonds childish and dum? But that kan be proved with a man who knows hundert times mor as I do. Ther is lots we kan lern if we hav to. I kud lern to be left handed when I was 80 yers old and I kut lern to be por when I had reached a long life and I kud lern to git along with one eye and I am ful satisfy if the dor opens to heven for me. Por and left-handed and one eye. I wud not have much to brag bout.

With luv to yu al.
Johannes Johnsons

142.
Mister Republican
We old peepel when we meet we talk old penshuns. I wish to tel of a nabor of mi furst home that got a penshun. He had a strip of land that folowed the sekshun line and the hiway bout a mile long and not an eigth of a mile wide.

On top of the hil wus a hous that a Finlander left. How old it was nobody nowed. That was what this newly married peepel moved into. The roof wus bilt out of logs, laid tite together and two feet of durt on the top. And the fireplais on the midel of the floor and a two feet opening for the smok to go out.

One day the ladi was working. She thot she herd her man holer to her to kum quik and yust as she caim out thru the dor the roof kaved in. And I hapin to kum. I was a kid and kaim a few minits after. And she wus siting on a ston krying. And her man kaim frum the fields and she told him she herd him holer to kum out and he said, "This is the happiest day I hav ever lived. "Yust think if yu wud hav bin in ther. I wud never hav a chance to talk to a pertier or beter ladi than you are. I luv yu and God twice as much today as I did yesterday. And now we wil hav a new hom".

And then the man kaim that owned timber land kros the rode and said he kud hav all the timber he wanted for nothing. And in a few days he started in. He bilt a nice hous and a barn and woodshed and everi log that went into the bildings he karied hom on his sholders.

And his land was so ful of ston so 30 yers later he had a fence round the hole farm that was three feet high and three feet thick.

And the Kroun Prince kaim thru that rode and he noticed that fence that stand strait as a line and he asked if he got al that ston frum the strip of ground, and he tol the man his 30 yer stori. And so the muther tol him to sit doun and hav sum homebrew and she gaiv him sum in a wuden kup. And when he drank it out he luked at the kup and ask who maid that kup and she said, "Magnus does it evenings when he aint got anything els to do."

And he said, "If yu giv me that kup I wil send yu sumthing that is beter for you." Then she said, "I wil do that, but who are yu?" He said "They kal me Karl on the 4 courners." And in a kupel of weeks thay had papers from the castel of Sweden that ther taxes were paid as long as they lived and $200 crown in penshun and a gold bage that he had orders to kari outsid his kote to show that he was the best worker, both in Sweden and Norway. This was when Sweden and Norway use the saim king. And I tel yu, al men, that it pays to be gud to both the wife and the farm.

With luv to yu al and if half of yu that owes me muni wud luv me I wud not need to be hungri. I am always,
Johannes

143.
Mister Republican
I was goin to giv yu readers a Christmas greeting, but the Swed gits behind both Christmas and mid-summer, so I am goin to tel yu that I bin in Red Wing for 61 Christmases and the furst Christmas I kut kordwud for 60 cents a kord, but if sumbudi wud hod me up in the wuds thay wud have hundert dollars out of mi inside vest poket.

I thot that was a gud scheme so I keep it up for 30 yers, but if I borrow ani frum the vest poket I paid that bak furst. The sekund Christmas was a shoemaker, lasting green lether boots, if I remember rite, for 28 cents a dozen pair, but they liked the Swede and in six munths I had six men working under me and mi pay was $7.50 a week.

But I lerned I had to pay bak to mi inside vest poket so I hired out to a hous bilder for $1.25 a day and than I started to saiv muney for mi furst home. Now we wil skip three or four Christmases and this Christmas I walked frum East Fourth street on Sorins' bluff to a strawstack and filled two matresses and karied them home to lay on the flor for mi Christmas frends to sleep on.

Them days both the churches and the home was full Christmas. Now ther is the beer parlors and the piktur shows. Now we wil yump ten Christmases. Then I use to bi turkeys bi the dozen and not ani skinny ones, eether, and giv to mi hous renters. Now I kud not bi a blakburd and I didn't hav to kari straw frum Sorin's bluff for mi Christmas frends to sleep on. One laid on the table and we talked over both King David and King Solomon and they didn't brag so much on their last day.

The oder laid bi mi feet and I said to him, "Yu got it gud." And he wigel his tail and that meens yes. I tol him yu aint got so mani Christmases to remember and he wigeled his tail and was satisified with the world.

And here I was siting with a teer in mi eyes and expecting a big krowd to kum and see a old goob that is her today and we don't know tomorrow. I seen so much in this world so I shud be satisfied, but that is the last Swede do to giv up. That tuk them over 30 yers to lik the Germans, but they did it and if that shud hapin again if mi naim is ani gud I wil put mi naim on furst.

I don't like what they are doin to the Jews in Germani. And God is gon to protect them like He did when He tuk them thru the Red Sea and when He told the sun to stand stil til they won the batel.

They got no rite to be meen to the Jews if they are smarter than them.

With luv to yu al.
Johannes Johnson

144.
Mister Republican
I red in the best buk in the world that we shal figur up our hauls and bisiness bekaus we hav to die. And not a rode kan be bilt round deth. The mor rodes we bild and the wider we maik them, the sooner peepel will die.

And now we wil settle up with the best man in our home town. Akording to that buk we wil forgiv yu for giving $75,000 to the Milwaukee railroad to kum in rond the bluf and bild a cheep stashun. We will forgiv yu for giving $50,000 to the railroads to the claypits and spoiling the hold Hay Creek valle. And now we kan ship the clay cheper in cigar boxes than on the railrode.

We will as also forgiv yu for bilding a rode kross the Island that kost us $100,000 for the farmers to bring us kord wud and we wil forgiv yu for the bridge kross the river that kost $85,000.

And yur name instead in both ends of the bridge for the honor of al of us. For to forgiv yu for giving away that bridge is a hard yob, when the trafic shows us today that our city wud be tax free yust as wel as Prescot. And I wil also forgiv yu for puting the swiming pool on stilts in the mud pond.

And giv our children's flesh to the mosquitoes that grow so big on the Mississippi. And we ask eech other what kan be the price. We wil forgiv taking out the Roman work at the Auditorium and maiking it plain so it wil be eesier to keep kleen for the janitors.

We wil also forgiv yu for putting our winter kole in one big pile and pressing the landing into the Mississippi. Al is forgiven-old and new-even when yu bot a stone crusher that could not crush sugar lumps and a snowplow so big we kud not put it.

Now it is up to yu to forgiv me. I live a longer life than the most of yu and mi life is ful of mistaiks. But I wil menshun three. I tuk the advis of an educated man and kut a hous in two. That kost me $2,200. And I married a sekund time without asking God or anyone else and that kost me yust as much. And I worked thru a full and long life, save muney and giv it to dedbeets in both Red Wing and Wisconsin.

And I am now like a rat that maid her hom in a church.

And now to yu, Mister Republican, plees let this leter under yur rolers and I will serv mi last days yust as wel in the courthous as in the por hous and they are both mi frends.

With luv to you al.
Johannes Johnson

145.
Mister Republican
A few peepel that likes to reed mi leters stik with me and you that hate them wil forgiv me. I got lots to tel yu and sum I wud not tel yu-it is to bi big a shaim for me-but I kan start it when I use to tro stone on wild duks wher the city hal stands now. And when I use to sit aside of Auditorium and drink water for mi helth at 4 o'clock in the mornin' and meet gurls that had two hair braids hangin on their baks. And I use to grab one in each hand and turn them fais to fais and yu kan guess what I stole. And I ask them if I kud see them home. And they smile like an angel. Then it was the time to liv. Ther was mor truthful luv than what they use now in the kalf stals in the beer parlors. We use to walk 4 miles in Wisconsin for a meeting. And ther was mor fun to walking in thos days than to riding in a thousand dolar kar now. We kud go to Hay Creek, Spring Creek and Bell Creek. And it luked like a paradise and wher ever yu see a farmer and his wife they had a smile on their lips when they were sitting on spring two feet higher than the wagon box. The stars in the kaliko dress sparkled like the Bethlehem star and they didn't have eether red led *(lipstick)* in the satchel on the trip to Red Wing.

Now days they have to go to the barbershop and kut the hair off that shud support the big kord that holds the hed up. Now them kords stand bair like a telephone pole and they hav hot irons in their hair and a cupel dozen klamps so they luk like a mouse that fel in a kold soup ketel and the finger nails painted blak and we know that is a big sign.

In the old days it hurt awful if a fingernail hapin to git blak. When a ladi hav kut her hair ther is no more left in this world that she got rite to be proud of akording to the wurd of the Bible. I tel you yung folks yu shuld talk mor to the old goobs and read that old book that lays on the shelf-probably kovered with dust.

Johannes Johnson

146.
Mister Republican
Seventy fiv yers ago ther wasn't no particular in Red Wing. When they bilt the furst post office one korner was to high and the bos tuk a yump on the top of the sil and the korner that was low he put a skul of an oxen under and nobodi maid ani complaint. And when they bilt the first potteri they put it in the midel of the street and no complaints for 40 yers. And that was the best bilding eve bilt in Red Wing for the taxpayer. Yust tink of how mani that wer fed, clothed and educated bekaus of that faktori here. So they kan feel proud today. And so long as the government wud alow them they paid their worker in gold.

And if they kan git mor of them bildings they kan put them on top of the swimin pol and on the park way next to the Swede kastel.

I want yu to be proud of yu has got ani konectshuns with the potteri. Even if yu push the weelbarow. But that dam they maid to leev the water in Hay Creek I think is gud for turtles and muskrats. I remember when the citi maid one with Haks mil that kost $7,000 and that was gud for a cupel of yers for his duks to swim in. But yu kant see wher it was maid.

Ther is anoder thing they kan do to giv work. They kan improve that Indian face that the natur maid on the west hump of Barn bluf and put a pier under his jaw to sekur him for anoder hundert yers or mor. It is to risky for the one that does the most of our washings now.

And for thos that wants to sing. Ther is always sumthing to sing. And if he wants to kik that is the easiest yob of al. And I am thankful to al yu that asks for mi leters. It is the only plesur I hav got. One part of the peepul that we kal relief got (*MISSING ENDING*)

147.

(*MISSING BEGINNING*)

mi harness off and I am redi to be chaised to the por farm. The ax is set to the root of the tre and they are goin to fal.

And when the roof is gone on the farmer's barn he kant afford to hire relief peepel. So he wil hav to go bak to strat barns. And don't forgit mi luv to yu al.

Johannes Johnson

148.
Mister Republican
Wud yu plees let me rite a leter to the oficers of Red Wing? Some is ded, sum has retired. And I wil promis to bring yu nothing but the truth.

I was the furst man that started to talk to the owner of the land of Sorin's bluf to see and turn it over to a park for the yung men that fite for our kuntri. I am stil a owner of a strip the hole length of it on the east side of the bluf and it has the most artistic view on the Mississippi.

I bilt a hous on the point that kost me 3 tousand dollars after a drawing frum Norway-800 yers after Christ-and yu kud see it 20 miles frum Wisconsin. The lock on the dor was since 1600 and the hinges of the Furst Episkopal church in Chicago and I think it never bin broke open til it kaim on that dor.

The klok on there was since 1426 and the trunk wher the public kan hide their booze in was since 1500 and that wasn't ani use for the Red Wing booze honds to pik that open. I had ten instruments for the public to play on and a beter piano and organ than in mi home.

I had nother log hous 245 feet square with an oven in one korner and a 2 feet hole in the midel of the room for the smok to go out-a style after the furst finlander that kum over frum Sweden in 1500. I had a windo 16 feet wide and a table and bench the saim length wher the public kud sit and wit mi 20 dolar spi-glass and luk over Kolvil park and the hole length of Lake Pepin. I had the city water up so far as the big pump down by the river kud lift it and al the benefit I had was the water bill-$18 that I had to pay. I had a 30 feet platform for the public to dance on that hung in steel kabels frum 4 big oak trees-swings for the children. I had a parti that kost me $150-kook fum St. Paul and waiter frum Red Wing for $50 apeese. The Mayor and the city koncil were there and firemen-so mani that kud leeve the plais. One day about 400 peepel frum St. Paul was ther.

But now the flowers are falling off the Swede Kastel and I shal explain the fault-no police protekshun. Officers kudn't walk up the hil. I stud bak of a tree and see a boy that shot out 20 window lites and I grabed him and tuk him to the plice stashun and 15 minutes after I was gon they let the boy go home kaus his fader was a church member.

I had an old lime kiln 90 feet frum the level of the quarry and a 60 feet high tower on it which I used for a blacksmith shop and the boy broke in and used a big iron bar and got stones loose and droped them on the flor so it brok and al mi tools, kegs of powder and boxes of dynamite went down 90 feet and I haint luk from them since-eether hav the city oficer of Red Wing and not unkel Sam.

When I locked up the kastel the sheeting was off the wal, the sekund flor was gone-used for huts in the ravines. I had to risk mi life to git two boys out of a trap that they bilt themselves.

But no one hav thanked me for it-and not one mother. And I mabe saived a funeral in the family. I luv the naim on the bluf and I luv the big oaks that stand ther so mani yers and fite with so mani hard storms.

I piked out a dozen that I give the Bible naim the saim as al mi children, but they are al gone with only one with the naim of Abraham's Oak and she stands so far out on the point that relief peepel kud not reech it.

I wish gud luk to al that luk at her when yu pass Swede Hill.

I level out a plais with Abraham's Oak with intenshun that mi bones shal rest ther. I piked out stones for yers that lay ther waiting, but it never goes as yu think, but it goes as it hapins.

That hapin that I kud see 40 yers ahed of the oficers of Red Wing, but mi life had to be a failure. I stands now side of mi graiv, luking bak on a long life, ful of harm, not for being so meen, but for being to gud to peepel that wasn't wurth it.

Now if I got gud luk with this leter the tail wil kum after.
With luv to yu al.
Johannes Johnson

149.
Mister Republican
I wud like to send the tale end of mi last leter and the tale end is the saim as the ruder on a bot. Yu kan steer it rite against the roks. When mi bluf parti was to the end and Mayor Pierce stud between the two flags-Swedish and Amerikan-one kost 50 kroners and the oder nine dolars. He said to me "What return do yu wish for the gud time we had today?

And I said, "Yu are the one that are goin to git the returns. Yu are the furst mayor we had that climbed the bluf for the Swede and yu shal hav al the stony u need to secure a level park frum the Mississippi river for ten cents a load." That kost me that to keep a man on the rode.

I had thousands of loads redi to throw on the dray and I had thousand loads of grub to put on the mudi streets in Red wing. Th stone they tuk, and I tol them if they wud paive the rode on the hil they wud not need to pay the ten cents. But they said they wud not fix no privat rode. But the grub they haven't tuk befor this sumer.

One of the straw boses ask me if I kare and I said, "I giv Mayo Pierce thousand loads 30 years ago and they taik mor, they kan let me know." But insted to kleen up like they did on their side, they started on a pile 30 feet high so they wud not need to do ani kleening.

And the wild peepel that goes up ther. They drive in on mi land and play hind in go seek. And ther is lots of cover that is six feet high. If I had a half hundert yers bak on mi time-now is the time for the Swede kastel.

A few yers ago I borrowed a hous trailer to the city for their men to eet their dinner in when they working on the rode. When they was thru they left her out in Hay Creek in middle of the rode when I find her.

Johannes Johnson

150.

Mister Republican
I'm here again and I always kuk for sumting difrent to tel yu, but I dont expect to suit yu al, but I tri to luk out for Jens K so I git mi o.k. on the letter. And I want al the reeders to know that Mr. Grondahl hav bin gud to me.

I maybe hurt the feelings of sum of his customers, but both he and the customer probably tink I dont know ani beter and they know the truth. A man nowdays that dont know mor than the truth, he isnt much to brag bout, but I wil tel yu who is the wisest man in our town. That is the man that keeps his mouth shut. If I kud hav done there wud hav bin parks and a swiming pool.
I was a gud feler and started the park 20 yers ago, spent $2,000 of mi hard erned muney and al I asked for was proteckshun of the city. I stud bak of a boy that shot out 22 window lights of the Swede kastel I bilt and I brot him down to the city hal and 10 minets after I was gone they let the boy go home, bekaus his father was a gud church member.
How do the truth sounds to sum of yu reeders? And I got mor and that wil leak out of a man that cant keep his mouth shut. And those old quarries in Red Wing. We wil estimate them to 24 akres and up to 50 feet hi of solid ton. And al the nations of the wurld work there, but the most Swedish, Norwegian and German. How mani drops of sweat havent droped down frum the old men's cheeks? I wil guarantee enuf for the Lusitania and Mauretania to sale on. How do this sound to yu yung folks that know so litel of the hard life? Now yu kum in a tousand dolar kar and hear them wisper frum both south and north poles.

And yu follow the bal gaime in Spain and when the chiken yumped the pole in Jerusalem and the hole wurld is in yu eers. Let me tel yu, yur life is lik the Roman's life that wil hav to end and I wil advis both yu and me to watch our steps and ask God what he wants us to do. Today we got a new day. One kums after the oder. Why shudent we tri to be a new man and so both God and Roosevelt said we gitin beter.

With luv to yu al.
Johannes Johnson

151.
Mister Republican
Ve taxpayers had a conference in the east end of our town and ve al decided to tenk Mester Strusz for explain fur do public the rule and charges for the city ambulance. But plese dont tell who put the prices on. Dat wil be to big shame for our city, and I wil tel both minister and munshiners that's a sin and a shame to charge anyting.

If the one that need him isn't wort life tousand dolars and I am thankful to al that show the public de hole where the pocket-gofer lives. Dey aint got no right in the taxpayers field.

Johannes Johnson

152.
Mister Republican
I want to tel yu sum of what I bleve so yu and me find out we dont bleve the saim. I bleve that taiks 700 yers to git that nice white pine trees bak to our kuntry. Three generashuns of tree to have to grow up and rot down and our kuntry hav to be forout both governor and game warden and for thos big trees in the south that didn't hav ani life seed for 400 yers I aint no bleve bout.

But I bleve that taiks 700 yers to bring bak those gud and honest peepel that us to liv in Hay Creek, Spring Creek and Belle Creek and other parts of our kountry.

Roosevet tried to bring them bak with law, but I bleve he got just as big yob as the whale when he was goin to swallow our profet. He had to kal on his bruder fish that had a biger mouth. I tink Roosevelt hav to kal on Shoemaker. His mouth is big nuf to swalo aniting.

Mi bleve is we por peepel kant live off listening to a big mouth with big gils bak of it to pres it out. We want work and a small pay and a blacksnake behind us to lern us to liv according to our income. I bleve ther is 2 ways to tri. One way is to set the government seal on the steemshuvel and tractors not to be moved befor al the por peepel and the mule got a yob and our government have to wer out loads of blacksnakes to maik them lazi peepel probisun brot to our kuntry start to work.

And one way is to start a world war and kil half of the por peepel and let the oder half luk on the new machinery that do the work and traid our swell riding away for a pair of crutches. This is no pleasant leter for peepel that aint got no work and peepel that want to snek their livin forout to work, but in the futur yu mite find sum truth in it but dont forgit mi luv to all of you who reed The Republican and want to pay for it and if yu kant borrow it frum yur neebors and keep posted.

Johannes Johnson

153. Thursday, December 7, 1933
Mister Republican
I got noos to tel yu. I got a yob, the furst for 15 yers and the furst time I worked for a boss for 45 yers. It's the best yob I had since I left my deer mother when I was 14 yers old. Now I am a old gub and a failure in bisnes but kan see gud when they got respect for old aig. I never thot we had to mani gud peepel in Red Wing.

I dont know how mani bosses we got on the yob because they all work, but one day one kum up to me and said "Dont yu maik to big hole in the bluf because of your aig. Yu are here to do so much as the next men, but what yu think yu kan do mor, dont maik us or Uncel Sam rich." So I maik a motion that whoever kicked and klaims he is misused giv him his time and dont send him to the kounty commissioner eether, and I shal be through tomorrow I will tank yu al for what yu hav done and if mi ship haven't stranded to klos to the parkway I wud meet yu al with return.

But al I kan do is to pray that both Roosevelt and me kan liv so I kud vote for hime oncet more and dont forgit mi luv to Hay Creek, Spring Creek and Belle Creek.
Johannes Johnson
154.

Mister Republican
Der is a kind of peepel that a menshun so little in mi leters that wudn't be more than rite they git their share. They had gud helth and they was onest and they pay their bills and thay had a gud wil power and thay went hed in this world got rich. And they helped lots of peepel and al luk up to them and both rich and por know them.

But there kums a time that they find out they help to mani. The poketbuk got empty and the bankers went to see them and their best frens didn't kum round for munths and their wives got ugli and the children isnt satisfied and son-in-law and muder-in-law havnt showed up for munths.

The luv of the home is gone and the chairs in the parlor is hard and the church benches aint ani beter, but dont giv up, the sun are bak of the clouds and we liv in hope for beter days and I wil send advis freely. Be onest when yu ask for county help, be onest when yu bi a drink of moon and be onest when yu go to church. Yu hav read about two and tried to lie in the church and they had to carri them out both ded.

Tomorrow is a new day. Start over new and pray for those that cheat yu out of the most of yur money and tel yur wife yu are glad that sumbudy hasn't taik her, and our children got just as big eyes as we and we ar goin to git long fine those short days we got left.

With luv to yu al.
Johannes Johnson

155.
Mister Repubican
I menshuned in mi las leter that I discover so mani gud pepek in our county and ther is lots mor if yu reeders want to help me to luk them up. I got an onest way that I wish we wil tri to find them al. They are needed and they wil be mor needed.

I and lots with me wish that al officers in Gudhue Kounty and al managers and klerks of al kinds that havnt had no kut in their salaries for the last six munths are goin to giv nothing less than 10 dollars kash to a fund when Roosevelt's funds are empty. We promis Roosevelt to do our share, and if we dont he wil be after us with the iron wip and with lots of helpers. Let us pik out a gud-luking and Christian ladi to see them al and put their naimes down so we know where we got them.

Ther is a time now that we need return for to help them to their office. Government help is gud and kounty help for widows and smal children, but that sounds bad for man that kan walk forout crutches. There is sumting we men kan do in return if they let us use a weel barrow. Three yers ago I kumenced to ask The Republican what bekum of the well barrows but they al tol me they are beried forever. But those that hold the sermon over the weel barrow, they are neebors to me in the sand kut in Hay Kreek and we got 100 of them der and how mani we wil git in Spring Kreek and Bell Kreek we wil find out in the futur.

The weel barrow are goin to maik broders and sisters of the Mexican peepul. The swell kars hav maid bankrobers and kidnapers of mani. And yu foks that didnt git no yob in Hay Creek kum out and luk at the krowd-that wil do yu mor gud than 3 yers in high skul. And al that got a yob, ther is beter than yu that feel to gud to ask for help if they need it.

With luv to yu al.
Johannes Johnson

156.
Tuesday, December 19, 1933
Mister Republican
I naimed myself as reported for Roosevelt's driveway in Hay Creek and I wil report that I tink we wil hav a beter road to Hay Creek and Hack's old mil than they hav between Jericho and Jerusalem.

And the traffic is big now. Thousands of old new cars-one whelled-meets in the hour and I hant herd of a kolishun yet. Not one radiator leeks and al the water they tails is a milk kan a day for both the kar and the drivers.

And we havnt used mor grees than there is in a Jack rabbit and the drivers improv for everi day so we kan turn around on a ten cents piece and there is to bad if they hav to lay off such a gud man. Now ole-new kar dont go so fast as the bank robbers and kidnapers but we dont need to mov the ded slough in the park and maik a graveyard side of our swimming pool when they are ded.

I wil sooner see a por man walk on crutches than see him ride in a swell kar and beat the groceri man and the one that keeps roof over his hed. Dont the truth sound bad when I kums out of a axe handel?

I also want to report that no Christmas present wil be accepted by me and wil tel yu the reason. Yu dont owe me ani, yu have giv them everi day, yer after yer, and now I am so old that I dont need ani and I feel bad bekaus I kant giv yu ani bak and those monies I ern to Hay Creek I got to sav for taxes on mi bak lot, so the city dont taik it for taxes and ad it to the park and kumplete their wish, and if that wasnt a way to kum to heven without to be perfect ther wouldnt be mani there.

But let us al tri to liv a beter life the kumin yer and end the old yer with forgivness to eech other and taik the first step on the road that goes direct to heven. I tink there is mor peepel in heven frum Damaskus por house than frum Jerusalem's tempel. Yu reeder kan tink that over thru the Christmas season and I wish yu al gud luk.

Johannes Johnson

157.
Friday, January 12, 1934
Mister Republican
I listen to a smart parti that seems to no al the mistaiks our kuntry maiks and they ask me wich was the biggest. I wil anser yu al wich I tink was the biggest. When we tuk the religun out of our public skuls. The sekund mistaik was when we tried to lik the Germans. We kan kil a beehive, but we kant lik them. An I bleve the religun hav civilized the wurld and the religun hav bilt milyuns of barns for the kattels comfort and hog houses with dri straw.

But when we git karless with the religun the rats and skunks got karless with the hog hous. Now we hav to rot down with the hog hous.

I hav seen much in the last 50 yers, but I hadnt seen one siner that kry over his sins and promis a beter life. Now to yu that want to help God and Roosevelt to beter our kountry, go bak to the religion. He kant use ani oder. Our kuntri is split in parts, one part wants to liv off the government and one off the state, one off the kounty and off the city like Hager and Wakuta and the part ther is left getting too old and tired out and the kreem they produce is without value.
What wil yu reeders do with the truth that kums out of the axe handle? I spose buri it side of the swiming pool. Yu kan buri both Ford and Studebaker ther, but yu kan not buri the truth ther. Truth was befor the sun kum up and the truth are going to be after the sun refuses to giv us the light.

With luv to yu all.
Johannes Johnson

158.
Saturday, February 17, 1934
Mister Republican
I see sum man lening on the shufel in mi gang working for Roosevelt today. Yu know how sum peepel are sneeking round. I kud heer this wasn't satisfy I wasn't laid off like they was and I dont blaim them eether and they know everithing bout the officers in the kort hous and how they run the money that's given to us por siners. Yu kan yust as wel taik mi report furst. I am in the sekund site and I kan heer when they whisper and mi deer mother lerned me to tel the truth. I havent seen or herd nothing bad bout the oficers in the cort hous. I know they are going to sel mi property for tackses next spring, but they aint their falt and they aint mi falt eether, but the falt is to them that kud pay me and wudnt. And I feel mor sorri for them than I feel for myself. That dont maik any difernce to me hundert yers frum now, but it mite for them.

And so far as the oficers on the rode is concerned, I am on the 4th yob and nobody told me to hurri up and I aint got mi slacker yob eether. But I am treeted gud and I tri to maik so big a hole in the frost as mi side man. But if I was 20 yers back of mi life that wud be the easiest yob that I had in mi life.

And I am thankful to al that put a gud wurd for me so I got the yob. And I wish I kud stay so when the banker taiks mi property they dont hav to pay mi taxes out of there own money. I didnt ow anibodi when I kum to this wurld and I don't like to owe ani when I leve, but ther is now mi bigest battle, but to late are the siners going to waik up but if sum of mi frend want to pay a flower on mi coffin, kum now.

I like to thank yu, but when I am ded I cant tank yu, but today I kan send mi best luv to yu al. I think both yu and me are best off if we eat when we got and beg for the rest. Al gud peepel isnt ded yet. From Adam to now, yu never see so mani gud peepel as there is rite now. And this kuntry got the most of them, but dont ask to much. If Rockefeller shud put on a parti for al in this wurld and satisfy them al I wudnt give 5 cents for his bank akount. I hav bin to gud to kroks and I am bout 2 yers hed of our kuntri. Put that in yur poket and remember I luv yu al.

Johannes Johnson

159.
Mister Reppublican
I wish to talk to al onest and peepel with gud memories of our city. Do yu remember a big burch tree on the rite hand going east 7th street with a big sign nailed on "Go Clausen for groceries and carpets" and below a small sign "go to Longset for fli powder?"
I use to go ther Sunday afternoon as a neukumer and sit ther and wish I kud maik muney to bi me a lot and bild a small home but that didnt grow up rite away, so I talked to a frend that had a few dolars saved and he rented the lot for $10 a yer and I got the yob to bild him a small hous and he lived ther a few yers and he tot the plais was to kold.

He hated to se al the farmers that kum frum the east freeze their noses in frunt of the hous so he moved his hous out of ther and for yers that was nown as Betcher's pastur. Yers went bi and with gud behavior and 15 and 1 hours a wurk a day I save muney enuf to bi my living place and I started to be sik with th saim sikness as sum of the Swedes got when they kaim to this kuntry-proud-and that goes always befor a fal.

Peepel kal me the "king of Swede hill". So when I laid out the fondashun I laid it out 46 by 66 and I thot that wasn't to much of a king. And when I kum to the porch the old burch tree was in the way so I giv orders to kut down. But then mi wife kum and said, "bild as yu plees, but I am the bos over the burch tree" and we chewed rags for a few minutes and I said, "if yu dont giv me ani reason that wil go down" and she said, "that tree is going to watch yu when I am gone," so that burch tre has watched me better than the chief and al the poleesemen in Red Wing. That only tuk a nap once and that was when I married the second time.

Do yu remember when I imitate what they kal the Swede castel on the bluff? But that was like a old hous on the highest montin in Norway and no record of when that was bilt. But they find out that was muvd up there 800 yers after Christ. And when the Swedes and Norwegians was frens and used the saim king, the king muved it down and put six-fot cornice on it and covered the ruf with koper. So that wil last longer than the one I built and no skul kids is goin to ter that down. Ther Norwegians and Swedish lion sleeps with open eyes.

Do yu remember when I had the Swede parti on the bluf? City koncil and the bankers was invited and I had kook frum St. Paul with kost of $10 and waiters frum Red Wing with a kost of $5 and one barel of bock beer frum Remmlers and wines frum Norway and France and nobody was drunk and I paid a dolar and haf a peece to bring up cripples to be with us. An the mayor didnt feel ani biger than the cripples.

I had one log hous like the Swedes had tousand yers ago with al kinds of relics, grinstones and spinning weels frum Sweden, spi glas so I kud see the flies on mi fren's nose in Colvill park. I had swings for the children and platform for the dancers. I had al kinds instruments to play on. I had beds for the sik and I had nothing to gud for the public and al was free.

So far as I know I was the furst one to menshun to git Memorial park wher ther is now.
What onor and thank yu hav I got? I had that al that want to sneek out of site and hide in the brush and I want yu al to know thatit was mi hard erned muney I spent. That wasn't gut herted muney. That wasnt city muney or Uncel Sam's muney.

Now I se I was failure in bisness to be gud to the publik, but I got the hope yet to git mi last wishes thru. I wish to git the park fence on the esterly line and turn mi point of the bluf to a graveyard fre to everbodi and I like to be the furst one and if God givs me the time I like to dig mi own grav. But ther is not much time to spair and to yu peepel that dont want to reed mi leters, the generashuns that aint born yet mite want to reed it. And to yu Republican if yu return this leter, I wil do like the meat market. It is mi duti to deliver the truth so long as I am her and I want yu to know I luv yu al, but I dont think the saim of yu al, but we are frens yust the saim.

Johannes Johnson

160.
Mister Republican
A haf hundert yers ago I was working truthful, kut kord wud for 60 cents a kord and busted and split and karied it into the wudshed and piled it under the rafters and got one dolar a kord. And I was square with the wurld and I tink I lived the life God liked. And I jumped and was hapi as a robin.

I had sunrise brekfast on Barn bluff and supper on Sorin's bluf and I kud walk ten miles in Wisconsin to a prayer meeting. I slept like an angel on straw that was growed inside the city limits. I moved into me furst and mi best home in the wurld when the sun shone thru the wal on the kradel and the child wud smile and I thought he wud be a king for our kuntri.

Now I kum to the sekund term in mi life when I growed up like a sunflower and bekaim an owner of 22 homes in our town. And I was rich and the peepel thot it wudnt be right to pay me no rent. I was rich enuf but that maid an end to mi sekund staig in life.

Now I am in mi thurd. Mi home stands like a forgotten kastel, mi furnishur haf to be moved into the barn and I had to go to the side hil with mi rabbits. And yu know how they jump? But this isn't the most importance that I want to tel yu reeders.

But frens that did me nothing but gud, I wudnt lose for the hole wurld. They tuk a jump lik a rabbit and al the reason I kan see is that I lost the big Merican dolar. Yu reeders and frends shudnt put a stone on the burden-its hevy enuf-and so yu dont fal. Ther are lots of big trees falling nowdays and lots of smal have to sufer from the bigger trees' fal.

With luv to yu reeders.
Johannes Johnson

161.
Mister Republican
I tried to be acquainted with a Big and Stylish bird but I couldn't. I throwd wheat in his way, but he let the wheat lay and scratch me on the feet so long as I could walk. He looked high and swallowed frogs and squirrels when the small bird was singing, and picked up the wheat. I heard about a bird in th e'old world' – an elephant and a nose horning had a fight and they both were equal-so they both had to die, and there come a bird flying and took them both and brought them to the nest to feed for the young ones. That must be a bigger bird than the one I throwd the wheat to.

In the 'old world' they had big men too. One that they called Goliath. He stood in the front of a big army, dressed in iron and sword six feet long. And the army in the front backed up seven days and here comes a sheep herder that went to meet him. And he laughed and said, "I'll give you to feed for the birds." And the sheep herder said, "I'll meet you in the name of God." And he bent down and picked up a stone and throwd to him. And he fell and he took his own sword and cut his head clear off. That was the end of that "Big Bird".

And the 'old world' had another 'Big Man", that they called Sampson. They couldn't do nothing with him, so they hired a good-looking lady to fool him to tell the truth. The first time he told her a lie and forout a sword he grabbed a jawbone of a mule and he killed 700. So the lady started in again and petted him on the cheeks and kissed him and you know you can't keep on lying for a good-looking lady. He told the truth. And they got him and they stuck out both eyes and he had to pull a flour mill so long as he lived. God never let a tree grow up so high so that aint got a place to fall. And if Johannes Johnson have fell down-that aint no wonder. And I will tell some of you readers when you have keep roof over head of so many that haven't paid, you are falling too. And I had nothing when I come-and I take nothing when I go. And if there wasn't a life after this, the life woldn't be worth living. And to you readers that think my letters are childish, I don't care, if the right one reads it.

With luv to you all,
Johannes Johnson

162.
Saturday, March 3, 1934
Mister Republican
If there is ani of yu reeders that wants to no how I git along thru the winter so far, I never lived no helthier munths than tho 4 munths that went bi. I never worked for a beter man and they al kal him Roosevelt. I never worked with ani beter partners. We are like we wus in life saving boat for the next shor. I kum home like a dog that chased a rabit al day, fire up a 12 rum hous for 2 kats and myself and if the kats hasnt stole mi super I eat and go to bed and I never need to be fraid for kidnapers, but sum time I git a nitemare, so I git a awful kramp so I hav to fite for a few minets, but hundert yers frum now they aint goin to hav any power over the nitemares. Roosevelt are making a harness for sum financiers so they hav to put their own load. We Amerikan peepel hav walked thru our sweet appel orchard and stepped into a desert where we find lots of thisels. If yu and me are the furst let yu and me jerk up the roots so thos that kum after us kan find the best way out. Desert meens no rain and if one that got the power lock up the sky, what kan yu do with yur 160 acr farm? And what kan Uncle Sam do with dams that kost so mani milyun dollars to hold the water back in the Mississippi river. That wudnt be water nuff for a goat. Hunderts of lakes in our state drying up. Who knows if that isnt a warning?

We git so smart in religun so we mite git a chance to tri out what ministers God answers. I seen that the ministers had a big conference and 90 per cent didnt beleev ther is a hell. I wunder if they didnt belong to bael when they pray for rain in olden times, but I beleev what mi mother told me when I use to sit on her knee. And I beleev a time in kuming when yu and me are wiling to taik the spoon in our rite hand and thank God if he fil it.

And dont forgit mi luv to all the reeders. When I throw water on the goose I hav to throw on them all. I dont know who likes it when I leeve yu reeders, I leev yu for gud and shal not bother yu no more.

Johannes Johnson

163.
Mister Republican
Hav yu never thot of that our kuntry has the most respkt for the ladies of ani civilize kuntry on erth? So thos that got the power over our kuntry must hav red the Bible and when God maid Adam, He luked him over and He feel gud over His work, but He said that wasn't gud he was alone so He giv him a wife and that must be the best that was given to the erth. Thru her our Saviour kum and if yu dont thank God for yur wife yu aint wurth havin one.

What wud heven be forout the sun and the morning star? What is a home forout a mother and a wife? I wud advis yu men to think it over. If everything isn't so korect as yu wish, yu know what yu got, but yu dont know what yu git. If yur lips git sore put sum salv on, keep them shut for a whil, and wil tel yu for sure, the ladies is just as yu tret them and so are yur neebors to. Pin this up side of yur kitchen stov so it that hapin yur man has to fix their own breakfast so he kan luk it over to.

With luv to bot man and wife.
Johannes Johnson
164.

Tuesday, March 13, 1934
Mister Republican
Wen yu rit a leter in the paper yu hav to rite what yu think if yu dont want to be a piker and wen yu rite what yu think yu git lots of enemies and few frens. But I want yu al too know that yu are al frens to me and I got not a bad wurd to say bout one of yu. Mi beleev cannot suit al of yu and yu al got rit to do as yu please. My beleev is the furst job our city shuld do is to lay of al our oficers and al that hav a steady job to our city and the county should folo us and state shud folo the county and the government shud folo the state.

In yers our oficers hang together lik a net and everi time they meet they put a mesh or two more in the net and befor we know of they got to al the shepherds and the suckers in the net so ther wudnt be no fish left to lay the egs.

The Red Wing horses gitting boney and we bot lots of gud feed and alfalfa hay so he shud travel the most on his hind legs, but I think ther is to mani lines conected to his bridel and al pul and want him to go his way, but wen yu git the line konected to a bone pile yu find out the hors got tangeled up in the line and chokes.

I wish yu wud do like the big ocean steemers when they know they got to sink-saiv the children and the mother first and let the oficers hang to the line. They are the ones that steer the ship. The captain goes last. I hait to be mayer in Red Wing and sit down and O.K. what the oders do. If I dont they git mad. One king and one fader in our home is nuff. How do yu lik to git into a big family where they is al kings?

When they bilt the tower in Babel they had so mani boses so one kudnt quit. The saim when they bilt the swimin pool in Red Wing. I beleev in Napoleon's idea. One king in heven and one on the erth. One hed kook in our kitchen and the oder kan peel potatoes. They us to kal me the King of Sweed Hill. If ther is ani left that kal me that I dont know. They tret me lik a king and if they kal me Lazurus in Sweed Hill be so kind as the dogs: lick mi sores and to thos that feel hurt of mi leters, talk to Roosevelt bout it. He is mi judge and whatever he says, I will holer amen.

With luv to yu al.
Johannes Johnson

165.
Saturday, March 17, 1934
Mister Republican
I wil taik a short time off and talk to yu if yu please want to listen. This is important to me and when we want to tel sumting from the hert we want al to listen. I see the warning on mi 76th birthday. I luk thru the window to the west and I see Mt La Grange lik a montain of gold in a ocean of al kind of color. I luk for frends and here is 2 cats that wiggle their tales and wish me gud luk and ask for brekfast.

And I got plenty time to luk bak and think over mi life that went bi. The furst I thot of was when we moved into our new home. I was lait when I kum home and I holer for mi wife and she said, "I am here. But the time wil kum when yu holer in this big hous and I aint here."

We kan forgit thos things when we smok cigarets and drink beer, but the old age wil sneek on us like a lion that we think is sleeping and nothing goes so fast as geting old-just lik yu turn yur hand over.

And to yu older peepel, what is lif? Nuthing but worri. Haf of mi life I work hard and wuri for not giting por. Old age is to die. We kan not run away frum that so I wud advis yu al to liv a life that is rite and wish to see another birthday and find out how yu boys giting long. And I wil not forgit the Republican. The only plesur I git of mi life now is to tel yu the truth and that sound bad lots of times, but don't forget mi luv to all the reeders of the Republican.

Johannes Johnson

166.
Mister Republican
Let me and yu that got the chans go bak 50 yers ago and rethink over our life. That mite be gud for us. We are not to the limit and we got to expect our biggest enemi what we kal death. Let us think over our best lie and se where we are now. Do you remember 50 yers ago when we use to go to church 3 times Sunday? And in the midel of the wek walk to Trimbel for a prayer meeting. Do yu remember when yur furst gurl or boy maid a speech in the Sunday Skul?
Yu feel lik yu was lift up haf way to heven. Do yu remember when yu kut kord wod in Wisconsin for 60 cents a kord and kud aford to giv a dolar in kolecshun? Do yu remember when yu walked miles to se a sik person and if yu had a dolar yu giv him the haf? Do yu remember when yu kud send a five dolar bill to South Afrika to feed sum that told them about God? Where are yu and me today?

I wil tel yu where I am. I am pushed in a korner of the world, siting krying over both mi sin and bisness. In the front of mi rod is a ston wal of kut stone and in the bak is a opening where I luk for the morning star. What is the life for the person when we git old? We kan talk with the angel's tonge but nobodi listens to us. And when yu are captured by deth yu are gud for about 2 weeks. Then yu are throwed in the forgetness heep. But don't forgit if the sky is kloudy the sun is bak of the klouds and if the evenin of our life are dark, the seed put in our bodi for a new life is ther. That is so small that no professor found it yet.

And to yu reeders that think I am dumb to menshun God in my leters I will tel yu I wished ther wudnt be a leter accepted of a mail carier if God's naim were not in the leter. And so long as I talk nuthin but gud about Him, I got the ful rite, but yu kan talk bout me and tel the truth, but when yu talk ani that isn't gud bout God, yu are teling an untruth. So far as heven and the world went, he did nuthin but gud.

With luv to yu all.
Johannes Johnson

167.
Wednesday, April 11, 1934
Mister Republican
I herd so mani stories bout that ston that rol down from the est bluf of Red Wing and did damage on mi neebor's hous. They use to kal me the king of Swede Hill and if I was a king and lived her for over 50 yers and owned haf of the bluf, I must know sumthing about it and I wil be responsible to tel yu the ruth so yu dont need to ask ani oficers that dont know anything bout it. In the frunt of mi point and half of the park's point was a rode bilt by Carlson for ston bisness with a ston wal 7 feet hi to suport the lower side of the rode. The yung boys use to go ther and rol sum down. I holer to the boys and I report to the poleece, but both the poleecemens and the boys was free. I sen them 2 stones that was dangerous for mi neebor's properti, but there was brush and small trees in the front, but when Uncle Sam kleened the bluf, kut down the brush and the homely trees and ther was not suport for eether small or big stons and start us neebors to now they was ther.

And for 25 yers I kan guarantee ther is the furst ston kum to the botm of the hil but we wil forgiv both Uncle Sam and his oficers. We al do mistaiks, but the bigest mistake we did was when we licked the Germans and if we hasn't done that ther, that ston have never kum down. And I wish that yu oficers wil do to my neebor the saim as yu expect him to do with yu and if yu dont, yu wil hear it later on and dont forgit I luv yu al.

Johannes Johnson

168.
April 27, 1934
Mister Republican
I sitting here tinking and that kosts me nothing and it seems that's about al we git to do. I kan yust as wel tel yu reeders sum of what I tink about. Wen I tink over what pay I got for being gud to peepel in Red Wing ther is a wunder of there isnt a big krows in hel. But suppose they kan bild adishun to that just as wel as we bild adishuns to our prisons every oder yer.

We wunder that our kuntri loses the water, but we didnt lost that. That went to nord and south pol and turn into ice. That is where a hole lot of onest peepel went, but they wil kum bak and the big ice pols at the north pol wil melt and kum in small drops frum heven and the onest peepel wil follow them so we will hav soft water and a frend is always beter when he kums bak than when he leeves. But sum of them stay long.

I bin waiting for sum a haf hunert yers, and the reason is they owe me muney and I bin to gud to them. And that has bin mi bigest trubel in mi life. God wants me to help the ones that tries to help themselves and I didnt do that. Now I am poorer than the one I helped. That pays to ask God how to with the big American dolar when he gives it to us.

But I wish to tel sum of yu what I wish yu wud do. Stay home frum the pichter show one evening and frum the kar ride one evening and pay me that much on yur old akounts. I need it to bi me stale bred for brekfast. Dont the truth sound shaim for both of us? We did both of us absolutely what God didnt want us to do and we both hav to huri to git our forgivnes.

And the ardest wurds I rite in mi leters is "I luv yu al", but I want yu to know that the way sum of yu live, I dont luv, and to help peepel that dont tri to help themselves is the saim is as to throw perls to the hogs and yu know yu kant git a hog fat of perls, but they are nice for the milynaires to luk at, but I dont tink they are no gud for the klam. If they was they wud al hav them.

Johannes Johnson

169.
Mister Republican
Dese is the time when the time is here that never bin here befor. No spring, no leeves and no flours. That we never seen befor. How wonderful dont the world look to us if we stop and think. How perfect isn't al that has a new life and grows. How perfect isn't the one that planted the furst time and told it to kum bak in the spring.

How about yu and me? We are plant, brot to this world by the saim Master. So are the Kanada thistels. Now to yu profesors, understand it if yu kan. I kant. But we was both maid perfect. And we are both there to meet a fal. How bout the fal? Hav yu seen a flour of Kanada thistle wurry bout the fal the midel of sumer? The last 50 yers the Kanada thistle and human beings went in kumpuny and the most shows the saim flour and in the fal they brek with the roots and follo the wind and the seed maiks a desert of the best kuntri in the world.

I read in mi best buk that God gaiv orders to Adam to kill the thistle, if they kum from Kanada or Sweden and He didnt giv him no caterpillar tractor to do it with eether. I wish that yu farmers of Hay Creek and Belle Creek wud start in and when yu kum to town, go thru our korthous. They grow in the mortar joints even there. City Hall, even in the fire station where they got medicin to choke fire. And when yu drive home, luk in yur skul houses to be sure.
With luv to al that keep the Kanada thistle away from the dors. Sum of us hav lived a long life in roses, but sum of us are choked to deth by Kanada thistels and to reeders that mi letres hurt, I wil taik it al bak and I want to be yur frend and I got lots to tel yu if Mr. Republican will let me. He is now the busiest man in our kountry to keep the Kanada thistel away frum his dor and the big burd frum the fields, so the gud seed gits roots.

Johannes Johnson

170.
Mister Republican
I never no of a yer in mi life that I lik as gud as the last yer. I git nothing to gud for muney and al try always to git it, and now I am afraid that the devil is doin to git me to steel it. We got to hav muney for to live. The only place to live forout money is the poor hous and I feel sorri for thos that hav to keep it up. I wish that Roosevelt wud giv the farmer a rest and let the milyonair do it. He dont need to pay $200,000 a yer to his lawyers and judges.

If we liv a life that the One wants us to do, who brought us into this world, we dont need them. Let us start at home and maik housklening after the sandstorm and ask God for rain. We got lots of por roofs in our town and we want to find out wher they leek so we kan fix it.

Mi last driv for muney was I investigat the saloon and that kosts me fiv cents eech plais and I coudnt see how I luked when I put out the fiv cents. A long ruf bord shelf kovered with old newspapers and a haf dozen kandi bars and a few boxes of Kopenhagen snuf. Not a table or a chair, but stals al round the wals like we had in Sweden for the calves. We thot ther was sin to put a rope on a calf. Yu know if a calf feels gud he dance.

I straightened mi neck and luked over the top and I see a nice yung girl with a cigarette between the finger, but the fether in her hat was missing. I think probishun got that and if ther was a gold pin in the hat, the lawyer got that. But I wil tel yu gurls if yu luk for a gud man that kan and wil suport yu, dont luk in them calf stals. Luk Sunday morning by the church door and yu stands a beter show. Now my investigashun was maid, I kud see that the saloon shud be fixed up, so I went to Remler and bot al he had left and I bot tousand dolars wurth for less than 20 dolars and I hauled truklods and trailer lods and horse lods and that tuk me a hole week to straighten it out and now I found out I am a loser so it luks like it is the last of mi busness in Red Wing.

Now I feel sheep and I am willing to sel it for the saim as Wisconsin sold the wud 50 years ago- $2.50 a kord and I wudn't be stingy in the measure eether.

Johannes Johnson

171.
May 17, 1934
Mister Republian
The ruler of the world sends us the time when He wants us to be gud one to the oder and He wants to know what we wud taik. He giv us only two rodes to go and he tol us where we are landing. Ther is bout time for us to stop, luk and lisen and holer to the one that kan help us. If we dont, he kan send a sheep herder to tel us what He are goin to do. And let the high professors sit home in their roking chairs and dreem how the world are running.

We never seen wise men that didnt hav to die. We never seen so gud doctor that cud cure himself from dying and we havnt seen so big sinner that God cant forgiv if he meens what he is talking about. We kant expekt God to taik us to heven when we liv lives fit for hel.

Yu kant expekt me to rite leter that al Republican reeders like, if I telling the truth. I kant expekt the whole Red Wing to cri if I hav to go to the por farm. That wil be sum standing on the korner and hollering "That is gud nuf for him," and they dont lie when they say that. And those that holer furst wil be thos that use to be mi best frens and owe me the most money. And sum got the plesur to see me go but ther is a rode frum the por farm to heven and ther is a road from a king's castel to hel and we kant kum to eether place forout to be on the rode.

Pik out of mi leters what yu tink is gud and send the rest bak to me and I wil pay the saim mileage as our county pays and dont forgit I luv yu al.

Johannes Johnson

172.
Monday, June 4, 1934
Mister Republican
God put us in a time when he wants us to stop and think what is best for us to do when we got strikes in both east and west and no parties satisfied. Who of us got rite? We al reed about one some two thousand yers ago that was a helper and a frend to the por. What kredit did he git for to be a frend to the por? He was spiked to a kross and had to die. Isn't that a wonderful way to land in heven? Fifty yers ago when we had 90 cents a day we never thot of to strike and knock onest peepel down with basebal klubs. We was thankful to both God and the one that gave us the 90 cents. And we was satisfied with a pair of oxen and a lumber wagon to ride to church Sunday morning.

Now that they got to be a $1,500 tractor with a soft spring seat on it and a Pakard kar to go to church, but the most goes to the dance hal or the beer parlor and kral into them kalf stals and kum bak with a bent axel and a sore hed and the devil shaiks his chains and waiting to git loose for a short time what he has promised and git his harvest, and according to the life peepel liv now, he wil hav a big one-so big that wudnt be peepel left to kover his part with dirt.

If they wud put up a strike for peepel that aint got no yob and got a luvin family to sport and see tham hungri and see the taxes so far behind that they ar going to be driven off of their luvin hom, how do you like to be one of them? Yu had a big salari for so mani yers-more than twice what yu are wurth-and thousands yust as gud as yu that be glad to taik yur yob for half the pay yu got.

We kan liv off litel. We see proof of that but we kant live of nuthin and yu that had a fat yob for so mani yers, why dont yu giv yur bruther a chance to liv? What wud yu think that wud be recorded for yu to answer for sum day? There is sum that had a small yob for 20 yers of our litel citi. Why dont yu step bak and let sumbodi hav it? There is yust as gud and onest as yu ar. The world wud never last long nuff to destroy al onest peepel. Thur must be sum left. And yu yung peepel wil se the saim as we old peepel see now. And yur time wil go so fast so you don't know befor yu git what we kal too old so nobody wil answer yu when yu talk to them.

With luv to both yung and old and I am thankful to al that want to reed mi leters and to you that hait them and I hope yu are educated nuf that never was a Swede profet.

Johannes Johnson

173.
Thurday, June 14, 1934
Mister Republican
How did yu like it when yu had flour mils along the creeks 4 or 5 miles apart and yu kud go ther with a load of grain and kum back with nuf feed for yur family, yur chickens and pigs and yur pastur luked like a paradise side of the creek? And both the rabit and robin was happi. Yu used to plant kabage and harvest gold dolars. Yu use to seed barley and harvest beer. Now yu bi beer and git rice. Now yu seed gut wheat and harvest Kanada thistels. Yu use to marry a por girl and git a rich ladi. Now yu mari the rich gurl and git a squaw.

The furst bil yu use to pay was the taxes. Now yu kant pay them at al. Yu used to grab for the big Merican dolar Sunday morning for the church collectshun. Now we aint got small enuf muney so yu stay home. Yu use to ask yur father how to run the farm. Now yu ask the kounty bord if they would not taik him to the por hous. Yu use to bi white rings and bels for yu horses. Now you kant bi them shoes. Yu used to buy wide gold rings for yur wife. Now yu kant bi her teeth, so she has to shew meet wit meet.

Yu use to wash clothes in rainwater. Now yu hav to go haf way to hel to git water and yu use to use hand power. Now yu steel the power from the sky and stil yu expekt God to let it rain.
Yu use to luk for beter company than yu are yourself and work hard and try to git a home on a bluf to show both yu and oders that yu got a nice home. Now yu dont want to own yur home. Yu want to borrow it and hide where the tods and snaiks like it. But we al want a swell kar on the konkrete rode. I am fraid that lots of us are goin to taik a shortcut and land in that plais what our deer mother warned us for.

This dont meen al that reed The Republican, but if the shue pinches forgiv the old por Swede. I meen wel and I want to be a frend to yu al and mi leter mite be reeded when neether me nor Republican isn't here. The sheep are in the rye field starving. Now they got too mani herders.

Johannes Johnson

174.
Wednesday, June 20, 1934
Mister Republican
I sitting now tinking what wud be the best for us old peepel to do. We work hard a long life, saived al we kud and brot children to this wurld that luk in our hands for mor and the mothers hart is tender and we loosed al we had and we are in the red where ever we go. If we go to our city where we worked hard for haf a hundert yers and practically bilt our city up, the answer wil be yu are to old-we kant use yu. If we go to the bankers to boro money for our taxes and they wil taik our home, bekaus we vant pay.

And her we are lik a jak rabit on the prairie and we wil be chased wherever we go, so I thot it over and the best we kan do is to die. Ther is no more fun for us in this world and let us be prepaired for the next world. Ther is one that wil bring us to the next world where we never git to old.

And I wil also let yu know what I tink wud be the best for our kuntry that got so on the bum that need repair mor than in Hay Kreek. We got to start in the Capitol and chais out al the lawyers furst. The Capitol is bilt for the farmers and not for the lawyers. We got 65 per cent lawyers ther now and they are al smart. If a farmer hapin to sel a sak of rutabages to a ded beat and want a lawyer to kolect, he hav to plant 4 akers next yer to pay the kost.

Ther is two kinds of bankers. One kind is satisfied when they git the value for other money and their percentage and they want to help us. They dont want our property. Do yur bisnes with them and tip yur hat to them and tel them nuthin but God's truth. And ther is one kind, smart as a kowboy. If they git the rope around yur nek they certainly like to pul. And what ther is mor to say bout lawyers and bankers that's gotten down in the kronicle that's more to depend on than Johannes Johnson.

And if yu want to maik ani mor improvements on our kuntri, maik the ded beats pay the bil and taik the kars and truks off the roads and bring the railroads bak side of the river where that use to be and the old and yung wil hav a yob and we al wil be happi. If yu put a yung teem on yur breeking plow yu will spoil both the team and the field.

But if yu use an old ox teem yu wul be sure. If yu put yung boys in Congres yu wil spoil the hole kuntri, but if yu put Hay Kreek farmer in ther, yu wil turn our kuntri into a heven.

With luv to yu al.
Johannes Johnson

175.
Mister Republican
I kan not quit to brag bout yu and I want to tel yu the reason. Whan the kat gits both paws in the rat trap she got to holer and the only way yu can stop her is to kil her or help her out. And the saim with me. Al I got left of 55 yers hard labor and $30,000 wurth of property is that I am the saim as the cat in the trap-I kan holer.

Plese let me holer for a while yet. If I dont die, I kan be a profit forout to be wurth a milyon dolars and I want to talk to the saloon peepel furst and if yu dont taik out yur calf sals out of yur saloons that wil be prohibishun inside of 2 yers and yu be forout yobs and to yu and yur kalfs nothing to drink.

And to yu ministers, if yu dont quit to pat on the shulders on your church members that sit in the frunt seet and let them do as they plees, yur church will be elmpti and sum day a krew wil kum and ter that down. They aredi started in. Yu dont want that and yu know wel that God done want that. Ther is beter to turn in the creek than in the river.

And to yu profesors and doctors that is so smart so yu kan lead ministers like a lectrician kan lead the lite, remember both yu and yur customers am the losers in the end if yu go against nature. God wants onest things in our kuntri and he wants onest man on the por farm and he wants onest ladies in our homes that feeds the kat so well as her husband.

With luv to yu al.
Johannes Johnson

176.
Saturday, June 23, 1934
Mister Republican
I rote so mani leters and forgit the most importance and that is to thank yu al gud ladies that helped poor sikly ladies that got ther hous ful of children and maibe a man gud for nuthin. I want to tel yu I think yu ar on the rite rode to heven and dont luk for ani oder rode. When yu kum to the last river that yu hav to kros yu wil be karried over with wings and yu wil be paid for every glas of water yu giv to a sik lady or her children.

But be sure to not do as I hav done-help dedbeats and krooks and think they are por. That is the rode to the por farm and if we dont walk up the rode, wil go frum the por farm to hel. Por people are those that pay their bils and starv and feel shamed to beg, so I wud advis yu gud ladies to talk to yur neebor lady if she kan afored to folo yu on the saim rode. Ther is plenty rum and plenty to do and yu mite be mor blessed to bi a por ladies' son a pair of overhauls than to bi yur own son a thosand dolar kar.

Yu dont need to spend lots of money on yur son to be a gud onest man-gud for the hole world and gud for the next world, but to be a bank rober wil kost yu lots of muney. To go to heven kosts nuthin, but to go to hel kosts lots of money. Al rodes goes to Jerusalem, but only one goes to heven.

With luv to al that are on the rite rode.
Johannes Johnson

177.
Mister Republican
I talked to a wel-edukated man the oder day and he said ther is no use yu write in The Republican. Yu are so far behind us the yung generashun, so we al laff at yu. I told him I know, but I see a time in the future when yu and me is goin to be both like. And that is when we are both ded. You knowing about Jupiter and the moon and eklipse in the sun and moon. They are doin to die with yu and my knowing about Abraham, Isaac and Jacob-I dont think they wud die. I mite talk to them sum day and yu kan talk to Jupiter and the moon and tank him for the law he rote for us and I wish that Roosevelt wud take it into our kuntry.

We taxpayers wudn't need to pay $10,000 for a trial for a murder and bankrober and kidnaper and then feed them for 20 years. Mi bleeve is that God don't wans us to do that and we condemn and taik away haf of the lawbreakers Moses did, that wudn't be one man forout a job in our kuntry. And we kud al pay our taxes and pay ten cents for everi dolar we ern to the church and we kud al be happi and want to live up to the law. And the farmers an the ground kud rest everi 7 yers and everi 70 yers al bonds and morgages wud die forever. That luks like Roosevelt kummence to luk up Moses law and starts to figure on seven.

Johannes Johnson

178.
Mister Republican
One mor leter from Swede Hil to keep mi promise. Bout 50 yers ago a man, even a koncil man named Carlson, bilt a retaining wal on the nord side of Sorinn's bluf for a rode. But the rode never was used and it has bin a playground for meen kids for these yers.

A yer ago when Unkle Sam butted in to help us por peepel, the bluf was ful of working men and officer that kud tel how mani stars ther wer in heven and how mani kernels of sand there is in the shore of the oshens. But they did not know nuf to leev the tres that was a suport for the stones. They kut the trees down in front of the stones and shake the bluf with dynamite and powder and a stone kaim down witih speed of one hundert miles and hour and struk a hous on the oder side of the street and maid damage for $75.00.

A luving oficers kaim down but they kudnt do aniting but they had a warning for a yer ago.

Mi father used to tel me "right is right and what isn't rite is going to be right." But we are livin in a time when everting has to be rong to sound right. Edukashun gits so strong so it seems they wil tri to git God out of heven to show us who is boss. He had to step down once to maik the Jews behaiv. And only one kud see Him and he had to luk thru a cloth. And the montans He steped on shuk.

I think He will luk thru the dor and tel the Germans to behave when he kums with the poisonous airplanes to sweep us off the erth. Germani is mor educated now as when they fot the Swedes. And Germans and Swedes is the best pals of ani kuntry on erth. They skrewed off the loks of dors to giv the Germans when they needed them for shells.

With luv to yu al.
Johannes Johnson

179.
Mister Republican
Ther is a pleesur to liv when yu are yung and strong and gud-luking and al see up to yu with a smile and yu bleve yu are the king or queen of Spain, but time flies-the winter cums soon. In the fal one of them yu carri under yur hert mite git kroup and one diphtheria and one hapin to git a broken leg and when the winter kums and yu are old and tired out the one that yur hert pounds the most for wants to throw yu out in the snowdrifts because yu aint styllsh enuf and yu are always in the way. And yu aint got anything to giv the kuming generashun and yu are not wanted ani longer

How do yu feel now? Don't you tink a rabbit's got it gud? He kan krawl into a hole and nobody knows anything bout it. Nobodi needs to spend ani money for flowers and wet the hankerchief with alligator teers. No bisness store have to be close to show the honor, no bel have to strike in the tower. Al is quiet and the rabbit is gone forever. The rabbit lived his life acording to the law God gave him. I wil sooner taik mi edukashun frum a rabbit or a sheep than frum a professor that leeds me on rong way.

Mi leter mite hurt sum of the reeders, but I am sure that it wudn't hurt either the sheep or the rabbit. And I wil promis to sing a verse next time of another song.

Johannes Johnson

180.
Friday, July 13, 1934
Mister Republican
We got lots of impruvments in this world since God sent Adam out to farm and we trow lots of it away that we wud be wise if we pik it up. If I dont maik ladies mad, I wil menshun sum. You remember yers ago we had a blaksnaik at the Training skul and they used it to and they threw it away and put on ladies silk gluves and they used them for mani yers so now they got both Sauk Center and Stilwater ful of them and they git a big expens for the peepel.

My neebors got a poni for nothing that a hole lot of horse deelers giv up and few yers after, I ask him what did yu do witih that poni that luked so gentel? He lift up the blaksnaik and said "I used this but I used it rite and I kud git mi boys yust as gentel if I kud use it, but wife wudn't let me." The man that invent the blaksnaik was a wise man but the man that invent the steem shufel was a fool. The blaksnaik kan maik a president, but the steem shufel kan taik the yob away for thousands of peepel.

And now, ladies, I kan see little dust in yur eyes, but I kant see a log in mi own eyes and I mite be blind. I kan see when yu stand by the saloon counter and shake dice and drink beer, but I kant see myself. If we wudn't hurt the business, I wud advis both yu and me to quit and go to the church. I know we both are welkum ther and they kan maik use of the five cents we want to spend. The five cents keep up the saloon and the churches. Now ther is up to yu and me. To stand by the saloon counter and drink beer that aint the bigest thing.

To rob banks and steal children and kil peepl isnt either, but to not do what we know is rite, and dont accept Christ as our Savior that is the bigest sin.

With luv to yu al.
Johannes Johnson

181.
Mister Republican
I had vacashun on Wednesday and I went down to the malt hous to see the most wonderful work we hav had in our town, and a 50 yers friend kame up to mi side and said "How do this luk to yu?"

I said that luked to me after the appel tuk after Eve tuk the bite, but kan yu tel me if that is God want lerns peepel to be so smart? I don't think so.

I think ther is the devil's teaching and he got us alredy dumber than a rat. A rat is satisfied when she gits nuff for the winter, but the malsters want for ten yers. I wud advis the malsters to put out the cow stals of saloons and chase them yung pretty gurls out. They shud be home with ma and help her peel potatoes, and chase the bedbugs out of their father's bed who has to wurk so hard if he hepins to git a job.

The calf stals and the yung gurls are going to bring probishun bak and to bad for our kuntry if we let the yung girls and the strikers run us.

Hav yu ever herd that the strikers is satisfied? Hav yu ever herd a farmer that gits nuf pay for his eggs? Hav yu ever herd of a Swede that is perfect? Ther mite be few Irish, but they tel it themselves.

But I luv yu all and if you reeders klose mi mout that face yu see in the front of Barn bluff is goin to taik mi place. And sum things I hav told yu, yu kannot buri when yu buri me.

Johannes Johnson

182.
Friday, August 2, 1934
Mister Republican
I am old and disgusted and tired out and got a new scheme to git to the penitentiary so when I git bak to mi home town I git a fair yob so I kan maik mi living and meet mi taxes. I bin living with yu for 55 years.

I had yur water since yur furst main pipe was put in and I dont own yu for more than yur last bill and that is not for me. That is for them than I am responsible for. I ask for to wurk it out but I get refused. I had yur gas and eletrish since yur furst pole was raised and I giv free ground forever for yur poles. Yur officers and company of Red Wing is forgetful, but I am not. That hav to be answered for sum day and yur officers of Red Wing that giv a steady yob to peepel that got $5,000 in the bank and let hundreds of children starv-yu got to answer to.

There is a time kuming in our future when we al is goin to be called up and answer for ourselves and both yu and me wil find out the wurld kan git long forout both yu and me and Roosevelt, the best and most wonderful man in the world, he wil find out he kant lift his bodi and kary himself and he kan not kary our big kuntry, but he kan try and I kan try to tel sum of the reeders the truth.

And to yu reeders of the Republican won't yu plees tell me what gud that did our kuntry to go up to hi in that balloon that kosts us taxpayers one milyun dollars? How mani quarts of milk wud that bring to hungri children? And how mani pair of shoes wud that bi for kold feet for next winter? We must hav a wunderfull God that knows al this and be so quiet. I reed in mi best bok that in olden times that He had orders to waik up and giv His peepel the rite.

With luv to yu al.
Johannes Johnson

183.
Thursday, August 23, 1934
Mister Republican
I want to tel the reeders that I hav grown to a time when I hav to sel the antiques that I gathered up for 55 yers and I invite yu al, but special to the rich. I mite got sumthing that yu want and yur neebors kant git. I got stones from Sweden and Alaska and a miller's ston frum Bell Creek, and I want Red Wing to have this furst chance and if sum of yu that gather up mor muney than yu kan eat up and know that yu kant taik it with yu when yu die. I wil giv the best view of the Mississippi river that I refuse tousand dolars for one akres and wil fil the furst story with antiques frum the furst seller.

The world goes so fast now that wud be wise to saiv it and show to the peepel that kum after us. And sum there is interested shud kum quick befor the klub fals. The sail wil be open frum 2 to 4 in the afternoon for two weeks and if ther shud be sumbodi that wud hav their name recorded for the after world, kum and we wil talk it over.

With luv to yu al.
Johannes Johnson
184.

Thursday, August 30, 1934
Mister Republican
There is 3 plaises that wud do yu gud educated peepel to folo up mor than yu do and dont be surprise when I tel yu. That is the church, the saloons and the graivyard. Who of them plaises improves the most on the past 50 years? I bin her al the time and so far I kan see the graivyard is hed of the 3 and I am proud over the muney I invested ther. Neether dedbeets or bankers kan taik it. We got a plaise to rest til we git called on. But when we want to go in to a saloon yu know we lose the bokbar. Probishun tuk that. Let us talk with a luking glass, maybe we kan discover our daughter in the kalf stalls side of the long wals and if we want to go to church, let us taik the Bible with to see if the minister reeds rite.

And if we want to go to the graivyard let us think over if we are redy to meet the One that is going to waik us up. And He is not going to ask me who cheeted me, but He want to know who I cheeted.

The nicest gift God let on this earth is a grey-heded person that lived a kleen life. That was the reesun God saved Sodom so long as He did, and I tink ther is the reesun Red Wing is saived today. Taik away al that beleev on god and the world wil turn into a desert, and the Mississippi river seems to giv us a warning now.
And to yu peepel that feel sory for I menshun religun in mi leters and I got yust as gud rite to talk gud bout God as ani minister in Red Wing. And yu shal not expect to meet al ministers in heven. Yu shal not expect to meet al bankers ther that boro yu muney in heven, but those that said no, they stands a gud show. Yu shall never kondem salvashun armi religun for piking up frum the gutter and beg clothes frum yu that yu wudnt use. They may cloth one that goes to heven when yu hav to stand outside in yur nice clothes and holer how gud yu bin to the peepel in Red Wing. And the one that tends to the dor don know yu.

If ther is a heven ther must be a dor to go in and I never herd of more than one that got throwed out and we kal him the divil and that was bekaus he got proud, so I advis al Republican reeders to be satisfy where yu are and not be proud.

With luv to yu al.
Johannes Johnson

185.
Thursday, September 27, 1934
Mi furst words in the Republican shal be Mister Republican. Those wurds is esy to day, but mi last wurds in mi leter, "I luv yu al" that is so hard, so I hav to leave it out sum time. One day a man krawl out of a calf stal and said "I like to reed yur leters, but ther is nothing to them mor than the truth and that shows yu got no more edukashun than a mule."

That is truth, but for mi part, I sooner hear the truth from a mule than to heer a lie frum a professor. So I beter tel the reeder how much edukashun I got and that isn't a lie eether. I forgot the Swede and English I never lerned so yu know that kant be so much to mi leters, but I don't think yu wil lose anything 50 yers frum now if yu reed them. Yu rite me a leter and kal me a mule and I wil anser yu and kal yu a professer. If yu kan kal Roosevelt for judge and Shoemaker for witness and I think that both Roosevelt and Shomeaker wil let the Swede live if they isn't so smart as the Irish.

A feler asked me the oder day which parti I liked the best-Republikan or Democrats? And I told him "I don't know. They are al old like me and nobody wants me. And he said which church do yu like the best? I like them al. I think that's a shaim that they ter down so mani nowdays. When we had churches and tended to them we had plenty wurk and muney, but when we ter the churches down and bilt dance hals then we al got por. I never brag bout mi children, but I feel proud of oder peepel brag bout them. Yu know the appels don't fal so fast frum the trees. I never brag so truth ful bout mi wife til after she left me. I never brag bout the big Merican dolar when I had plenty of them. Now they are big as a plate and kant git them in mi poket, but the time is soon kumming when the milyunaire makes half penies for us and keps al the big bils in safety.

I think that Roosevelt do al he kan, but stil a wurld's panic kan be stoped in one day. I believe go after the milyunaire with the blaksnaiks. They got the por peepel's muney. I believe ther is one way to heven and one way to hel and lots of ways to the por farm and I wud advis yu al to find out which rode yu travel and don't forgit that wurd that was rote down in our best buk thousands of yers ago too lait are the sinners goin to waik up.

Johannes Johnson

186.
Monday, October 15, 1934
Mister Republikan
I got bad news to tel yu. I had to hav an operashun on mi hart. Mi hart hav bin to soft for mor than half a hundert yers. Dedbeets tuk al they kud and others tuk their shair.

Now I am to the gait of the por hous and kiking. I dont want to go in.

I tink I paid more than 50,000 dolars tackses in our town and I bult hunderts of homes for por peepel and sum of them are rich today. I trow mi votes for mani oficers in our town and kounty and state, but I cant see no return, but I wil taik the trute to yu. And yu kan do with me what yu want to.

I thank yu al, but befor I leev, I want to tel yu oficers yu shudnt bot a biger snowplow than yu kud pul. Yu shudnt put the swimming pool in a mud pool when yu had plenty rok to put it on. Yu shudnt taik the contract yourself. Yu shudnt examin the buks for nothing. We was able to pay. That isnt rite to kut the tale of a dog after yu sold the dog. Let the byer do that.

Yu shudnt giv a stdy yob to a man that got plenty muney in the bank and let the tackspayer sit hom with a housful of shildren hungri. And ther is a hole lot mor yu shudnt hav done, but if yu did the best yu no yu are excused and we are gud frends, but I wud sooner be a prisoner in the kounty yail than a tackspayer in Swede Hill. And if sum of yu wants to se me don't luk in mi swel hom. I room with the rabit in the bluf and I wil thank God so long as I kan tel the trute and walk forout crutches.

Johannes Johnson

187.
Mister Republican
I want to rite a leter to yu ladies that are so gud to the por peepel and sik peepel and even to the church and the ministers. How hapi the wurld wud be if they were al lik yu. And if yu wish to be just as gud to the peepel we bring up in this wurld, I wish to giv yu mi advis when yu start. Disconekt yur radio and pay more atenshun to yur children.

The oder idee is to stay home with the children and sho them the kros on the church and explain what it is ther for. And when yu go to church, luk yur ministers rite in the eyes. Yu know he kan see if yu kum to church to hear him or kum just to show yurself.

And the third thing yu ladies kud do, and I know yuk an do it, is to trow out the calf stals in the saloons. Yu don't want yur daughters to krawl in one of them and maik luv for a glas of beer. It is beter that they shud stay outside of the counter or sit down bi a table lik they use to do, and 50 yers ago they used to go to church to pik out their luvers.

And that luv yu maik up in church yu kan taik with yu into heven, but what luv yu maik up in the picture show and in the caff stals in the saloons is only an imitashun of the reel thing and yu hav to leev it outside the dor of hel for sumbudi els to be phooled with.

There is 2 side to everiting-the saim with luv. This is mi bleef and mi freewill staitment.

With luv to yu al.
Johannes Johnson

188.
Thursday, November 15, 1934
Mister Republikan
I been fixing old foundashun and shingle ruf in dis town for more than a half a hundred years and I make some pour ones myself and I got de experience but I aint got educashun vat wud keep the rane out. I lived in this town when our kuntry was the richest kuntry on the earth and dat wasn't long ago eider.

It's dat poor foundashun or ruf dat's leaking. A kloudburst is over our ruf and the new improvements of the sewers is washing our fundashun out. What footing are the young generashun going to have ven we tear down the churches an yu al know that religun is the only ting that civilized the world.

Yu can keep on an build danse halls and dress haf naket. Roman did the same, but dat vas befur da fal. Yu can let yur 1 years baby creep on da top of the saloon korner and play wid him and yu can let yur fifteen yers old gurl sit in the calf sall smoking cigaretts but vat condishun are yu lay for demm? An fur yourself when yu git old and mebee can't turn round in de bed wid out help. Ve better stop boat me and yu and tink it over. We never come to Jerusalem or Hager, if we don't start. An yu no ve got a big bil to pay to our government. Ate hundred and forty dolars a yer for evry family in United States. A educated newspaperman tol me that yesterday. An edukashun have made us tacks-blind. To dolars for a pig an ve hav to feed him so pour dat we kan't git the hair off. Ve go to a small candy store to chirp a box of matches. Haf of de sidewalk hav to be covered wid lysense.

If we shute a mudhen, de game varden tak the meat. An ve git de guts and fedders. Adam and Eve live in a free kuntry, if de snaks haven't cum rund. Now do snakes crawl in de grass, so ve can't see dem. An ve pay dem a high salry.

Wid luv to yu al.
Johannes Johnson

189.
Thursday, December 13, 1934
Mister Republican
I vant to tel yu that I was invited to 6 plaises for Thanksgiving diner so I thot over wher wud be the rite plais to go so I ent bak of Rattle snaik bluf and I certainly had a gud dinner and I met friends that was 10 yers older than I am so I mite git chance to send yu a few leters mor.
So far as mi bodi, I got no kik kuming. I got mi own teeth-the roots anyhow. I never bother a dentist, but the barber I bother 2 or 3 times a yer and we had a kinda hard batel, but that went over and I got mi furst liking to git since mi muther kudn't lik me and I got the furst rober to meet, but I seen lots of krooks and sneeks, but ther aint no mor to git-the theif said when he tuk the dor.

I never need to paint or kut mi fingernales. I use them to scratch over mistaiks in mi life, but ther is 2 I kant scratch over. When I kut the hous in 2 and married for the sekund time. That wud taik a long handled shufel to do.

But time wil heel up al mi sores and I invite yu old goobs that use to as childs walk bak of rattle snaik bluf to kum now. That wud supris yu yust as much as a man that never seen Red Wing for 50 yers. That wud taik Uncle Sam more than 10 yers to bring it bak where it was yers ago.

Wacouta was a paradis for the furst settlers and ther is now. Ther is a king in everi home. All they are fraid of is the gaim warden and I think gaim wardens is hired by rich yelous peepel that dont like to see the por peepel liv. The gaim warden thinks ther is beter to be a king with the hogs than to be hogs with a kin king. Wher I use to sit and fish in 10 feet of water is big timber now. Mr. Natur hav made the plais for gud mani homes and Mr. Natur is going to taik them bak.

Wise are the man that bilt his hom on roks and use gunny saks for curtains instead of to kover up the windows with mortgage. Yu never git por for what yu giv away, but for what yu throw away.

With luv to yu al.
Johannes Johnson

190.
Thursday, January 10, 1935
Mister Republican
I sitting here by myself and tinking how mani por peepol we got in Red Wing this Christmas. I know we got 2 kinds, one kind that is use to be por al their life and they are so used to it that they help themselves to be porer and porer and they got just as much paint on their cheek as the rich and just as small heel on their shoes. I wish they wud taik Martha Washington stiles so rich peepel kan trak them for the next yer.

And then we got the older kind that dont use to be por, but that kaim so quick. They had gud jobs but they losed it. They maybe had muney in the banks but they met a bank rober.
What kud the por felow do? He didn't hav the honor to rais the hands up for a half a hundert yers savings. Do you feel sorri for him? That wud be better for that man if he never had a dolar. He wud be more used to it.

I know a man that used to bi a dozen fat turkeys and giv his frends Thanksgiving and Christmas also. Now he kant bit a blakburd. How do yu think that man feels? I wish that they who are so religious wud visit them por peepel and talk nice to them. That wud help them lot and I dont think they wud beg for anithing. But if yu wud giv them a lift that wud maik yu both happi. We shud feel sorri for the man that wants to help himself and kant.
Giv us a yob. We kan do sumthing if we kan walk forout crutches. We kan live off little but we kant liv off nothing. Listen to that, you, that we giv a gud yob to do what God wants yu to do.

With luv to yu al.
Johannes Johnson

191.
Saturday, April 20, 1935
Mister Republican
What hav we got the most of in our kuntri? Oficers and edukashun and bils that arent paid and RELIEF. And what kums next? Old men frum al direkshuns of the wurld that kum and kut our trees off, grub the stumps out and maik our kuntri a paradise.

And now they are siting on the edge of the graiv and haven't got muney nuf to leev for their burial. And they were wurth from $10,000 to $100,000. They are the ones I feel sori for and the reason is that I am one of them. But I want to tel yu that strip us naked on the side of a cold graiv, yu shal hav yurs kuming in the futur. And yu kan laff and hunderts of leters that I hav ritten, but think of this befor yu throw it away. I wish I kud liv ten yers mor and tel yu sumthing bout what God wants me to tel yu. And I wish to not put a blak spot on mi old aig for al the hard labor I imagin in our city.

But if this leter shud hapin to be the last I am ritin, rmember to do to oder peepel like yu want them to do to yu. And yu kan be sure I never wil quit ritin in The Republican before I hav to do it. He is one of mi frends I hav left and he dont kare how old and homely I luk.

I always hated the jail and the por hous and I tried a long life to wurk myself away, but when I wok up I had one hand in eech gait and now, do as yup lees. I try to luv yu al.

Johannes Johnson

192.
Mister Republican
I bin busi for kupel weeks thinking over mi old aig penshun, how to use it and where to use it. That wil bring me more money kleer than when I had $30,000 properti in Red Wing. We old goobs wil be sitting pretty and we kan taik goodbye of the bankers and say helo to the hole wurld. Our children dont need to taik mortgage in our property for to saiv sum for themselves. This is the best that hapins since Moses and Solomon was the leeders for the peepel. I never had the 7th year off and I didn't git mi 70 yers off when al shud be scratched off the buks and I shal be a free man.

I feel sorri for yu yung folks that krawl into a bak stal and drink a few glasses of beer when we old folks go to our meetings and pay out our last 25 cents to be a member and tri to pul this through. That mite kum a day when yu yung folks kud liv off yur old man's penshun and we old folks expekt yu to know so much-we had yu in skul 20 years.

Taik yur koat off and help us. Yu wil fee beter when yu see yur father beded down in flowers and that day wil kum. I, for mi part, see the penshun so far away as the moon, but I see the por farm close by but the one that brot me into this wurld, He owes me the living and that's up to Him what He wants to do. And he feeds the hawks. Why shudn't he feed Johannes Johnson and if that shud be long between the meals a hungry stomach always brags of the kook.

Everything taiks time. It tuk the Swedes 30 yers to lik the Germans but dont forgit they was likked.

With luv to yu al.
Johannes Johnson

193.
Mister Republican
I wish to tel yu what I wud do if I was Roosevelt. I wud hire Mussolini to kum to our kuntry for six munths and find out what he kud do and if I as Governor Olson, I wud pik up al old gubs that grub up our kountry and giv them a chek for $30 a munth so long as they live. They are wurth that and that aint's so mani left.

We ain't quite satisfied to go to saim places as they taik the old horses. We kan grub if ther is anything to grub. We kan plow just as straight as a yung man but we kant maik so mani rounds. Fifty yers ago they kud use a man so old that there growed moss on his bak. But now he hav to be yung and gud luking, educated so high so he kan tell whats bak of both the moon and the stars, but they never ask if he kan maik an ax handel or feed the pigs.

I also want to tel what I wud do if I was the mayor of Red Wing. I wud taik away thos targets that stands on the korner to protect the banks. That is too risky a yob. The bank robbers luk for them furst. Dres them up in a farmers overhalls, buy them a $15 old Ford and maik them drive in the allies 8 hours in the shift. Yu wud be surprised to see what gud wurk they kud do.
We always see the policeman, but if we want them bad, they are hard to find. If they had a farmers suit they kud git along beter with peepel that's got a bean on.

Talk nice to them and they wudn't need to use the klub and ther is always a case that a drunk haits the kap and the brite butons.

And don't plees don't hait me for these leters. This is mi blev and blev lot that isn't the rite thing. Do like the most of them do, forgiv me.

Johannes Johnson

194.
Tuesday, June 4, 1935
Mister Republican
I got a bon to pik with sum of yu, but I hav got lots of luv to send to sum of yu. But them that I send luv to are yu that don't owe me anything and those that want to pay me and kant-and yu that kan pay me and wudn't. Are yu goin to keep me out of heven? God wants me to luv yu just the saim, but I kant. And forout lov nobody gits into heven. Reed your Bible and then think it over.

There are 2 kinds of sikness that are just as bad and ther is luvsik and jelosy and they are twins. One has got golden hair and the oder blak. But they are both as strong and brav and they luk deth right in the fais. And they kan turn a flower garden over into a ratelsnaik patch. And they send hunderts of ships into the bottom of the sea. And they fli higher than the sky, but they kan never slack the stars. Ther is the limit.

Ther is lots we kan do in this wurld nowdays. But God sets the limit. Mi limit is set, but I got lots advis to giv yu yung peepel. But I hav went so far in this wurld that I havn't got one to be afraid of. But yu yung folks with the one that draws the straw to a stack and not pul one off. And luk out for al company that wans to brek up a home. That is moor katching as smallpox and yu know if yu liv over yu git a mark for life.

With luv to the most of yu.
Johannes Johnson

195.
Mister Republican
Rich and por hav always bin in this wurld. Way back they are menshuned. Abraham Isaac and Jacob. They was al wel to do and a man named Job. I tink that God like him the best, but the devil was so jelous so he went rite up to God and try to be a tattle tail and God said, "Have yu put any attenshun to mi man Job? Do yu think he is onest to Me?"

"That is nothing to brag about," the devil said. "Yu know yu giv him half of our kountri and 300 gud onest working men and lots of children and the best an nicest women on erth, but let me handel him for a while and wodn't cal him Job ani longer."

God said, "Handel him as yu want, but do not hurt him."

He ordered the litning frum the skies and he tuk the lov of Job's wife away, so she asked, "What yu got now for serving God?" But he said, "When we got so much gud of God, why shudn't we stand sum of what we think aint so good? He giv us what we got and He tuk it bak."

I wish I kud said the saim. God giv me 22 properties in this town, but dedbeets tuk the most and the others tuk ther share and that's to hard a yob to say, "God bless them."

But if yu readers want to feel bad for sumbudy feel som for thos that use to karri a tousand dolar check in ther pockets and kant change it for a chiken and if yu want to investigate in frenship, wurk and save al yu kan for 50 yers and when yu are tired out, maik a aukshun, advertise gud so al yur frends kan kum round, hire yur frend for the auctioneer and a few says after yu know what frenship meens in this wurld.

I reed bout the onest frend to al, but they crucified Him 2,000 years ago. But He said He wud kum bak and He is needed now. Both Roosevelt and Olson wil hav a gud helper but that wil kum a time when the devil kant do nothing. They wil be al paralyzed. I wish I kud liv to see the day.

Johannes Johnson

196.
Mister Republican
I tink we keeping on long nuf to maik one machin after the oder that maiks hundert days' work in one day. We have now to start in an maik one after the oder that feeds hundert men a day. A traktor is nice to sit and smok on and when he gits hot an giv him a pail of water and yu kan rol a oder cigarette and go, but what kums out behind the traktor aint so gud for the ground.

Don't you think that the ground gits tired to giv you 60 bushels to the acer? Wud not yu git tired if yu keep on a long life and giv to a gud frend and he never said thank yu? I am now in the evening of mi life and fiv out of ten I did business with for the past 20 yers bin deadbeats and I want to luk yu al in the faice and tel yu I am tired. I want to hide six feet under the grond and to al you that's bin honest to me and al that begged muney frum me and al that wud pay and kant pay I wish I kud liv hundert yers more with yu.

The world is a paradis to liv in if we was al onest, but after we got the electricity to the steem shovel and the kurling iron that burn our paper dollars before we git it into our pokets. We don't git chance to ask our wife what she needs for the children. She hav to tel it to Roosevelt or sum of his officers that maybe never brot up a child.

We bilt our corthous twice to big few yers ago. Now ther is ful of officer that we never figure bout and needy peepel that holer for work and that luks sum time that sum peepel yust play with them. We clered and bilt up our kuntry with grub hoes and wheelbarrow and railroads kum puffing long. And yu showed the weelbaro to us kuple yers ago. Check them off and keep yur books cler.

And to yu, mi best frend, The Republican, don't thro this leter in the tub. I promis yu a nicer leter the next time.

With luv to yu al.
Johannes Johnson

197.
January 3, 1939
Mister Republican
If a person had lived a long life all days haven't been alike. If in the blooming of our life the sun shines and we see the world like a paradise and we hear thousands of birds singing. We don't have no seeding or no harvest and no hair that have to be curled and no cheeks that need painting and we woudn't trade our suit with the Pope in Rome or the Queen of England. We are satisfied and thankful to the one that give it to us. But we, and I, and one of them. When the sun hides back of a black cloud and we see the sharp spark in the cloud that will kill everything that have got life if it drops from the cloud and strikes. I see one of them clouds not long ago. I was sitting in my home like an owl in a forgotten castle. I didn't have a dream for a week. If we can't sleep we can't dream. And all of my friends had vacations. They was on a trip. Some went to Alaska and some to Jeruselum and those that cost me thousand dollars apiece took good-bye and went to China. So the only way I seen was to take a walk. Nobody seen me more than the dog. And he followed after. I stopped at the High Bridge and looked at the West wher the sun leaves us in the night. But the clouds were just as thick. But I seen in the clouds both the sheriff and the bankers and I know they don't have no Mother's heart. And if they did the bank would be a failure. The Mother's heart is only for small children. So I looked at the East where the sun used to say "Good Morning." But I couldn't look through Barn's Bluff. So I stepped up on the railing to see how deep it was to the water and the dog started to cry and wanted to go. And I said "Go"-I will follow you." And he went to the place where I used to buy the stale bread and when we was through I said "Go, I will follow you". And he went to Dutch Town where we used to get the bone and I bought a big Norwegian herring and I had potatoes home. And I said "Go, I will follow you." And we both went home to Swede Hill and in a short time we both had a good meal. And I sit down and I had a rest and here comes an old man, so old that my friends wouldn't have him with on their trip.

And I started talking about the black cloud. But what I told him he said, "That could be worse." So I said, "That seems to me if I starve to death, that wold be good enough." If that happened you should thank God. Starve and freeze to death is the easiest death we got. You talking about sunshine-if the sun shines every day the world would dry up and catch fire and burn up. The most power the world got now is fire and we better all look out.

With luv to you all
Johannes Johnson

198.
Mister Republican
I am now to the end of the road and over the second limit of life. I have to do like millions before me. I have to die and I have depend on some of you that stay a little longer to bury me. But before that happens I want to talk to you men about the biggest shame and the biggest sin we did in this world. And that is if we have been mean to the ladies. The ladies have brought the world up to the "Highest point" and they suffered for every life they brought into the world. They have been the best workers in the church and in the hospital and rummage sales, and maybe, the ministers and the doctors forgot to thank them for. If some of the ladies had curly hair and painted cheeks they have been nothing but a hired girl for the children and the man, and the older the children get the more worries they have got. And the older the men gets, the more cranky he gets.

It is about time we talk it over. If you can afford, buy a diamond pin and put in your wife's hat, she is worth that. And if you can't afford it, give her a smile when you come and a smile when you go. And stay home all you can to help her to bring up the family to live an honest life through the world.

We men don't know what will happen to us in the future. Maybe, we have to do like Moses did when he looked at God. He had to look through a cloth. And if the ladies is going to have to pay for what they done in this world, they will look bright in the next world. But I don't mean all ladies.

But my wish today is-if I been bought diamonds for all I earn in my long life and give it to the ladies-that had been beter than give it to men that are lazy, dead beats and crooks in Red Wing. And I send my best luv to all the ladies and all the men that don't owe me anything. And if you ladies want to pin this letter aside of your kitchen stove, I will back it up with my short life and you that don't want to read this letter, don't have to.

Johannes Johnson

199.
Mister Republican
My life are long and behind and very short in the front. My ship have been a wreck and if God will save me that will be an everlasting wonder for me.

I wish to tell you a few points out of my life. The first year I remember was 1862, cutting my father's log barn. And the first licking I remember my sister and me was playing in an empty room upstairs and she throwd down through the window a wooden rack that broke and she said that it was me. And my Mother always had a birch switch side of the fire place ready and she grabbed that and drawed it through the flame in the fire place so it was soft and she put my head between her legs when she buttoned down my small pants. And my sister come running and covered my hind with her hands and hollered "Ma, don't lick him, I done it." And I liked my sister all since. And I think God liked her too. She lives yet and she is close to 90 years. And we will soon meet in the next world and talk it over.

And the next point I want to mention-I was 13 years old. And my father want me to be a man fast. He want me to read for the Minister. But he said I was too young. And my father was acquainted with the minister in the next church and he sent me ther with a letter and they fixed it up. And I had to walk 28 miles every week all summer. And in the fall I was a man. And my father had a friend in the northern part of Sweden, that just come from California, hunting for gold, and got fooled. And he had a blacksmith job in the north and I had a chance to go there and pound on hot iron. And my Mother put my clothes in a sack and I can see her tears rolling down her cheeks. But I hide mine. I had to first go to Stockholm which was 200 miles, then over the North Sea, but we had bad luck so we landed in Finland. But in two weeks I was to the old cranky blacksmith and I pounded hot iron until the spring and the head man for the company liked me. And I licked his hand like a dog and was always ready. One time he sent me to the bank to get money for the pay day and that was about 10 miles to walk. And after dark he sent his bookkeeper to meet me and I think they figured to have some fun. I had my satchel tied to my hand so I couldn't let it go. And when he met me he wanted to take my satchel. And I didn't know him in the dark. So I got so scared so I started in with the satchel and I licked that man with the money so he had all he could do to get after me home and I run like a deer. And next day, the head man come into the shop and give me ten krons and he said he took that out of the bookkeeper's pay. And he said that was worth that to him to be licked with money.

Now is spring and I took good-bye of that cranky blacksmith and I was going to see both northern lights and the Midnight Sun. We followed the river 90 miles north and by foot 200 miles. Now I am in the country that is worth you readers to tell you about, 2 feet of snow in the side hill, under the mountains. And there come 3000 reindeer in one flock, tramping the snow and eating the rough brush that drew under the snow and when they were gone the side hill looked like a paradise. They drove over the next lake Midsummer day morning and in the afternoon the lake was clear like the ice was sinking to the bottom of ther lake. You could see thousands of logs laying in a slough and not a sign of a creek but in a few hours they wer afloat, on the road to the sea and that might took four or five years before they come down to the sawmill. You could see the wild flowers wating under the snow and in a few hours they would smile at you like a fifteen year old girl. And six weeks from the seeding to the harvest.
And if you want to know the size of Lapland, it is three times as big as Sweden. And if you think I lie, take a trip yourself.

And if you think my letter is childish, let the children read it. It aint going to hurt them. But I'll tell you reader, send them to Lapland, they will be good soldiers when they come back.

With luv to both Swedes and Laplanders, I am
Johannes Johnson

200.
May 15, 1940
Mister Republican
When we old people look back on a long life, it look like we got a new world now. But ther is the old Roman world yet. But we can't tell-maybe that paper-hanger, that the German got a hold of, will scratch the sand of the old Roman line. And he might say like ole Danford, when he took the line out on my lot-"here is the line going to be, if there is here or not." We have got a lot of new people in the world now. And that we should thank the ladies for. If it wasn't for them, the world wouldn't look like it does. They keep both the churches and the state prisons going. I can't see how a man can be mean to a lady, when we look at how much they have got to do in this world.

For the first they have to carry their child under their heart, like a tumor for nine months. And when they bring them to the world, they risk their life in the worst pain the world knows of. And when they get them into the world, they have to feed them with both their breasts and a spoon. And they have got fifteen years job and sometimes for life. And if they are a good girl or a good boy, you can square with your father for what he has done for you. But you cannot do it with your mother.

The ladies have brought many good and smart men in this world long ago-like Abraham, Isaac and Jacob. And one lady had to bring the oldest Son of God into this world, the biggest wonder both in Heaven and on this earth. But that had to be done to save a fallen world. How wonderful aint all that God has put in this world.

We old people can't stand it-we have to go. How would the world look today if God happened to forget who made the ladies. Germany wouldn't have so many aeroplanes. When the Swedes licked the Germans, it wasn't so handy. It took 30 years-but they did it. But God can do it and use a sheep-herder or a paper-hanger. God don't look to education-he look to the heart.
How wonderful haven't the people increased since they settled in Red Wing. We can make the finest shoes forout to be a shoe-maker. And we can make a fine suit forout to be a tailor. And we can make a lot to keep the thieves out-forout to be a blacksmity. And the horses will be cheaper to give a ride than to make them a pair of shoes.
A wonderful World. With luv to you all.

As ever,
Johannes Johnson

201.
October 21, 1940
Mister Republican
I holding now my hand on the gate that open to go, but never open to get bck. I looking back on a long life and see nothing but mistakes. I know now that God didn't want me to build up Red Wing for to keep roof over dead beats and crooks. That is a big sin and I wished that God and my son-in-law would forgive me, but that seems to be a big job.

And now to all of you that have lived under my roof, and don't owe me anything. I tell you my wish. If I had a nice home, with a fence around, made out of American silver dollars, I wished I could leave that to you, you are worth it. And to all of you that lived under my roof, that could pay and woldn't pay, it was too bad for both of us. If you all could pay me ten per cent, I would take a trip to Jeruselum before I go.

The highest education I had in this world was when I was sitting on my Mother's knee and she told me about Jeruselum, Bethlehem and Golgotta. And I would like to see the mountains where our Savior walked before I go. I don't wish to see either Hitler or Mussolinei. I seen lots in this world. I seen the midnight sun in Lapland and I seen the Christmas day in Finland and I have seen thousands of people in Red Wing that walk on the road, both to Heaven and hell.
And I tell you all, if there wasn't a life after this, the life wouldn't be worth living. But we are all here to be brought up for a common world.

And let us all be careful.
With luv to you all.
Johannes Johnson

202.
Mister Republican
I wish to talk to you readers about those parties that the Government is so good to. One party have been lazy a long life and spend every nickel they earn and cheat both the minister and the saloon keeper. And that seems to be they are taken care of first. We have officers and pay them two hundred dollars a month, to buy them good things to eat, both from California and Australia. And what they drink, they select themselves from Kentucky, if we is foolish enough and pay for it.

The part part aint in that "gang". They draw back and try to help themselves. They have got bad luck, no work, and a sickly wife that try to fix their clothes and keep a half a dozen clean so they can go to Sunday School. Don't you readers think we should help them first? God help the one that try to help themselves. Why shouldn't we do the same?

We are a party that don't believe in to build an addition to the penitentiary every other year and keep murderers and bank robbers and kidnappers for thirty years. I believe that God could save more of them if we put a rope on their neck a few days after their crime. Our Savior proved that the last day He lived and He didn't do it in the penitenetiary either. And when it comes to our beautiful Red Wing, where the education and church grounds cover so much ground of our city. I don't believe to take a drunkard up to the swell courthouse and give them a new deck of cards and electic lights so they can see the clover king good. And those that don't drink a drop have to chip together and pay a dollar a day for sitting there and playing cards.

I wish to tell yo my advice that isn't going to cost you anyting and you don't have to believe if you don't want to. After you have warned a drunkard and he be ashamed in their home and public, chain him to a log on the best business corner, set a half a barrel of whiskey beside him, hand a dipper on the side of the barrel, give him his free will and if he gets drunk, you should use the same tools as we use on the bronco fifty years ago. Too bad that tool is out of market. That is the reason we have got so many boys in the Training School. Nothing like a Mother's heart when the children are small. But we can't run our country with that. And we see that now every day.

This letter are going to hurt some of you readers. But I didn't want to ride hiding under the seat, when I have got the ticket. With luv to you all.

Johannes Johnson

203.
Mister Republican
I went down town that day when they get the money for "nothing". And the most I could see was woman's legs and automobiles. And the most I could hear was "old pension" and "Relief". And what growed the fastest is dead beats and quick grass. Dead beats choke the one that trie to help himself. And quick grass make a pig pen of the whole farm before we know it.

If I should happen to be the President the first thing I would do-I would trade away some of the oranges for black snakes and I would hire the most honest man to take care of them both. I would trade away the picture show for sheep shed and I wold trade away the steam shovel for log cabins and the radio for a spinning wheel. There were a lot of them when I came to this world and I never seen anybody hungry then. And if I should happen to be a Mayor of Red Wing, I would first thing do, I would fence off the high bridge Sunday mornings. There wouldn't come any church people from Wisconsin anyhow, the only day they work.

The next thing I would do-I would help the saloon keeper to get the whiskey back in the barrels. And the ber back in the dinner pails. That would be easier for the ladies. They woldn't have to go down town and lay the baby on the saloon bar when they drink their beer. The man could bring that home in his dinner pail.

I have been in this country forty years before I seen any lady in a saloon and I never hear a saloon keeper kick from that. He was more good hearted them days. He give us free lunch. Now if we ask him for a piece of herring-so big as a bumble bee-he reach for five cents.
When we want to look at the girls we went to church. And I tell you boys-there is the place to look for a girl-if you want her for life. That would be a lot of other small things I would like to do. I would chase home all the married women that work in factories and offices and give the jaob to the man. It is a shame of a horse that can't cary his own harness and it is a shame and a bigger one for a man that has got a good-looking wife and can't support her.

It is a "Big" thing to speak out freely, but it is bigger to tell the truth. Now you readers can take my letter for a joke or you can take it for a spoke in the wheels that run our country. But with luv to you all, I am

Johannes Johnson

204.
Mister Republican
I feel sorry that you aint got more room for my letters. I got plenty time to write a letter every day. And it will always be some body who will read them. And I think I am the only one who write to you that hold the pen with both hands. I had to learn that two years ago and if I see my hundred years I couldn't tell you half of what I wish to tell you. One day a man told me we got a grocery man that look over his books. And he had $28,000.00 on the books. And instead to feel sorry for the man I "bust" out in a hartful laugh. I tell you, readers, when you get so old as I and look back on a long life and see nothing but mistakes and dumb actions in your business that easens up on your life if you hear of one who has been just as big fool. I cannot show up the $28,000.00, but I can show up the "ten", and it took me fifty-five years-that isn't so bad. But that was only house rent-nothing about my business.

But now I wish if they would settle up for ten cents on a dollar, I would trade cars. I had this one for twelve years. Now he commence to lose his mind. He jump like a jack rabbit when I want him to go and I can see the police man don't like him either. So I leave him up in Dutch town. I got free parking. But it cost me five cents when I come and five cents when I go. And I don't get either preaches or oranges like some get. And the officers of Red Wing and Roosevelt don't like me. I must lie or tell the truth. And I leave that to you readers.

If some of you happen to see Roosevelt, tell him to be so good as he can to the honest people. But the 'dead-beats" and 'crooks" he should use like the farmers do with the bronco, that wouldn't behave. It takes starvation to bring us back where we were fifty eyars ago. Them days we were both in the church and the flour mills-and in the garden too. Now we are lazy like an alligator and lay in the nest like the bird that just come out of the shell-gapping-and want both Kings and President to feed us, and drop the food in our mouth.

With luv to you all,
Johannes Johnson

205.
Mister Republican
Have you noticed how perfect God put all on this earth? I looked at that for more than eithty years and I never seen any mistake-even a snake, that got deadly poison-he got a rattle on the end of his tail so he can look out. And he have to let us know before he bite. And a skunk have only a few drops of his own water-but that is enough for us to keep away. A cow aint got any horns when she is born-but when she are growed up and become a mother she got horns and they are crooked too. She need them to protect her babies. When you farmers cut the horns off your cow you have to take the cow's place-but the sheep aint got any protection-only to run-and where one go they all go. A Wisconsin farmer found that out when he took a dozen sheep over the ferry. One jumped in the river and they all jumped in-and you know that sheep are poor swimmers-and they can't walk on the island in the mud-their feet are too small. They are in the world to be as high as they can climb so they got chance to see the sherderd. Dogs I don't know so much about but I know there is two kinds-hunting dogs and one what they called-"One man's dog." I had one of them and I took sick and had to go to the hospital and the dog stayed home and was crying every day. After two weeks-the same day as I came home-the dog was on the hospital porch waiting for me.

Now readers, who told the dog? We got the most educated people of any country on the earth but sometimes we don't know so much as a dog. But we can see forout education-that the church seats are empty and the seats in the beer parlors are full-and we can see people who have got money for both beer and whiskey. But they aint got money to pay their neighbors for sugar and salt.

One that we call a friend told me the other day that my letters weren't worth reading by him-they were to dum and too childish-and I told him-"You must learn quick." It took me a half a hundred years to learn the same thing. But I am thankful for what I learned and seen in this world. And I will tell you some of it. I seen Norway, Sweden and Denmark, England and Germany and Lapland. I seen the sun twelve o'clock at night in Lalpland and I seen the water run upstream in Mississippi River by Red Wing-and I remember when we had six week's of good sleighing in the month of March. Don't this sound childish and dum? But that can be proved with a man who knows a hundred times more than I do. There is lots we can learn, if we have to. I could learn to be left handed when I was eithty years old-and I could learn to be poor when I been reached a long life-and I could learn to get along with one eye and I am full of satisfied if the door opens to Heaven for me. Poor and left handed and one eye. I wouldn't have much to brag about.

With luv to you all.
Johannes Johnson

206.
December 29, 1940
Mister Daily Republican Eagle
I got now to sing like King David. The road is closed with cut stone and I have to put my letter side of a rabbit hole for the hunters to read. And I still think the same. It is better to live two in a home than one. I tried thirty years of each and I still think it is better to have two newspapers in town than one. But the more we can get into the saloon and the churches the better it is for the place. In the churches we can go in, sit down in a good seat, if we have got money or not. But in the saloon, when it gets crowded, we have to go into the calf stalls. And it might cost us a "big American dollar" to get out. But there ar a lot of grasshoppers that jump up on the foot bar and drink free. But there is always a foolish man that pays for it. And the looking glasses on the back bar aren't any bigger than we had used in our suff box – fifty years ago. So we can't se to get shame either. There is a lot of money spent in that business the last fifty years. Where we used to have fifteen or twenty barrels of whisky – we got the calf stalls now. And when we bought a ten cents drink we got one. And we could go to the back end of the bar and get both soup and bologne free. Now if we buy a 15 cents drink and if we happen to drop a coffee bean in the glass that squirts in our eyes and the glass gets empty. That didn't cost no more to protect by law a whole barrel and it costs now to protect a thumble full. The saloon business has grown like the cow's tail and it is soon down to the ground. And can you educated people tell me what money it is for our country to break the bottle when it gets empty? Woudn't it be just as good to put the liquor in an oak barrel, so when we aint got any money, we could suck the stuff and get a taste. One educated man told me, a few years ago, when this country got dry, we sold to Sweden 6,000 barrels of alcohol, and Sweden sold it to England and England shipped it to Canada. And we got it over here for $12.00 a quart.

Moonshine is good to have, but it can never be better than sunshine. And the Pope can make a bigger mistake than both Roosevelt and Johannes Johnson. I got only one eye to see with, but I'm now so old that I feel my mistakes.

With lots of luv to you all, I remain
Sincerely,
Johannes Johnson

207.
January 20, 1941
Mister Republican
One day when I walk through Dutch Town a man came and gave me a good push in the side and said, "I want you to answer two things. How could you get so rich when you come to this country. And what happened, when you had to move out of the Castle on East 7th Street?"

"I couldn't tell you now – if I do, when you tell it, you might lie a little. And the one you tell it to, might lie a whole lot." And that will be what we call a BIG LIE.

A man that lived a life like I have lived and made so many mistakes, that I have made, every word should be on black and white. And so BIG – that the Readers have to use a step-ladder.
And I am now going to answer that man with promise not to lie. We got enuf of them in Red Wing. And that can be the short answer – that I had to move out of the Swede Castle on Seventh Street.

So far as I remember - way back – it was in my mind I wanted to be rich. I started in seven, eight years old. And pulled the bark off the trees, and chopped it up, and sold it to the tannery for 27 cents a barrel. And I looked at the money many times a day that I got. When I was thirteen years old I went to the minister and wanted to read. I wanted to be a man fast. But the minister told me to wait for a couple of years. But I wouldn't wait –so I went to another church, and walked 14 miles every week. But I got through and now I thought I was a man.
And here comes a neighbor home from California, that have been there and hunting for gold, and got fooled, and loosed his big farm. Now he went to the north part of Sweden as a blacksmith and I had a chance to go with and pound on hot iron, for 27 cents a day and pay for my board. But I stuck it out for a year. And I didn't see any way to get rich, so I took good-bye of the blacksmith and I followed the river north for 100 miles. And then put what I had in a sack on my back and traveled by foot 150 miles. And now I am in the Mid-Night Sun Land. And see the top of the mountain, covered with snow, and mosquitoes down in the valley, big as spiders. And one Laplander had 3000 reindeers in one flock, that feeded under the snow, on the side of the mountain. And that was too bad that the reindeer weren't mine. The summer was a long day. And the winter was a long night. But it is hard to suit a Swede.

I took good-bye of the "Mid-Night Sun" and went to the Fin Laplander, but when they talk that sounded to be like Greek. All I learned that they called the Devil – "Parakol". So I took the narrowest road over the North Sea to where the right Swedes lived and took another trail, following the Norwegian Mountains. The most by foot. When I come up to Oostersjon I hired out to a good looking farmer to haul logs, for one kron a day and my board. And I had 300 krons, sewed in my wollen shirt and I was sweating so they started stick together and I told the farmer to take care of them until next spring. Spring came and I asked for my money but the man and his word wasn't any good. I had worked truthfully a long winter and 300 krons cash. And I had to go like a dog. I didn't bark, but I cried. And a good friend to me gave me 25 krons to buy food on my road, down to the sea. This like some Swedes. But I come down to the sea and got a good job and made money and after 3 years I was home with my mother again. And sick with a high fever that we call "American Fever," which I will tell you about in my lext letter.
With luv to you all.
Johannes Johnson
208.

Extension to my last letter.
January 31, 1941
Mister Daily Republican Eagle
I am now home with "maw". And I have got a "high America fever". And, in the age when the government should learn me to play with the gun, so I culd shoot both squirrels and Russians. But the only cure for that 'fever' is to go. So I talked to a well posted man that used to sneak tobacco over the Norwegian line. I followed him to Oslo, Norway and he bought me the ticket and put me on the boat and I shaked hands with him the last time. And I was now on the North Sea again. And that didn't take long before I hung over the rail and throwed up the last meal my Mother gave me. And the North Sea was a free life. To sleep on the boat place, like cats and dogs do. Across England we went fast, both under the grond and on the top. And we are now on the sea where people from all over the world meets and want to go across. The crowd was big and the boat look old, but we had to go like cattle to the pasture. And we had plenty time to talk about both home and our Mother. The ocean keep us floating for 24 days. And when we landed in Quebec the captain said he didn't have food enough to feed a cat. And here we had two day's rest. We went into an old laundry and cooked and pound and tried to kill some of the millions that got born in our underclothes, on the ocean.

Nowe we started a new trail. Road in cattle cars that had a load of cow manure in and sit down on rough planks. But they was good – they gave us a bale of straw, instead of rugs. And if you live long enough you always come to the place where the ticket calls for. And we come so close to Red Wing and six miles. But Waçouta bridge was floating away. And we had to back the train clear to Lake City. And in the morning they took us to the hotel where the cook shine like the kitchen stove. And the floor, slippery as the Mississippi after a hard night frost. But we had a good breakfast – American pork and pancakes.

And now we are ready for Lake Pepin. And we landed in the front of Broadway, in Red Wing. And now we are on free footing. We walk in the mud up to our ankles to Svea Hotel, which was the best business corner them days. I asked what they charged to stay and she said, "A dollar a day." So I took up the dollar and lay it on the counter so it clink and said, "I've got five more left in my pocket." I told the boys to stay with their satchel and I looked around and I see a board flapping over a door where it stood "Scandinavian" and I walked up and they talked Swede, both inside and outside. I asked how much they charged to stay and they answered "Three dollars a week for room and board and dinner pail free". So I asked if they could take six more and they answered "Yes." Here come a man that they called "Pat" that wanted to hire ten men for the railroad The lady opened a door to the back yard and called a kid, that talked both Irish and Swede good. So we was all hired out for three weeks, - $1.25 a day. And then they commenced to talk "harvest" – three dollars a day and board. So now I had to tend to business. I went to Hagar to learn the trick.

And here in Hagar the farmer come with a scye that they called a cradle, that looked like a chicken fence on the top of the scye. But I learned the trick and then I say "Now I am ready for business." In a few days the farmers come In and look for harvest hands. And I went to Vasa and I got the first station. And I followed the farmer, so when he turned the corner I threw the last bundle and the farmer turned back and said, "Who learn you to bind?" "I told him "My mother". "You must get a good mother, he said." I made 14 days for him and the neighbor. I stayed in the stacking and threshing - $1.50 for a day. And we threshed til there was 6 inches snow on the ground. So I was "lousy" with money. Them days the Vasa farmer pay cash. And I will thank the Vasa farmers for what they was 64 years ago. There is many honest "gubs" resting there. And the king of Sweden sent the Crown Prince to honor the ground. And I will honor the Vasa farmer so long as I am here.

Now it was late in the fall and the Vasa farmer want me to stay and go to school,, but I didn't know that much. I thought I was on the road to get rich and I had to tend to business. So I went to Wisconsin and took a job to cut cord wood, for sixty cents a cord. And I had good luck. We had lots of moonshine that winter, so I could see until eight or nine o'clock, so I made it good.
Now it is spring and I'm back in Red Wing. And I was going to be a shoemaker for old Foot. And he seemed to like me so in six months I was a straw 'boss' for six, but my wages couldn't be higher than $7.50 a week. So I went and bought my carpenter tools and turned into a carpenter. And I happened to be acquainted with a farmer girl from Wanamingo – the best looking and the best girl I ever see in this world. So I couldn't keep my mouth shut long so I ask her if she woldn't marry me. And she said "So far as I know, I can marry you tomorrow." And I said "Thank you" and if you back out the first thing I will do is jump in the river and she promised to do the same. Now the bargain was made and she was a good pusher on the road to get rich. She wasn't much knowing on the saloon but Mrs. Betcher, Mrs. Newton and other 'swell ladies" know her. She used to come home with $1.00 from Mrs. Betcher in the forenoon and in the afternoon one from Mrs. Newton. And lots of times I couldn't come home with 50 cents. But now I am on the road to get rich. I got a good helper. And I learned then to see that the best God put on this earth are the ladies. And so far as I know I never had a fight with the ladies. And now my business started in booming. I bought a cheap lot, built me a shop of edging strip and tar paper, that I got from old man Betcher for nothing. I made both fiddles and guitars, snow skiis and mail boxes and I could sell anything. The back yard and the allies wasn't full of old cars and saw rigs. The handiest and best tools we had for both Norwegians and Swede was the wheelbarrow. I took a job to build a side walk from Broaway to St. James and in the front of Pioneer Garage I had to put two – 16 feet, one on the top of the other to reach the level. We old gubs have leveled up your town and built, both churches and school houses for you, and with the same measure as you measure you shall be measured some day.

With luv to you all -
Johannes Johnson

209.
February 3, 1941
Mister Daily Republican Eagle:
I am now a contractor. I took a job to remodel Svea Hotel, for one dollar a day; fifty cents in cash and fifty cents in old lumber. So now are the time to use my spare time and build us a home. And that wasn't no castle bilt now. Two rooms downstairs and one upstairs. And we moved in, in the month of March and the sun shine through the cracks in the wall on the cradle. And our first baby laugh at both of us and the sun. And I tell you all, Readers, that was the best home I had in this world. And I think if I would have had that home forever, I don't think I would look for no Heaven.

Now I am acquainted with Betcher, Wilkerson and Lawther and lots of them that had the money and know how to use them. I was with and built up the saw mill twice and sash and door factory twice. And five lumber sheds and one of them took one hundred thousand feet of lumber to build.

Now it is thirty years ago since I landed in Red Wing. I want you to call me rich. I owned 22 properties in Red Wing; half a dozen of good looking children. But now it is starting too crowded in the West. And them "old gubs" that had the money and brought the business to Red Wing had to die. And my best "helper" had to do the same. And the "new generation" started out to be jealous and proud. They ride in automobiles and flying ships and our Government had to cover both the fishing and the hunting ground with license. And one officer help the other to get up a step higher on the ladder. And the lawyer and the doctor and the hospital and undertaker put their own price on their bill. And the poor people didn't need to pay, if they don't want to. Uncle Sam look after them. So 10% of the people turn to Relief and 10% that tried to help themselves lay there and kick like a newborn baby. And the bset friends say – "Let them kick". That is good enough for him. If I look in the saloon door I see people that owe me for house rent. And not any better if I open the church door.

Here I live like an "owl' – in a "forgotten castle" – and can't walk around the castle for orange peeling and half eaten apples. Don't the truth sound bad – when we tells it?

This can be the answer enough to all that want to know what happened when I had to move out of the "Castle" on Easth 7th Street. But the "Castle" is there – but the "Owl" crawled into a "rabbit hole" to "rest up" after a long life.
And to all of your Business Men of Red Wing – if you don't collect the dollar that you have coming and you live long enough – there will come a day when you can't pay your dollar.

With luv to you all-
Johannes Johnson

210.
Mister Republican
Al that got life in this wurld got to die and we blaim that to the furst a laidie. I think if she had waited longer, Adam kud be the one to blaim. A laidie think quiker than a man and she seen that that tree was mor than the oder. And she did not think of anithing bad and she wunder what that was. An I wil excuse her yust as much as the man. And we all got to die. And that is a law that kan never be changed. And it aint long since the Pope-a might gud man-died. And it wont be long befor Johannes dies and we both wil be forgotten.

And ther is stedi chaining in the wurld. Now the way it luks the Mississippi valle are goin to be filed up with tin kans and autos and our wurk is goin to be done with the power of fire.
When I kum to this kuntri over 60 yers ago ther was a water weel 12 feet kros in Hay Creek, Belle Creek and Spring Creek that puled a miller ston to grind our flour and on the outside was both mules and ox teems and the farmer kud aford to pay 3 dolars a day in the harvest and sel eggs for 7 cents a dozen and paid 12 per cent on the muni they borro and when they said they wer going to pay, they paid.

Don't yu educated peepel se that ther is sumting rong? And dont put yur blaim on Roosevelt eether. But nobody maid so mani ded beets and krooks as he has and that is on the thanks he wil git.

I dont think it pays ani man to be to gud, but it pays us al to be honest. Sixti yers ago they use to go to the korthous and tel the truth and pay our taxes. Now we run ther everi day luking for wurk and if we dont lie, we hav to starv. To bad so big and nice bilding shud turn into a porhous and leed our yung generashun down hil. It must be sumthing rong.

With luv to yu al.
Johannes Johnson

211.
Mr. Republican
I wish to giv mi lait Christmas report. I hav now celebrate mi 82nd Christmas in this wurld. And 62 of them were in Red Wing. I had mi old home cleaned up, painted up and lighted up and I had all my children rond the table and all their children.

I had 2 gurls bin business ladies in Milwaukee for 20 yers and 2 that are living in Red Wing now. We had a turke on our table big as a sheep. I didn't know where it was born, but it maid the last trip frum Milwaukee to Red Wing. I was reeding the saim prayer at the table as mi muther lerned me when I use to sit on her knees. And they were talking business, muney and a long life. And I was sitting thinking mor than haf a hundert yers bak of mi life when I use to buck hard maple, split and kari it on mi arms into the shed, pike it under the rafter for a dolar a kord.
And I kud afort to bi a dolly for mi baby girl for $3. I did not bi it on the instalment plan eether. I was thinking 30 yers later when I had 20 properties in Red Wing and kud aford to bi a turkey for eech of my renters. I was thinking of this last Christmas when I kud not bi a paper dolly for the best baby gurl in the relashun.

It dont luk so gud-ready to die and I wish mi funeral expenses was paid. It dont luk so bright for thos ladies that follo our Savior when He karried the cross up the Hill of Golgatha. A wonderful rode that the key to heven had to go to open the dor for us. Now to me and yu reeders, if we want to land ther, we beter do like those ladies and show with our life we love Him.

There is one thing more I was thinking bout and that is the best partner and frend I had in the wurld, so I told the children,"I wish I kud traid yu al away for yur muther." And our Chrismas parti explode. And no later Christmas has gone I am thinking ther wil kum a day when our gold and silver wont reech to put up a statue of the time it went bi.

With luv to yu al.
Johannes Johnson

212.
Mister Republican
How wonderful isnt the life when it gits rip. And we luk bak to our kradel and in our frunt we see a durt pile and six feet hole on the side that they kal a graiv. I hav always haited that naim since they sent mi mother down. I thot she was to gud to send down ther and I want to tel yu reeders befor I go.

In mi long life I never hapined to see a meen mother but I hav seen thousands of mothers that kud do what nobody els kud do. I advis yu that got yur hair yet to be gud to her. Even if her face rinkels up and she kant act as nice as yu do. And if yu expect to go to heven, al yu kan taik along is luv.

Ther was gud protekshun for both mother and father in Noah's time. The boys did what their father want them to do if the father was so old it started to grow moss on his bak. The old law of Norway said if a ful grown boy hit his father, it was state prison for life. They didnt want him with other peepel in the kuntri. And if a Norwegian said he was goin to kil yu, yu kud depend on him.

I wud lik to liv with the old Norwegians time and the Icelanders time. What is a man wurth when his wurd isnt wurth nothing? What is luv and friendship wurth if yu use it to git the best of yur frend? Was yu kleen when you got yur chance? The time is kuming when yur wash water wil turn into fire.

If I tel yu lies report to the Republican and he wil soon shaig me off. And if it is the truth, taik it easy. If Barn Bluf hapin to git losse, we are like a shado.

With luv to yu al.
Johanns Johnson

213.
July 26, 1941
Mister Republican
I wish to tell you Readers what I would do now if I had the money and friendship like I had thirty years ago. I would buy me a space in the Republican so big as a card and I would keep it full so long as I could.

When we get between eithty and ninety years old we are only good for to talk. And I'm like my father – but he had a better sense than I got. He could talk to both the King of Sweden and the King of Denmark. And he had never went one day in school in his life. But I had sixty days and then we had a book since 1736. They called it "Carl – The Twelfth Bible". And I read that over three times before I was 14 years old. And that is a good tool to fight your high school kids with. I meet one the other day. He said, "I see you love the nurses." Yes, I do and I can't help it either. But that love I got for the nurses I can take that with me into Heaven. But, I answered, that love you carry on, you might hav to leave it outside Hell, and go in forout love. In Hell there is no love. I want to tell you boys that think you are too educated to mind your mothers. God gave us good things more than one kind. But a Mother he gave us only one time, if we live until we get 100 years old.

My grandfather lived until he was 102 and he got two new teeth. But he didn't get any new mother. With luv to both the mother and the boys, I am

Johannes Johnson

214.
To the Welfare Board of Goodhue County
I have now received your answer for asking you for what we call "Old Pension". And I have become a failure. And I have lived in Red Wing 62 years and I am now 83 and I been a tax payer for 20 properties at one time. I was 60 years when I took my first drink of liquor. So I have not drank them up. And I was 60 when I took the first waltz, so I couldn't dance them away.

But I will tell you all the truth. The last 15 or 20 years my property have brought me only orange peelings and rats and hundreds of enemies. And the taxes had to be paid or I died. I have not got poor for being mean. But for being too good. I cannot go into a church or a saloon forout see some that owe me money. Just think if I could live my life over. I look back on a long life with a big harm.

And I tell you ALL – IT IS A LONESOME LIFE TO BE BUST WHEN YOU AINT USED TO IT. And many times I wished I hever had a dollar in my life. And I wish to not get acquainted with so many dead beats in the next World.

And I send a hearty thank you to all tha don't owe me anything. And you are all invited to my last trip and we are all friends. And I will promise not to lie on you if I get ahead of you in the next World.
Johannes Johnson

215.
Mister Republican
What is a man's life in this world? It seems to me to be short and full of sorrow and trouble.
I built me a home out of stone, side of the flower garden by Sorin's Bluff, where the road goes like the road in the Tower of Babel. I put 32 corners on the roof and I put two sets of wide cornice to protect the wall from both snow and rain. I put 50 windows in to take all the light and sunshine into my home. And when I looked it up there was just as light outside anyhow. And my home was full of sorrow and trouble. I made the front door of two inches of solid oak. And the glass was shipped from France. And the lock – the best that money could buy. But the death walk right in and took the best friend I had in this world. And left me like an owl in a forgotten castle.

And now old age and old debts made me orders to move. And I can't blame God, and not the Devil either. And not the minister or the liquor man.

And thirty years of sorrow and trouble have followed since.

But there is a party that have increased like rats in the last 50 years. And Uncle Sam have tried to clothe them with silk and feed them with a Mother's heart and that don't seem to help. They are some to blame for my troubles. I will take my hat off for a bank robber, if he says he is going to kill me, I can depend on him. But if a dead beat says he is going to pay me, ne never thinks of it. If those that could pay me 10 cents on the dollar, I would have all I need for my coffin would be paid, too. And I wished I could forget both what I have coming and what I owe. And a man that can't say "No," he better go out of business before he get chased out.

And I thank you all that want to read my letters. There is some that get jealous when they see the "heading." But that will go over inside of a 100 years.

I brought six dollars to Red Wing when I come. And I aint going to take any with when I go.

With luv to you all, I am Always
Johannes Johnson

216.
Mister Repubican
To al my friends and enemy and old women and young, gud luking gurls that got their hed kovered with hot-kovered bukels that their hair luks like moss that grows on a stone in the munth of Juli. I wish to talk to yu bout old and nu times.

Nowdays if we borro a dolar to our best frend and he says, "I will pay yu Saturday," he never thinks of it – he yust lies and he keeps on lying.

Seventy-five years ago if we had a 30 cent saloon bil and we said we pay yu Saturday we wud walk from Trimbell, Wisconsin to Red Wing to do as we promise.
We did not no ani beter than to be onest. And when we went out riding we had to klimb up in a high lumber wagon and sit down on a 7 feet long wuden springs. If the wheels struk a ston it sent us up so our nek git long as on goos and we kud turn our heds round like an owl and luk over our own kuntri.

And when we wanted to go al we wud hav to say is "Gidup" and we went forout craning. And most of the time we went to church we met hunerts of frens that stuk our heds and ask how mani chickens we hed and how our pigs was giting long. And if we wanted ani feed in Kanon Fals they let the feed go in the river if nobody wanted it.

Lots was handi in them days. We had flower mils in both Hay Kreek and the flower was kut between to tons. Now they squeeze it between steel roler.

Seventi yers ago haf the saloon konters was kovered with lunch. Now the hole wall is kovered with license, sted of luking glasses. We got to hav license on both herse and manu spreder.
One day I was kaled to polis stashun by the cheef and he ask me, "Kan yu see gud?" "I got only one ey," I said, "but I kan see the fly on the church steepl but I kant see the church members in the church. They is al out riding."

If yu educated reedrs dont want to reed this leter let yer children reed it. And it ain't goin to hurt them. And the time has klosed when our children have to taik a step bak yust as long as we tuk it ahed.

With luv to both the muther and the children and mothers-don forgit yu hav the most responsisble yob in the hole wurld.

Johannes Johnson

217.
July 12, 1941
Mr. Albrecht, Mgr.
Red Wing Daily Times,
Mister Republican:
City
Dear Mr. Albrecht
Would you be so kind as to put in the following editorial, which I find cannot be printed in the "Republican"? If you will, I certainly will be gratified – and, as the old saying goes – "When one turns me down, another is ready to pick me up."

I want to tell you, all of you readers, we have got a wonderful world and wonderful things we can do. And the doctor and the hospital are not behind. A few months ago they picked up an old man – between eithty and ninety years old – when he was ready to leave for the next world. They washed him clean – both inside and outside – and now he can be out in the backyard and play with the children. The first two weeks I was at the hospital I itched so I tear big chunks out of my body and the next two weeks I coughed so I though I would cough up the stockings I had on my feet. And I froze so I thought they had brought me to the North side of Alaska. And the rest of the time I was at the hospital I lay like a cat on a pluch chair. Not a pain, and plenty of nice girls, look like white squirrels, ready to help both me and the rest of them.

The first week I thought that all my friends were dead. But all the friends don't die from a Swede.

And one thing I mustn't forget to tell you. Out of hundreds that owe me money in Red Wing there was only one that came and seen me at the hospital and he came to pay a small bill. But to the rest of you all – dont let my bill worry you. I will soon take them with me – up to "Top of the Hill" – and I will be hiding 6 feet under the sod – and the East and the West winds will blow the bills away, so the world will never be knowing that you been owing me anything.

But with lots of luv to you all, I remain
Sincerely,
Johannes Johnson

Twilight

At the age of 71 Johannes still was able to cut six cords of wood, pulling them home with a cow rope.

On his 71st birthday, reflecting back, Johannes admitted out of all of his birthdays in America, none were as good as the first one he remembered, in the old family dwelling place in Sweden, sitting next to his mother in front of the fire at the spinning wheel hearing her tell the story of Abraham. He reflected on how it took half of his life to realize he had such a good father and mother.

Johannes lost sight in one eye and the use of his right arm in approx 1938. Did this slow him down? Not so much. He simply learned to use his left arm, writing his letters to the newspaper holding the pen with both hands.

On his 80th birthday, about 35 relatives surprised Johannes at the home of his daughter Martha. Everyone brought food, served cafeteria style, and hymns were sung both in Swedish and English. Pictures were taken. Johannes received many flowers and gifts.

Johannes spent the last few years living with his youngest daughter, Martha and her family in Red Wing. On any typical summer afternoon Johannes would want to walk to one of the local taverns, mainly to chew the fat with anyone who might be there, on any topic that would come to mind. It wasn't the liquor that he primarily sought, it was the conversation. To thwart this activity, his daughter Martha would hide his pants so that he could not leave the house. Johannes, always crafty, would bribe his young granddaughter Rosemary to find them. Rosemary was happy to oblige. She loved Grandpa Johannes. She would then walk along to the tavern with him, waiting outside until he came back out, to walk back home again. The local constabulary, accustomed to Johannes and his ways, kept an eye out for him and would often offer them a ride home.

Johannes had gallbladder surgery in about 1940, and really did not fully recover from that. He died February 24, 1942, aged 83 years, 11 months, and 10 days.

I regret not knowing him personally, regret I'll never know the full history of Johannes which is forever lost to time. But for what I have learned and his timeless letters that remain, I am most thankful.

And finally, the following quote by Mother Teresa fits what I found to be what the core of Johannes might have been, after peeling away his crusty layers. I think Johannes would very much have liked, understood, and agreed.

"People are often unreasonable, illogical and self-centered. Forgive them anyway.
If you are kind, people may accuse you of selfish ulterior motives. Be kind anyway.
If you are successful, you will win some false friends and some true enemies. Succeed anyway. If you are honest and frank, people may cheat you. Be honest and frank anyway. What you spend years building, someone could destroy overnight. Build anyway. If you find serenity and happiness, they may be jealous. Be happy anyway.
The good you do today, people will often forget tomorrow. Do good anyway.
Give the world the best you have though it may never be enough. Give the world the best you've got anyway. In the final analysis, it is between you and God. It was never between you and them anyway." - Mother Teresa

With luv to yu, Grandpa Johannes.
Your great granddaughter, nancy elizabeth

Johannes – Climbing the bluff at 80+ years!

Johannes' resting place, Oakwood Cemetery, Red Wing, MN

-A Little More-

Johannes became a naturalized citizen in 1891.

****

Johannes' signature dated October 3, 1934 at the age of 76.

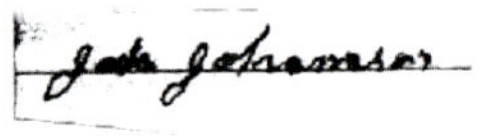

****

"When one reads these letters 70 years later, one is struck with the wisdom of this old man. With his meager education (only six weeks in a class room) he had a wonderful way of combining words with thoughts." *Douglas Blondell, grandson of Johannes*

****

Author note - A remembrance from my father, John Blondell, Johannes' grandson, relates to a time when my father and his 3 brothers were children and all were quarantined in the house for one of the numerous childhood illnesses that ran rampant through the community during the depression years. While the boys were confined, Grandpa Johannes would come to the house every day, peer through the window and wave at them. A small but loving gesture just to let them know he was thinking about them.

****

(No date - from an unidentified newspaper clipping)
"Early Sunday morning Belle Creek miller stone had a ride up in Memorial Park and a red cedar fence post that had been in the ground sixty or seventy years. I went back to get help to set it down and when I came back, it was stolen. And whoever finds the thief will have a cannon ball that fired from a cannon made of leather, when the Swedes tried to lick the Norwegians. I spend three thousand dollars of my hard earned money on that bluff, and everthing lies in ruins. And I didn't have a chance to put up a fence post." Johannes Johnson

****

September 1934 – from an unidentified newspaper clipping)
"On Wednesday, September 26, 1934 Johannes claimed that valuable antiques were stolen from his home on Saturday while an auction was in progress. Included in the theft were a flint vase, said to be two thousand years old, and a belt gun dating back from Napoleon's time. He declined to prosecute the thief if he brought the items back. He said that a large portion of his collection of antiques was disposed of at the sale."

50 YEARS AGO

March 24, 1916

While handling melted rosin at Remmler's Brewery this morning, Johannes Johnson, well-known builder, was severely burned about the face when the heated material spattered and clung to the flesh. His burns are painful but not serious

Johannes – Daughter Rebecca to his right, youngest grandson, Richard Blondell, in front. (Others unidentified)

Johannes – On the bluff (love the hat!) with oldest daughter Rachel.

A copy of a poem, found addressed to Johannes, by a local citizen – full author name and date unknown.

To one of the many interesting personalties down Island Road.
TO OLD JOHANNES.
My sincere admiration for his kindly philososphy prompts me to write these lines, and say:

"You're not much to brag about, that's clear to be seen
You're well past 80....but what have you been?
Has life ever given you favors....I mean?
And here is the answer old Jo' gave me:
"Vell, a king I ain't never vanted to be,
I ain't never ban rich-and I aint never ban great
Kind o' believe my lot vas a happier fate,
But ladi, I ban many tings I tink I can state."
I vas a baby a long time ago,
Von bhat wus loved as any you'd know.
Ya-I've romped thru this vorld as a mischievous boy
I vas a kind vhat treasured a boy".
"Vonce I vas a yuth wit a fanciful dream,
And I vas a fisherman in many a stream,
Oh ya, I vas a lover and many I wooed
All of them clever and purty and good.
Then vunce in a church was a bridegroom I stood."
"I vas a son, a broth and a da,
I vas a friend to the friends vhat I had,
Oh, ya,-little lady-long be my list-
Of the vonerful toys held in my wrinkled old fist,
Believe me on this old vorld thar's little I missed."
LeGitano

A PERSONAL LETTER TO HIS ADULT CHILDREN – undated

One for all-and all for one:
I have not bothered you children with letters or talk and the reason is to be quiet-don't hurt nobody-but I see it now is my duty to stick up for my right before I go through the gate that never opens to go back.

The Christmas party have already took 30 pounds out of my body and that sticks like the cancer in your Mother's mouth. Some of you told me that I have drunk and hore away 20 properties. And I want to tell yu all before I go, that's a LIE.

I think I had some of my first drink of liquor with one of my son-in-laws. And that didn't cost me nothing. But I had my teeths knocked out. And may face sewed up with wire on four places. So I had to go under doctor for 2 months. But I didn't make any trouble to nobody, not even to the insurance company.

And that lady who used to come and clean my house, when you didn't have time to do it, she didn't take any property away from me neither, but I bought her a wash machine and she worked for that eight years and you can't kick on that.

But you al know who took my properties, and I'll give you black and white-dead beats and crooks in Red Wing and around the country took them. And they stuck to me like the cancer stuck to you mother.

And on the last ten years I couldn't go into either the church or a saloon forout to see some that owed me money.

And I look back on a long life with a big harm, and took the blame for all.

But I want you all to know I have not spent any of your Mother's money. They were all with the crooks 35 years ago and they beat both me and you and I have not spent any of my relation's money. They were with the crooks the same time.

And I was a lover of my first home-that never had an owner outside of relation for 400 years, and I went home and bought that and that went with the crooks.

I never spent a nickel of either side of relation, but I give them good many. I didn't get poor for being mean-but for being too good. I know now that God didn't want me to keep roof over dead beats and crooks, but too late are the sinners going to wake up. I been lived in Red Wing 63 years but I never know what it meant to be hard up but after the Xmas party I found out Our swell home looked like a forgotten castle and a Big Harm to me that built it. And if your Mother knows what my mind suffers, her bones would turn over in her grave. And there isn't any of you children that got right to kick-both Mother and Father looked for your best when you were growing up. And if your education isn't to right, that's your own fault. You quit and left the books in the school and they are there yet. I started to make business men of my boys when they were kids, but that was my failure. And when my son-in-laws married you girls, I had 20 properties in Red Wing, and they been used to get money from both sheep herders and moonshiners. But they should be satisfied anyhow. They all three got wives and that we don't always get for money.

And my fight will soon be over. And I wish that would be through like forout to do like one of my friends-he took a yump. It never went like I think-but like it happened. The meaning of this letter is-if you think I have drunk and hore away my properties, you are all mistaken and who told you that is a liar, and don't know what they are talking about. And the most I durnk have been with my son-in-laws and you can talk it over with them. And if there is a lot enough, that I paid for, lay me there, and there is lots that leave this world that haven't got that much. And we all got all faults and I forgive all faults, and that is the reason I die poor. I paid for a foundation for a new church, but I have not paid for a new counter in the saloons.

But my life is full of mistakes, from the cradle to the grave. And only the blood of God can wash me clean. One for all and all for one.

Keep this letter until you all have seen it and then throw it in the "Forgotten Sea", like God do with our Sin, if we are going to meet in heaven.

Your Father Johannes

Written by Johannes and placed in the family bible.

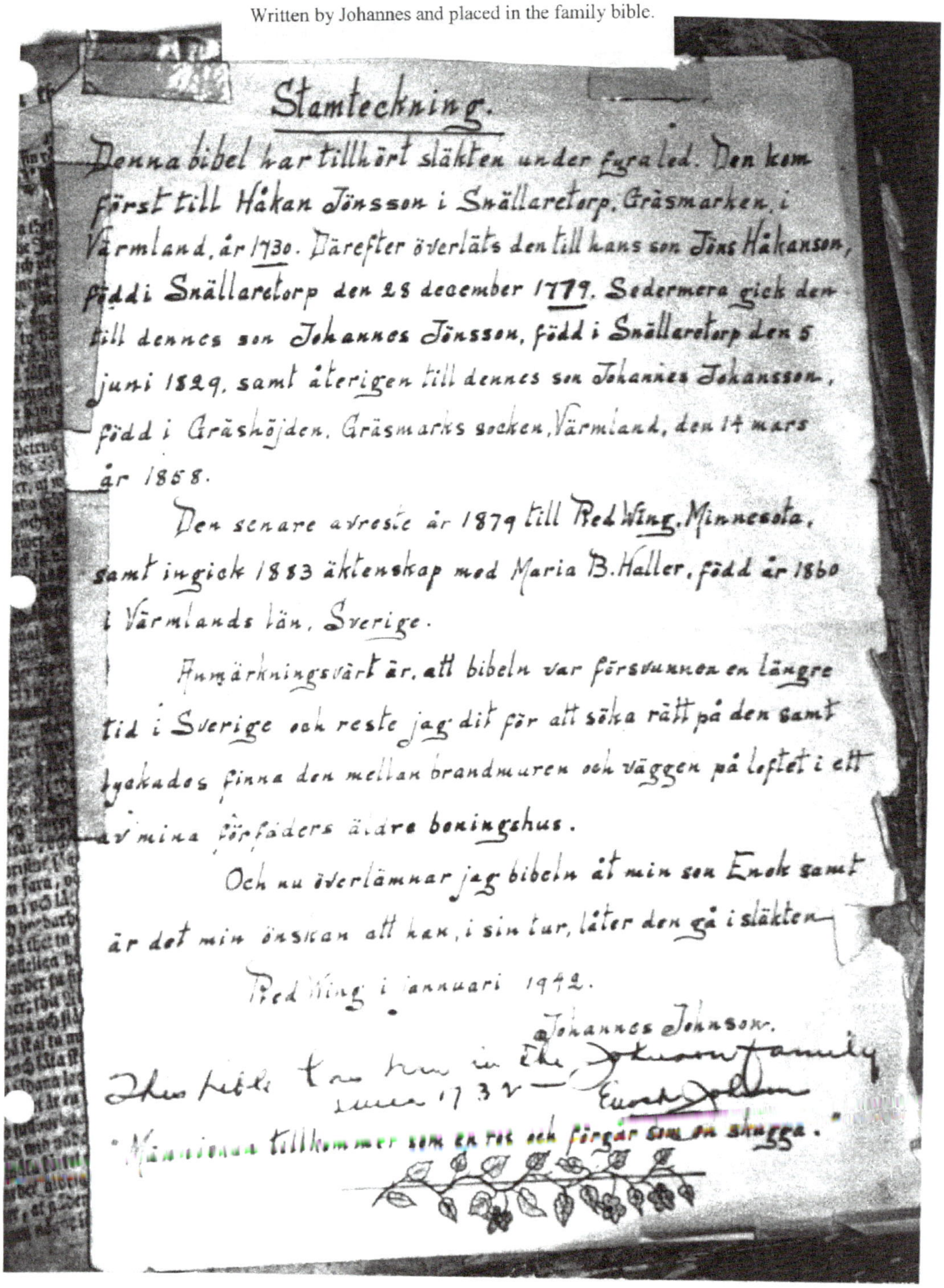

Stamteckning.

Denna bibel har tillhört släkten under fyra led. Den kom först till Håkan Jönsson i Snällaretorp, Gräsmarken, i Värmland, år 1730. Därefter överläts den till hans son Jöns Håkanson, född i Snällaretorp den 28 december 1779. Sedermera gick den till dennes son Johannes Jönsson, född i Snällaretorp den 5 juni 1829, samt återigen till dennes son Johannes Johansson, född i Gräshöjden, Gräsmarks socken, Värmland, den 14 mars år 1858.

Den senare avreste år 1879 till Red Wing, Minnesota, samt ingick 1883 äktenskap med Maria B. Haller, född år 1860 i Värmlands län, Sverige.

Anmärkningsvärt är, att bibeln var försvunnen en längre tid i Sverige och reste jag dit för att söka rätt på den samt lyckades finna den mellan brandmuren och väggen på loftet i ett av mina förfäders äldre boningshus.

Och nu överlämnar jag bibeln åt min son Enok samt är det min önskan att han, i sin tur, låter den gå i släkten.

Red Wing i januari 1942.

Johannes Johnson.

This bible has been in the Johnson family since 1732 — Enoch Johnson

"Människan tillkommer som en ros och förgår som en skugga."

Translation of page in the Family Bible.

This bible has belonged to the family during four (4) generations. The bible came first to Håkan Jönsson at Snällartorp (farm) in Gräsmark (Sweden) in the year of 1730. It was thereafter given to his son, Jöns Håkansson, born at Snällartorp farm 28 of December 1779. It later belonged to his son, Johannes Jönsson, born at Snällartorp farm 5 of June 1829. Then the bible was given to his son Johannes Johansson, born at Gräshöjden farm in Gräsmarks parish, County of Värmland (Sweden) 14 of Mars 1858.

The last mentioned (Johannes Johansson) went to Red Wing, Minnesota and was married to Maria B. Haller, born 1860 in the County of Värmland, Sweden.

Noticeable is that the bible was lost for a longer time in Sweden and that I went to Sweden to look for it. I managed to find the bible between the chimney and the wall, at the loft in one of my ancestors older house.

And now, I give the bible to my son Enoc and it is my wish that he in turn will pass it on to the next generation in the family.

Red Wing in January 1942

Johannes Johnson

"The Human is coming into being as a rose and perish as a shadow"